SpringerBriefs in Population Studies

Advisory Editors

Baha Abu-Laban, Edmonton, AB, Canada

Mark Birkin, Leeds, UK

Dudley L. Poston Jr., Department of Sociology, Texas A&M University, College Station, TX, USA

John Stillwell, Leeds, UK

Hans-Werner Wahl, Deutsches Zentrum für Alternsforschung (DZFA), Institut für Gerontologie, Universität Heidelberg, Heidelberg, Germany

D. J. H. Deeg, VU University Medical Centre/LASA, Amsterdam, The Netherlands

SpringerBriefs in Population Studies presents concise summaries of cutting-edge research and practical applications across the field of demography and population studies. It publishes compact refereed monographs under the editorial supervision of an international Advisory Board. Volumes are compact, 50 to 125 pages, with a clear focus. The series covers a range of content from professional to academic such as: timely reports of state-of-the art analytical techniques, bridges between new research results, snapshots of hot and/or emerging topics, and in-depth case studies.

The scope of the series spans the entire field of demography and population studies, with a view to significantly advance research. The character of the series is international and multidisciplinary and includes research areas such as: population aging, fertility and family dynamics, demography, migration, population health, household structures, mortality, human geography and environment. Volumes in this series may analyze past, present and/or future trends, as well as their determinants and consequences. Both solicited and unsolicited manuscripts are considered for publication in this series.

SpringerBriefs in Population Studies will be of interest to a wide range of individuals with interests in population studies, including demographers, population geographers, sociologists, economists, political scientists, epidemiologists and health researchers as well as practitioners across the social sciences.

Yoann Doignon · Isabelle Blöss-Widmer ·
Elena Ambrosetti · Sébastien Oliveau

Population Dynamics in the Mediterranean

A Demographic Convergence?

Springer

Yoann Doignon
IDEES UMR 6266, CNRS
Mont-Saint-Aignan, France

Elena Ambrosetti
MEMOTEF Department
Sapienza University of Rome
Rome, Italy

Isabelle Blöss-Widmer
MESOPOLHIS UMR 7064, CNRS
Aix-Marseille University
Aix-en-Provence, France

Sébastien Oliveau
MESOPOLHIS UMR 7064, CNRS
Aix-Marseille University
Aix-en-Provence, France

ISSN 2211-3215 ISSN 2211-3223 (electronic)
SpringerBriefs in Population Studies
ISBN 978-3-031-37758-7 ISBN 978-3-031-37759-4 (eBook)
https://doi.org/10.1007/978-3-031-37759-4

© The Editor(s) (if applicable) and The Author(s) 2023, corrected publication 2023, 2024. This book is an open access publication.

Open Access This book is licensed under the terms of the Creative Commons Attribution 4.0 International License (http://creativecommons.org/licenses/by/4.0/), which permits use, sharing, adaptation, distribution and reproduction in any medium or format, as long as you give appropriate credit to the original author(s) and the source, provide a link to the Creative Commons license and indicate if changes were made.

The images or other third party material in this book are included in the book's Creative Commons license, unless indicated otherwise in a credit line to the material. If material is not included in the book's Creative Commons license and your intended use is not permitted by statutory regulation or exceeds the permitted use, you will need to obtain permission directly from the copyright holder.

The use of general descriptive names, registered names, trademarks, service marks, etc. in this publication does not imply, even in the absence of a specific statement, that such names are exempt from the relevant protective laws and regulations and therefore free for general use.

The publisher, the authors, and the editors are safe to assume that the advice and information in this book are believed to be true and accurate at the date of publication. Neither the publisher nor the authors or the editors give a warranty, expressed or implied, with respect to the material contained herein or for any errors or omissions that may have been made. The publisher remains neutral with regard to jurisdictional claims in published maps and institutional affiliations.

This Springer imprint is published by the registered company Springer Nature Switzerland AG
The registered company address is: Gewerbestrasse 11, 6330 Cham, Switzerland

Preface

"La démographie en Méditerranée: situation et projections" (*Economica*, 2001) has been released more than 20 years for Plan Bleu. I am delighted to see a new publication on the topic, delighted for several reasons. First of all, it was a much needed and highly anticipated work on a part of the world that concentrates number of issues that are highlighted by demography. I am also delighted as this publication adopts a holistic approach, successfully achieving the difficult feat of producing a complex and changing territory. Finally, I am delighted as I know the team that has been working on this publication for several years and because this publication is a result of a long-term project carried out by the *Mediterranean Demographic Observatory—DemoMed*, which is attached to the University of Aix-Marseille.

The Mediterranean is a region experiencing global challenges. While some may have seen it as a "clash of civilisations" and others as a "convergence of civilisations", it is, in fact, a place of meetings and exchanges dating back thousands of years. Throughout the publication, the authors demonstrate the convergence of demographic trends in the various Mediterranean countries. The most recent statistics were used, although national statistics were not used as frequently, this was the only realistic option for conducting a harmonised analysis of the phenomena for the Mediterranean as a whole. The publication makes sure, however, to look at developments over more than half a century and does not shy away from projecting the possible future of the region.

The authors, in a rather novel way, sometimes propose sub-national analyses, which remind us that countries are not homogeneous blocks, and that certain regions on one shore are more similar to regions on another shore than to regions in neighbouring countries. The choice of conducting a global analysis, as opposed to focusing on certain specific places, has the virtue of offering a truly comparative vision and of putting each situation into context. The desire to go beyond the irreducible uniqueness of places runs through all the chapters. At the same time, however, the reading of the phenomena focuses on the particularity of certain countries or regions of the Mediterranean.

In a very fluid manner, the four authors begin by describing the settlement of the region as a favourable, but restrictive, geographical setting that welcomes a variety of populations with diverse, but ultimately convergent trajectories, with the exception of those where the political situation is particularly difficult (Israel, Palestine). This is followed by analyses of fertility, mortality and migration, classic themes in population analysis, which they use as a driving force to understand the transformations of the societies studied, both in terms of habitat (coastalisation, urbanisation) and social (gender relations, elderly care) or economical (windows of opportunity, demographic dividends) dimensions. These elements are all challenges that are fuelled by transition processes and population dynamics.

To fully understand the will that motivated this group of researchers and the originality of the angle chosen to produce this work, it is worth recalling that out of the four colleagues who wrote it, two are demographers, one a geographer and one (the first author) a disciplinary hybrid, which his doctoral thesis on ageing in the Mediterranean has already demonstrated. For more than 10 years now, the four of them have been in charge of the *Mediterranean Demographic Observatory— DemoMed* at the Maison Méditerranéenne des Sciences de l'Homme in Aix-en-Provence (France). This observatory brings together a network of colleagues from teaching and research institutions around the Mediterranean driven by the same desire to understand the changes taking place in this geographical area in the field of population studies. This publication brings together their expertise from the different scientific fields of demography, geography, statistics and sociology. It is just like them: diverse in its approaches, demanding in its methods, but also richly documented and illustrated.

It is therefore without hesitation that I recommend reading this publication, as its contribution to the knowledge of this part of the world is as essential for those who live there as for the rest of the world. The Mediterranean is a concentration of humanity where many phenomena that are in fact universal are played out and thwarted: declining fertility, declining mortality, changing family structures, ageing and also migration and development.

Demographer, Former Senior Researcher at the French Institute for Demographic Studies (INED)

Paris, France   Youssef Courbage

Acknowledgements

This publication would not have been possible in its present form without the help of various individuals and institutions, whom we would like to thank now. It is the result of work carried out since 2010 by the *Mediterranean Demographic Observatory—DemoMed—*within the Maison Méditerranéenne des Sciences de l'Homme (MMSH) at Aix-Marseille University.

We would like to thank its directors, Brigitte Marin and Sophie Bouffier, for all their support from the very beginning of the project.

We would also like to thank the staff of our parent institutions for their help and understanding, especially those from the MESOPOLHIS laboratory, IACCHOS (UCLouvain), the MMSH and La Sapienza.

We would like to thank all our colleagues and the students and trainees who worked with us over the years, particularly for their help with data collection and analysis, and with the logistics of the final drafting of the manuscript, especially Elise Lévêque, Quentin Godoye, Clément De Belsunce, Jean-Baptiste Cortese, Florent Kuntzmann, Marc Soler, Thomas Finiels and Claire Vandemoortele.

We would like to thank Ami Saji for her careful review of the final manuscript.

We would like to thank Youssef Courbage who has honoured us by writing the preface for this work. It is a testimony of which we are very proud.

We would like to thank La Sapienza University of Rome, the Maison Méditerranéenne des Sciences de l'Homme (MMSH, UAR 3125) of the University of Aix-Marseille, the Institute for the Analysis of Change in Contemporary and Historical Societies (IACCHOS) of the University of Leuven, and the MESOPOLHIS laboratory (UMR 7064) for their financial support, which has allowed us to publish this book as open access and, in turn, make it accessible to the largest possible number of people.

We sincerely thank Evelien Bakker, Corina van der Giessen, Aarthi Padmanabhan, Bernadette Deelen-Mans and Prashanth Ravichandran from Springer for their trust, patience and professionalism.

Last, but not least, we would like to thank our loved ones for all their support.

Contents

1 **General Introduction: A Study of Mediterranean Populations** 1
  1.1 A Book Addressing the Lack of Pan-Mediterranean
       Demographic Studies 1
       1.1.1 In Search of Human Unity in the Mediterranean 2
       1.1.2 The Mediterranean and Population Sciences 4
       1.1.3 A Lack of Pan-Mediterranean Demographic Studies 5
  1.2 Approach and Commitment 6
       1.2.1 What Do We Mean by the Mediterranean? 6
       1.2.2 International Comparisons Over Time 8
       1.2.3 Grid Convergence to Analyse Demographic
             Phenomena 11
       1.2.4 Data Used 11
  1.3 Structure of the Book 13
  References 14

2 **Spatial Distribution of Population and Urbanisation** 19
  2.1 Introduction 19
  2.2 Uneven Distribution of the Population 20
  2.3 Far from Determinism: Opportunities and Constraints
       of Mediterranean Areas 24
  2.4 A Very Coastal and Increasing Urbanisation 25
  2.5 Settlement Challenges in the Mediterranean 29
  References 30

3 **Sex Ratio, Age Structure and Population Ageing** 33
  3.1 Introduction 33
  3.2 Gender Inequalities in the Mediterranean 34
  3.3 An Ageing Population 36
  3.4 Ongoing Significant Differences in Age Structure Between
       Regions 37
  3.5 Implications and Consequences of Age Structure
       Differences 40

	References	41
4	**The Various of Demographic Transitions**	**43**
4.1	Introduction	43
4.2	Demographic Transition "Models"	46
	4.2.1 Type 1: Ancient Transition with Pseudo-Equilibrium in the 1970s (Spain, France)	46
	4.2.2 Type 2: Transition with Pseudo-Equilibrium in the Late 1990s (Cyprus, Montenegro, Malta)	47
	4.2.3 Type 3: Rapid Transition with Late Pseudo-Equilibrium from the 2000s Onwards (Macedonia, Albania, Kosovo)	47
4.3	Completed Demographic Transition with a Post-Transitional Decline Regime	49
	4.3.1 Type 4: Transition with Pseudo-Equilibrium in the 1980s–1990s (Italy, Portugal, Greece, Slovenia, Croatia, Bulgaria)	50
	4.3.2 Type 5: Transition with Pseudo-Equilibrium in the 2000s (Serbia, Bosnia-Herzegovina)	50
4.4	Completed Demographic Transition with a Post-Transitional Regime with Sustained Population Growth (Type 6: Israel)	50
4.5	Recent and Rapid Demographic Transition, Now Being Finalised	52
	4.5.1 Type 7: Transition Already Underway in 1950 (Lebanon, Turkey)	53
	4.5.2 Type 8: More Recent Transition (Libya, Morocco, Tunisia)	54
4.6	Possible Demographic Counter-Transitions (Type 9: Egypt, Algeria)	56
4.7	Recent and Ongoing Transition, Slower Decline in Birth Rate (Type 10: Jordan, Palestine, Syria)	58
4.8	A Diversity of Demographic Transitions Despite a General Convergence	58
	References	60
5	**Fertility Intensity and Timing**	**63**
5.1	Introduction	63
5.2	A Global Fertility Convergence	64
5.3	The Intersection of Birth Timing and Fertility Intensity	66
	5.3.1 Mean Age at Childbearing	66
	5.3.2 Fertility by Age Group	69
5.4	Specific Contributions of Age Groups	72
5.5	(Un)certainties for the Future of Mediterranean Fertility	75
	References	78

6	**Family Formation and Dissolution**	81
	6.1 Introduction	82
	6.2 Major Marriage and Divorce Trends	82
	6.2.1 Marriage	82
	6.2.2 Divorce	85
	6.3 Changes in Marriage	88
	6.3.1 An Increase in Age at Marriage	88
	6.3.2 Permanent Celibacy	92
	6.3.3 Summary of Family Models	94
	6.4 Conclusion	96
	References	97
7	**Mortality Profiles**	99
	7.1 Introduction	99
	7.2 Mortality at All Ages: Life Expectancy at Birth	100
	7.2.1 A Very Heterogeneous Picture in 1950	100
	7.2.2 General Convergence Since 1950	102
	7.2.3 Decreases in Life Expectancy at Birth	103
	7.2.4 Gender Inequalities	104
	7.3 The Different Mortality Profiles	105
	7.3.1 Infant and Child Mortality (Under 5 Years Old)	106
	7.3.2 Adult Mortality (15–64 Years Old)	108
	7.3.3 Mortality at Advanced Ages (65 Years Old or Older)	109
	7.4 The Health Transition	111
	7.5 Conclusion	113
	References	114
8	**The Mediterranean Migration System**	117
	8.1 Introduction	117
	8.2 Migration in the Mediterranean (1950–1995)	119
	8.3 Migration in the Mediterranean in the XXI Century	121
	8.4 Two Emerging Phenomena: High Skilled and Irregular Migration	125
	8.5 Conclusions	127
	References	128
9	**Population Dynamics and Their Components**	131
	9.1 Introduction	131
	9.2 Evolving Power Relations	132
	9.3 Natural and Migration Dynamics: Which Combinations Exist in the Mediterranean?	135
	9.3.1 Natural Dynamics: South and East	135
	9.3.2 Migration Dynamics: Sending Versus Receiving Countries	137
	9.4 Growth Outlook to 2060: What Can We Expect?	138
	References	142

10	Conclusions. An Overview of Population Dynamics in the Mediterranean	145
	10.1 Major Demographic Developments Since 1950	145
	10.2 An Assessment of the Book's Overall Approach	148
	References	151

Correction to: Mortality Profiles C1

Correction to: Population Dynamics and Their Components C3

References 153

About the Authors

Yoann Doignon holds a Ph.D. in population geography from the Aix-Marseille University, France. He is Researcher with the French National Centre for Scientific Research (CNRS), affiliated with the UMR 6266 IDEES (Rouen, France). He is too an Associated Researcher at the Center for Demographic Research (UCLouvain, Belgium) and at the UMR 7363 SAGE (Strasbourg, France). He has been a collaborator of the *Mediterranean Demographic Observatory* (DemoMed) for several years. He specialises in Mediterranean populations. His Ph.D. focused on territorial and spatial convergence of the ageing population in the Mediterranean. Additionally, he has been studying population decline in France and Southern Europe, and on spatial diffusion processes of demographic phenomena, especially family changes in Europe and fertility decline.

Isabelle Blöss-Widmer holds a Ph.D. in demography from University Paris I – Panthéon Sorbonne. She is Associate Professor at Aix-Marseille University, and a researcher at the UMR 7064 MESOPOLHIS. She is the head of the *Mediterranean Demographic Observatory* at the Maison Méditerranéenne des Sciences de l'Homme. Her current research is mainly on the demography of Mediterranean countries, in particular, the causes and consequences of demographic ageing examined at different administrative scales of the territories.

Elena Ambrosetti holds a Ph.D. in demography from the Institut d'Etudes Politiques, Paris, France. She is Associate Professor of Demography at the Faculty of Economics and affiliated to the Department of Methods and Models for Economics, Territory and Finance—Sapienza University of Rome, Italy. Since October 2022 she is research fellow of Mesopolhis, Aix-Marseille University, Sciences Po Aix & National Centre for Scientific Research (France). She is member of the *Mediterranean Demographic Observatory* (DemoMed). She has extensively worked on the demography of the Mediterranean countries with special attention to the demographic transition in Egypt and in Northern African countries and to population ageing and its consequences in Italy and in the Southern European Mediterranean countries. Additionally, she is an expert on international migration, with particular focus on migrants' integration, migration policies and demographic behaviour of migrant populations.

Sébastien Oliveau holds a Ph.D. in geography from University Paris I, France (2004) and a Habilitation from Aix-Marseille University (2011). He is the director of the Large Research Infrastructure PROGEDO (https://progedo.fr) and researcher at MESOPOLHIS, Mediterranean centre in Sociology, political science and history, France (UMR 7064, CNRS). As Assistant Professor at Aix-Marseille University, he has supervised several PhDs since 2010. His research focuses on the spatial analysis of populations. He is currently working in the *Observatoire démographique de la Méditerranée* (DemoMed).

Chapter 1
General Introduction: A Study of Mediterranean Populations

Abstract The Mediterranean region has been much studied by human and social sciences. The length of its written history, and the variety of civilisations sharing a common history (going back to the Roman *mare nostrum*), of course, go some way to explaining this wealth of studies. However, the Mediterranean has only recently been studied as a global study area, rather than as separate sub-regions. We note that there is a lack of recent general publications, or writings in general, providing a synthesis or inventory of the various demographic phenomena on a pan-Mediterranean scale. The aim of this publication is to provide an overview and detailed description of the demographic trends of the last 70 years for the populations of the Mediterranean as a whole.

Keywords Mediterranean · Population studies · International comparison · Demographic convergence

1.1 A Book Addressing the Lack of Pan-Mediterranean Demographic Studies

The Mediterranean region has been much studied by human and social sciences. The length of its written history, and the variety of civilisations sharing a common history (going back to the Roman *mare nostrum*), of course, go some way to explaining this wealth of studies. However, the Mediterranean has only recently been studied as a global study area, rather than as separate sub-regions.

1.1.1 In Search of Human Unity in the Mediterranean

The very word "Mediterranean" was coined in the eighteenth century and refers only to the fact of "being inland"[1] (Bourguet et al., 1998). The Mediterranean was little studied before the nineteenth century, owing to its lack of scientific significance. It was thought of rather as a space of division and separation between very different populations. It was not until three French scientific expeditions to Egypt (1798–1799), the Morea (1829–1831) and Algeria (1839–1842) that the Mediterranean became an object of study in itself. The research thus carried out attempted to give consistency to the Mediterranean area by seeking to identify common elements on both sides of this geographical area, which would make it possible to affirm the unity and homogeneity of the region.

The botanists on the Egyptian expedition discovered species common to Syria, the Barbary Coast and Southern France. Pyramus de Candolle (1820) considered the Mediterranean to be one of the world's 20 botanical regions. This led to the notion of a Mediterranean region, although it was not recognised as having any specific character. The Mediterranean was said to be a transitional botanical region between the three continents, along a north–south and east–west gradient.

It was not until the 1830s that a scientific discourse developed on the cultural unity of the Mediterranean, based in particular on ancient history (Roman and Philhellenic legacies). Thus, this geographical area is less and less perceived as a barrier or a space of division between civilisations, but as an interface linking the different shores, where the sea facilitates the exchange of ideas and trade more than the land (Reclus, 1876).

The Vidalian approach, prominent at the end of the nineteenth century, broke with tradition by positing that the physical homogeneity (climate and landscape) of the Mediterranean had an influence on the lifestyles of its populations. The sea is becoming less important than the land (Sorre & Sion, 1934). This idea of the Mediterranean as a human unit cumulates with the work of Braudel (1949). He was one of the first to articulate the concept of a Mediterranean world. He viewed the Mediterranean as a permanent place of maritime and land exchanges, which changes its meaning throughout history (Roncayolo, 2002). In particular, he emphasised the continuity throughout history, but also the homogeneity of the societies surrounding the Mediterranean Sea. Landscapes are considered as major elements of this homogeneity, in accordance with a certain geographical determinism of the Vidalian approach, which has been vigorously criticised (Péguy, 1986). However, Braudel deserves credit for taking on the Mediterranean and establishing it as an object of study in the human and social sciences.

---

[1] This text has been translated into English by the authors. The original text in French is as follows: "ce qui est au milieu des terres".

1.1 A Book Addressing the Lack of Pan-Mediterranean Demographic Studies

Other scientific fields have been involved in this question of the geographical, historical and cultural unity of Mediterranean societies. In particular, anthropologists have researched the common characteristics of social life, marking a coherence of the Mediterranean world. For example, Peristiany (1968, 1976) proposed the concept of "Mediterranean modes of thought". Pitt-Rivers (1963) compared the social structures of rural communities in several Mediterranean countries across the different shores. He argued that Mediterranean unity stems from geomorphological and climatic characteristics. Continuities over time would therefore be little affected by political or religious changes. Others identified concepts and values characteristic of social relations on both sides, such as honour and shame, the male virility complex and patronage (Albera, 2006; Peristiany, 1966; Tolosana, 2001).

These aspects can also be found in the field of history of the family. Peter Laslett (1983) proposed four patterns of family and household formation in historical Europe, one of which was explicitly identified as Mediterranean. Subsequently, the testing of this "Mediterranean model" quickly became one of the objectives of family and marriage historians in Southern Europe and the Middle East (Sacchi & Viazzo, 2014). Historians of the family have tended to dismiss the possibility of commonalities between Mediterranean marriage and family patterns (Sacchi & Viazzo, 2014). On the other hand, some have hypothesised a long-standing regional contrast between Mediterranean Europe and the rest of the continent, and a very long-term continuity of the different shores of the Mediterranean (Smith, 1990).

The human and cultural unity of the Mediterranean has been widely debated since the 1960s. Anthropologists criticise, for example, the relevance of human unity as an anthropological mirage and a sum of stereotypes of northern researchers, especially of British anthropology (Herzfeld, 1987; Pina-Cabral, 1989). Some researchers reject the category of the Mediterranean (Horden & Purcell, 2000) and question the very existence of the object (Kayser, 1996).

At present, there is a growing consensus that rejects the vision of the Mediterranean as a culturally homogenous area (Huebner, 2016). The human unity of the Mediterranean no longer structures the frames of reference (Deprest, 2002). Nevertheless, it is possible to recognise a certain scientific coherence to the Mediterranean without denying its heterogeneity. Bromberger and Durand (2001) believe, for example, that it would be a mistake to present the Mediterranean as the ultimate place of mixing and blending. Exchange, migration and spatial proximity do not necessarily imply merging. However, without speaking of homogeneity, they recognise a "family resemblance"[2] between Mediterranean societies and cultures. This can be explained by the circulation of ideas, human migration, a similar ecological context and monotheism. Bromberger and Durand (2001) noted that the Mediterranean is defined more by its differences than by its similarities. The specificity of the Mediterranean space would be defined precisely by these differences, neither too close nor too far away. The Mediterranean would then constitute a stimulating study area for "understanding the whole range of possible relations with the other

---

[2] This text has been translated into English by the authors. The original text in French is as follows: "air de famille".

which is neither too close nor too far, neither too small nor too big"[3] (Bromberger and Durand, 2001), and would ultimately be an implicit tension between unity and diversity of its characteristics (Von Kondratowitz, 2013).

1.1.2 The Mediterranean and Population Sciences

This overview, which is deliberately not exhaustive, reveals the extent to which the Mediterranean area has been the subject of much research and intense debate since the nineteenth century. Thus, in several social sciences disciplines (geography, history, anthropology, etc.), the Mediterranean continue to constitute a relevant study area. A specific field of research has emerged (*Mediterranean studies*), and there are research structures dedicated to it, such as the Maison Méditerranéenne des Sciences de l'Homme (MMSH) of the University of Aix-Marseille in France.

However, we note that this liveliness of studies and debates on the Mediterranean is almost absent from the population sciences, the scientific field under which this publication falls. The Mediterranean does not seem to be a geographical frame of reference for population studies. The latter are largely concentrated on portions of the Mediterranean area of varying size, but much less so on the Mediterranean as a whole (on a pan-Mediterranean scale). The national scale remains the most commonly adopted, with many monographs on a particular Mediterranean country or sub-national regions. There are also regional studies which deal with a specific region (in the broad sense) of the Mediterranean, such as the Maghreb (Fargues, 1990; Le Bris, 2021; Ouadah-Bedidi et al., 2012; Sebti et al., 2009), the Near East (Courbage, 2008; Fargues, 1995), the Southern and Eastern shores of the Mediterranean (Courbage, 1997, 1999, 2015; Fargues, 2000a; Rashad, 2015; Tabutin & Schoumaker, 2005), the Balkans (Deslondes, 2004; Lerch, 2018; Sardon, 2001), and the countries of Southern Europe (Avdeev et al., 2011; Doignon et al., 2016; Pfirsch, 2011).

Thus, compared with the numerous national and macro-regional monographs, there are relatively few pan-Mediterranean demographic studies (Anastasiou et al., 2020; Attané & Courbage, 2004; Carella & Parant, 2016; D'Addato, 2010; Doignon, 2019, 2020; Doignon et al., 2016; Fargues, 2000b; Fargues and Salinari, 2011; ITAN, 2015; Matthijs et al., 2016; Oliveau and Doignon, 2014; Salvini, 2023; Troisi & Von Kondratowitz, 2013; Wilson, 2005; Zagaglia, 2013). This is probably due to the demographic contrasts across the Mediterranean, which many researchers in the population sciences consider to be too great to constitute a coherent study area. Indeed, the shores of the Mediterranean are generally presented in terms of contrast: a declining, low-fertility and ageing Northern shore facing a fast-growing, highly fertile and young Southern and Eastern shore. However, this dichotomy does not take

---

[3] This text has been translated into English by the authors. The original text in French is as follows: "appréhender toute la gamme des relations possibles avec l'autre qui n'est ni trop proche ni trop lointain, ni trop petit ni trop grand".

1.1 A Book Addressing the Lack of Pan-Mediterranean Demographic Studies   5

into account the dynamic nature of demographic phenomena in terms of time and space. Mediterranean demography is in a state of flux, whether in terms of structures, dynamics or demographic behaviour: the rapid spread of declining mortality and fertility rates, the deceleration of population growth, the circulation of sociocultural or family models and ideas, etc. Consequently, the disparities that so well characterised the populations of the Mediterranean in the past are not necessarily of the same intensity today. By shedding light on the spatial dichotomy between the shores in light of recent demographic changes, it becomes possible to rethink the Mediterranean not just as a space of contrasts, but as an area in the process of homogenisation.[4]

1.1.3 A Lack of Pan-Mediterranean Demographic Studies

In light of these various elements, we note that there is a lack of recent general publications, or writings in general, providing a synthesis or inventory of the various demographic phenomena on a pan-Mediterranean scale. For instance, the few existing demographic studies on the Mediterranean as a whole often focus on a particular demographic aspect. At this level, international migration remains perhaps the most studied demographic phenomenon at the scale of the Mediterranean as a whole, as the latter is conceptualised as a coherent migration system (Ambrosetti et al., 2016; Wihtol de Wenden, 2019).

From a certain perspective, this lack of analysis of the demography of Mediterranean populations as a whole is harmful. Population is the foundation of many other socio-economic phenomena. Studying the population allows us to understand the intimate aspects of a society, such as the fact of dying, giving birth, marrying, migrating, etc. Often considered as basic, these phenomena are nevertheless essential for a detailed understanding of contemporary societies and their evolution. This understanding would be more than welcome in the case of the Mediterranean, at a time when there are various initiatives for regional integration and cooperation in the Euro-Mediterranean region: Plan Bleu, the 5 + 5 Dialogue, the recent 2019 Summit of the Two Shores of the Mediterranean, the Union for the Mediterranean, the NATO Mediterranean Dialogue, the Centre for Mediterranean Integration, and the European Institute of the Mediterranean (IEMed). By updating our knowledge of population dynamics in the Mediterranean, we would be able to generate interest and fuel discussions in several fields, such as the social sciences, geopolitics, political sciences, etc. This is all the more important when demography is used to study international relations. The clash of civilisations (Huntington, 1993) for example conceptualises the youthfulness of Arab-Muslim societies (against the ageing societies of Europe) as a determining cause of a war between civilisations. Today's demography is thought to be timeless, making political unrest and conflict in the Mediterranean inevitable at

---

[4] By the term "homogenisation" we mean a reduction of contrasts, not a perfectly similar situation shared by all Mediterranean populations.

the same time. The reduction of demographic contrasts is therefore a strong argument against the clash of civilisations and its conflicting predictions.

The aim of this publication is to provide an overview and detailed description of the demographic trends of the last 70 years for the populations of the Mediterranean as a whole. From this point of view, we are in line with the approach taken some 20 years ago by Attané and Courbage (2004) in their publication *Demography in the Mediterranean region: situation and projections*.

1.2 Approach and Commitment

1.2.1 What Do We Mean by the Mediterranean?

Firstly, we need to define the project's study area. The delimitation of the Mediterranean has been the subject of much debate, with no real consensus having been reached. First of all, it is pertinent to consider the Mediterranean Sea as the essential element of the Mediterranean area, especially as it is easy to circumscribe. On the other hand, the task becomes more complicated when it comes to delimiting the Mediterranean land: we know where to start, from the Mediterranean shore, but we do not know *a priori* where to stop. Thus, there are several delimitations of the Mediterranean.

The Mediterranean has a characteristic climate with the concomitance of the dry period and the hot period, and a very marked seasonal alternation. However, with a width of 3,800 km, there are great climatic differences, both in terms of rainfall and temperature. Indeed, the summer drought lasts between 2 and 3 months on the Northern Shore of the Western Mediterranean, compared to 6 to 7 months on the Eastern Shore (Clément, 2002).

Geographers of the nineteenth century choose to use the olive tree as the boundary of the Mediterranean. This tree is said to be a shared symbol in the Mediterranean as it is a gift from Athena to the Athenians, an idealised image of Abraham in the Old Testament, the tree that introduces the Light in the Qur'an, and a representation of justice and peace in many Mediterranean societies. However, the biogeographical and bioclimatic limits would be insufficient and too stringent (Roncayolo, 2002). They have the disadvantage of "revealing only one facet of the Mediterranean environment and would always be an imperfect approximation"[5] (Clément, 2002, 37).

Yves Lacoste (2001) proposed a geopolitical delimitation of the Mediterranean from Morocco to Turkmenistan and Iran, passing through the Caucasus region and the Gulf countries, and including the countries that are part of NATO (for example the United Kingdom).

---

[5] This text has been translated into English by the authors. The original text in French is as follows: "de ne révéler qu'une facette du milieu méditerranéen et constituent toujours une approximation imparfaite".

1.2 Approach and Commitment

Finally, other researchers, such as Robert Ilbert (2006), considered that there is no fixed limit between the Mediterranean and the non-Mediterranean. The Mediterranean would be characterised precisely by an absence of limits, since it would be a territorial space limited by edge and not by a limit.

In this publication, we will delimit the Mediterranean in the following way. A first simple geographical criterion is to choose the countries with direct access to the Mediterranean Sea. However, national borders changed during the twentieth century and problematic cases easily emerged, for example in the Balkans. At the end of the First World War, the Kingdom of Serbs, Croats and Slovenes, i.e. today's Croatia, Slovenia, Serbia, Macedonia and Bosnia-Herzegovina, was created and later called Yugoslavia. Until the period between 1991 and 1995, this country had access to the sea and could be considered Mediterranean. However, it is currently divided into several different countries. Thus, what are now Serbia, Kosovo and Macedonia would no longer belong to the Mediterranean region due to their lack of access to the sea. However, we believe that the Mediterranean character is not lost in the course of political change. Some countries do not have direct access to the sea, but are nevertheless extremely close: regions of Portugal, the West Bank, Jordan, Kosovo, Serbia, Macedonia and Bulgaria are often located less than 250 kms from the sea (Fig. 1.1).

For example, France and Algeria are considered Mediterranean. However, regions in the north of France are as close to the Mediterranean Sea as some regions of the Caucasian countries, Russia, Poland and Ukraine. Without extending the scope so far, we chose to include countries with at least a portion of their territory within 250 kms of the Mediterranean Sea. We made an exception with Austria, Switzerland and

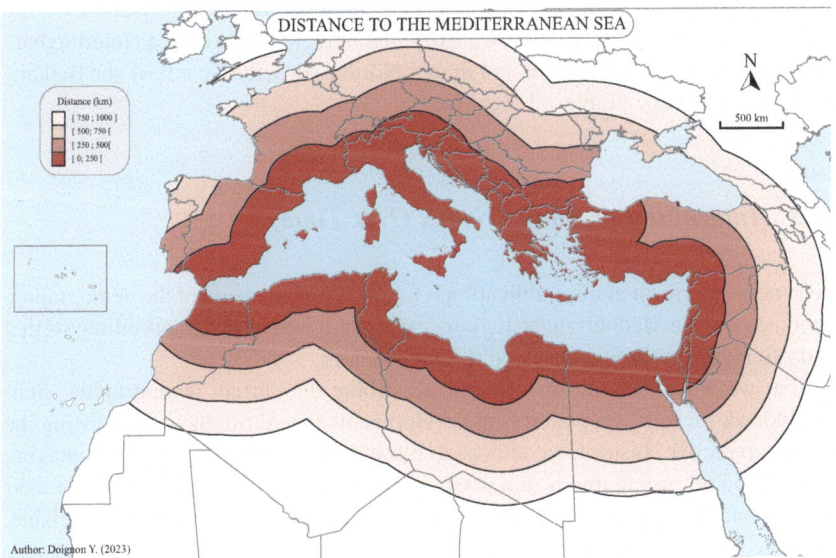

Fig. 1.1 Distance to the Mediterranean Sea

Table 1.1 Composition of the geographical categories used in the publication

SOUTHERN SHORE	EASTERN SHORE	NORTHERN SHORE	
North Africa	Near East	Balkans	Southern Europe
Algeria	Cyprus	Bulgaria	Portugal
Egypt	Lebanon	Croatia	Spain
Libya	Turkey	Montenegro	France
Morocco	Israel	Albania	Italy
Tunisia	Jordan	Serbia	Malta
	Syria	Bosnia-Herzegovina[a]	
		Slovenia	
		Macedonia	
		Greece	
		Kosovo	

[a] For ease of reading, we use "BiH" in this book to mean "Bosnia-Herzegovina"

Hungary, which are not oriented towards the Mediterranean. Thus, our study area consists of all countries with direct access to the sea, plus Portugal, Jordan, Kosovo, Serbia, Macedonia and Bulgaria. Andorra, Monaco and San Marino, located less than 250 km from the Mediterranean Sea, are not included in the study area as their populations are too small.

Mediterranean countries are commonly classified according to the shore to which they belong: the Southern Shore (African shore), the Eastern Shore (Asian shore) and the Northern Shore (European shore). We will use this categorisation for the representation of the data, to which we will add four regional clusters, an intermediate categorisation between countries and shores: North Africa, the Near East, the Balkans and Southern Europe (Table 1.1, Fig. 1.2).

1.2.2 International Comparisons Over Time

The general approach of this publication is to give a global vision of the demographic phenomena of the Mediterranean region. To this end, we have five commitments that we try to maintain throughout the different chapters.

First, we will not limit ourselves to describing the current demographic situation. Indeed, focusing only on recent developments would run the risk of losing the global perspective. Instead, we choose to place them in the long term, thus making it possible to put recent trends into perspective or, on the contrary, to underline their unprecedented character compared to past trends. Depending on the data available, our study will cover the period from 1950 to present day.

1.2 Approach and Commitment

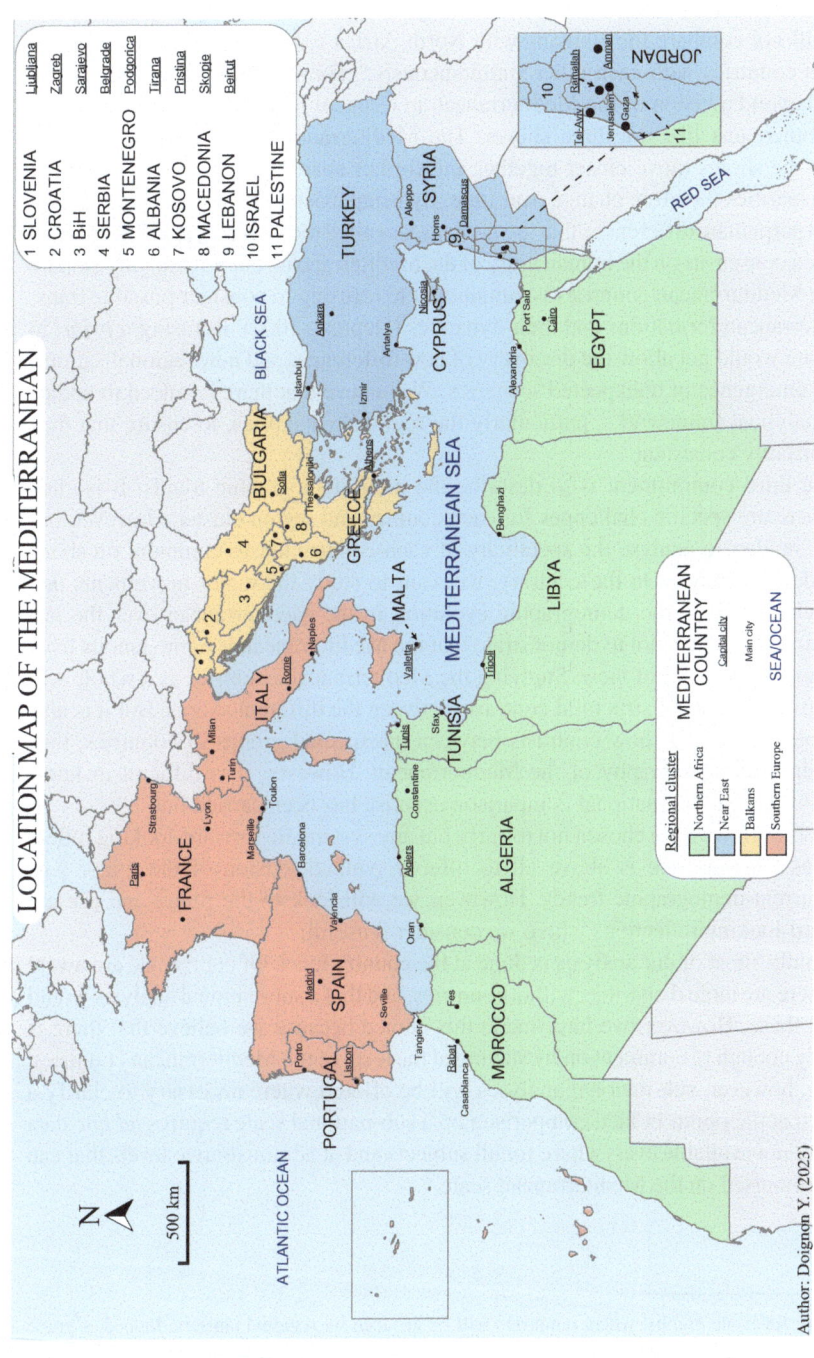

Fig. 1.2 Location map of the Mediterranean

Secondly, we will carry out a global international comparison of the Mediterranean. Our unit of comparison is the country, not preconceived regional categories. We will not compare the Balkans with North Africa for example, but all Mediterranean countries with each other simultaneously.[6] The interest of this approach is to go beyond a vision of the Mediterranean in terms of regional blocks that oppose each other, just like the three shores. The Mediterranean is a maritime basin in which the shores move closer together and further apart (Brunet, 1995). Contrasts and disparities therefore change over time. By using existing regional categories, we would perpetuate differences that are perhaps less alive today. It is true that there is no longer a consensus on the human unity of the Mediterranean, but refusing to compare all the Mediterranean countries is tantamount to refusing to consider possible trans-Mediterranean formations and their dynamics (Deprest, 2002). Refusing *a priori* to compare would not allow the discovery of new differences and new regionalisations, or the emergence of unexpected scenarios. We believe that there is a need to update our analytical frameworks, particularly the regional categories, to ensure that they are currently consistent.

The third commitment is to describe the main demographic trends. It is clear that there are specific challenges for each country and region cluster. However, our aim is neither to analyse the specificity of each country nor to comment on short-term developments. On the contrary, we want to study the major movements that have characterised the demographic evolution in the Mediterranean over the last 70 years. Our aim is not to demonstrate that the Mediterranean is homogenous from a demographic point of view. Studying the Mediterranean countries as a whole will perhaps highlight the structural contrasts between the different shores. But it is also possible that it will show contrasts between unexpected groups of countries, thus renewing the demography of the Mediterranean. However, it is difficult to know until this global international comparison exercise has been carried out.

Moreover, we have chosen not to carry out any systematic forward-looking reflection, as the objective is above all to offer a synthetic vision of the major past and current demographic trends. However, we will look to the future and present forward-looking reflections where we consider it useful.

Finally, most of our analysis is done at the country level. Of course, we are aware that there are large disparities within countries, and that a sub-national analysis would reveal these. However, we have made this choice because we believe that there is already enough to comment on by staying at the level of the Mediterranean countries. Again, however, sub-national analyses will be offered where necessary to clarify a more specific point. In fact, comparison on a sub-national scale requires *ad hoc* data that are not available everywhere for all subjects and at administrative levels that can be harmonised on the Mediterranean scale.

---

[6] Except for some graphs, where countries will be grouped by regional clusters. Indeed, a graph with 27 countries is difficult to read. However, the interpretation of these graphs will not be based on regional clusters, but on the countries as a whole.

1.2.3 Grid Convergence to Analyse Demographic Phenomena

To analyse the major trends of the Mediterranean countries as a whole in the long term,[7] we used the concept of convergence, i.e. the reduction of disparities and inequalities within a study area. We wanted to measure the evolution of disparities between Mediterranean countries. Have the gaps between these countries narrowed or increased? Are Mediterranean countries more similar today than in the past? However, lower disparities between countries do not imply an absence of disparities. Thus, observing convergence should not be interpreted as a deterministic process where all populations are destined to be perfectly similar in the short or long term. Converging trends should simply be interpreted as a reduction in disparities, not as a sign of continued convergence in the future.

The spread of the demographic transition in the world has led to a convergence of several demographic phenomena, such as birth rate and mortality (Wilson, 2001, 2011). It will come as no surprise that it is expected that there will be a convergence in the Mediterranean. However, our aim is not to demonstrate demographic convergence in the Mediterranean, but to analyse the extent to which this convergence is or is not taking place, and even to envisage cases of divergence. If there is convergence, our aim is then to analyse its intensity, pace, persistent disparities, etc.

Similarly, through the analysis of a possible convergence, our aim is not to prove any kind of demographic homogeneity (or unity) of the Mediterranean. We simply wish to highlight the converging and diverging areas, to provide elements for reflection on the fact that the Mediterranean is a more integrated demographic area today than in the past.

1.2.4 Data Used

In the absence of an integrated statistical system specific to the Mediterranean (Blöss-Widmer, 2019), we choose to use major international databases. Conventional demographic indicators are reliable for international comparisons as their definition is fairly widely shared. When analysing indicators such as birth rate, mortality or life expectancy at birth, we are not comparing incomparable things.

The main source of data for our publication is the *World Population Prospects 2022*[8] of the Population Division of the UN Department of Economic and Social Affairs. This database provides a wide range of demographic indicators for all countries around the world. Unlike a national statistical office, the UN does not collect data. It produces population estimates from existing data sources, such as surveys (national and international), population censuses, civil registration data, etc. A specific section

---

[7] See Doignon (2016) for a discussion of the concept of convergence and an application to demographic ageing in the Mediterranean.

[8] https://population.un.org/wpp/.

of the *World Population Prospects*[9] lists the sources used by the UN for each country. The quality data sources in some countries are scarce or incomplete, which makes demographic estimation even more difficult. In these countries, the data should therefore be interpreted with caution. The *World Population Prospects* thus consists of two parts: retrospective data since 1950, which includes UN population estimates, and population projections up to 2100. Moreover, UN estimates and projections have sometimes been criticised, in particular in relation to Mediterranean countries (Courbage, 1999). However, it should be stated that they have the undeniable advantage in providing good quality international comparative data over a long period of time, which is very useful when it comes to analysing major demographic trends, which is the objective of this publication.

In terms of territorial boundaries, the *World Population Prospects* considers current and UN-recognised states or territorial entities. The UN has therefore reconstructed the retrospective data so that it corresponds to the States (or territorial entities) in their current borders. This requires several clarifications in the case of the Mediterranean:

- Western Sahara has been considered as a non-self-governing territory by the UN since 1963. For this reason, estimates for this territory are made from Moroccan data sources, such as the population census.
- For the countries of the former Yugoslavia, the UN has reconstructed the demographic data of the Yugoslav period for each country within their current borders, using in particular the Yugoslav censuses which made it possible to distinguish the different territorial entities that made up Yugoslavia.
- Kosovo refers to the United Nations administered region under security council resolution 1244. For statistical purposes, the data for Serbia do not include this area.
- The Turkish Republic of Northern Cyprus is not recognised by the UN. Therefore, the data refer to the population of the whole island of Cyprus, without distinguishing between the two political entities.
- The UN considers Palestine within its 1967 borders. Referred to as the "State of Palestine" in the data, Palestine thus comprises Gaza and the West Bank, including the Arab populations of East Jerusalem and excluding Israeli citizens residing in the occupied Palestinian territories. Population estimates are based, among other things, on data from the Palestinian Central Bureau of Statistics.

In this publication, for the sake of clarity, we use "Macedonia" for "North Macedonia", "Palestine" for "State of Palestine", and "Syria" for the "Syrian Arab Republic". Similarly, for convenience, we use the term "country" to refer indiscriminately to the countries or territorial entities of the UN. These two choices are in no way an expression of opinion regarding the legal status of a country, its authorities or the delimitation of its borders.

When the *World Population Prospects* 2022 is not sufficient to study a subject, we use other international data providers to complement it. These are other UN

---

[9] https://population.un.org/wpp/DataSources.

databases (UNdata,[10] International Migrant Stock,[11] World Marriage Data,[12] etc.), and data from other international institutions (International Organization for Migration, WorldPop,[13] etc.), along with international surveys (DHS,[14] MICS,[15] etc.). The additional sources used are always indicated below the figures or in the text.

1.3 Structure of the Book

For a publication that aims to provide a global perspective of the population in the Mediterranean, we felt it was important to start by recalling how this population has been distributed in the area concerned. The second chapter therefore deals with settlement and urbanisation in the Mediterranean.

The third chapter focuses on the age and gender composition of the population, analysing the sex ratio of the population and the age pyramids of the Mediterranean sub-national regions.

The fourth chapter deals with demographic transitions, i.e. the evolution of birth and death rates. It proposes a typology of Mediterranean countries according to several characteristics of the process. It highlights the great diversity of demographic transitions in the Mediterranean.

Secondly, we wanted to take a closer look at each of the phenomena that make up the demographic transition. Thus, the fifth and sixth chapters analyse fertility and the formation and dissolution of unions respectively. The seventh chapter deals with mortality, with the evolution of life expectancy at birth, the decomposition of age-specific mortality, and an overview of the health transition.

The eighth chapter deals with international migration, where the Mediterranean is a migration system, which has undergone major changes since the 1950s.

Finally, the ninth chapter concludes the publication with an analysis of population dynamics, i.e. the evolution of the number of inhabitants in each country, and its components (natural and migration). It will also take UN projections to consider the future distribution of the population around the Mediterranean.

There will be a general summary conclusion, the main objective of which will be to take stock of the analysis of the demography of the Mediterranean countries as a whole and of the question of the convergence of this area over the last 70 years.

---

[10] https://data.un.org/.

[11] https://www.un.org/development/desa/pd/content/international-migrant-stock.

[12] https://population.un.org/MarriageData/Index.html#/home.

[13] https://www.worldpop.org/.

[14] https://dhsprogram.com/.

[15] https://mics.unicef.org/surveys.

References

Albera, D. (2006). Anthropology of the Mediterranean: Between crisis and renewal. *History and Anthropology, 17*, 109–133. https://doi.org/10.1080/02757200600633272

Ambrosetti, E., Strangio, D., & Wihtol de Wenden, C. (Eds.). (2016). *Migration in the Mediterranean: Socio-economic perspectives: Routledge studies in the European economy.* Routledge.

Anastasiou, E., Doignon, Y., Karkanis, D., Léger, J.-F., Parant, A., & Sahraoui, S. E. (2020). *Tendances et perspectives démographiques en Méditerranée.* Les Cahiers du Plan Bleu 21. Plan Bleu. https://planbleu.org/wp-content/uploads/2020/10/PLAN-BLEU-CAHIER-21-Tendances-demographiques-en-Mediterranee.pdf

Attané, I., & Courbage, Y. (2004). *Demography in the Mediterranean region: Situation and projections.* Économica.

Avdeev, A., Eremenko, T., Festy, P., Gaymu, J., Le Bouteillec, N., & Springer, S. (2011). Populations and demographic trends of European countries, 1980–2010. *Population, 66*, 9–133. https://doi.org/10.3917/popu.1101.0009

Blöss-Widmer, I. (2019). Pour une connaissance statistique de la Méditerranée. In T. Blöss & I. Blöss-Widmer (Eds.), *Penser le vieillissement en Méditerranée : données, processus et liens sociaux* (pp. 19–24). L'atelier méditerranéen. Karthala; MMSH.

Bourguet, M.-N., Lepetit, B., Nordman, D., & Sinarellis, M. (Eds.) (1998). *L'invention scientifique de la Méditerranée: Egypte, Morée, Algérie.* Recherches d'histoire et de Sciences Sociales,77. École des Hautes Etudes en Sciences Sociales.

Braudel, F. (1949). *La Méditerranée et le monde méditerranéen à l'époque de Philippe II.* Armand Colin.

Bromberger, C., & Durand, J. -Y. (2001). Faut-il jeter la Méditerranée avec l'eau du bain? In A. Blok, D. Albera, & C. Bromberger (Eds.), *L'anthropologie de la Méditerranée* (pp. 733–756). L'atelier méditerranéen. Maisonneuve et Larose, Maison Méditerranéenne des Sciences de l'Homme. https://www.researchgate.net/publication/32233079_Faut-il_jeter_la_Mediterranee_avec_l%27eau_du_bain

Brunet, R. (1995). Modèles de méditerranées. *L'espace Géographique, 24*, 200–202. https://doi.org/10.3406/spgeo.1995.3389

Carella, M., & Parant, A. (2016). Age-structural transition and demographic windows around the Mediterranean. In R. Pace & R. Ham-Chande (Eds.), *Demographic dividends: Emerging challenges and policy implications* (pp. 83–113). Population Studies. Springer. https://doi.org/10.1007/978-3-319-32709-9

Clément, C. (2002). Une mer des hommes: les limites du monde Mediterranean. In D. Borne & J. Scheibling (Eds.), *La Méditerranée* (pp. 28–48). Carré géographie 8. Hachette.

Courbage, Y. (1997). La démographie en rive sud de la Méditerranée au XXIe siècle: Changement de perspectives. *Espace Populations Sociétés, 1997/1*, 11–26. https://doi.org/10.3406/espos.1997.1786

Courbage, Y. (1999). *New demographic scenarios in the Mediterranean region.* Travaux et documents 142. Institut National d'Etudes Démographiques-Presses Universitaires de France.

Courbage, Y. (2008). Démographie des communautés chrétiennes au Proche-Orient. *Confluences Méditerranée, 66*, 27–44. https://doi.org/10.3917/come.066.0027

Courbage, Y. (2015a). The political dimensions of fertility decrease and family transformation in the Arab context. *DIFI Family Research and Proceedings*, 2015:3. https://doi.org/10.5339/difi.2015.3

D'Addato, A. (2010). Tendances démographiques, développement économique et mobilité des populations en Méditerranée. *Migrations Société, 6*, 13–30. https://doi.org/10.3917/migra.132.0013

Deprest, F. (2002). Notes on the geographic invention of the Mediterranean. *L'espace Géographique, 31*, 73–92. https://doi.org/10.3917/eg.311.0073

Deslondes, O. (2004). Les populations des Balkans depuis 1990: Aspects géographiques de la crise. *Espace Populations Sociétés, 2004/3*, 487–498. https://doi.org/10.4000/eps.336

References

Doignon, Y. (2016). *Le vieillissement démographique en Méditerranée: convergences territoriales et spatiales*. Ph.D. in Geography, Aix-Marseille University. https://tel.archives-ouvertes.fr/tel-01471133/

Doignon, Y. (2019). Transitions démographiques et vieillissements en Méditerranée: le Sud rattrapera-t-il le Nord? In T. Blöss & I. Blöss-Widmer (Eds.), *Penser le vieillissement en Méditerranée : données, processus et lien sociaux* (pp. 151–177). L'atelier méditerranéen. Karthala; MMSH.

Doignon, Y. (2020). Demographic ageing in the Mediterranean: The end of the spatial dichotomy between the shores? *Spatial Demography, 8*, 85–117. https://doi.org/10.1007/s40980-019-00054-2

Doignon, Y., Oliveau, S., & Blöss-Widmer, I. (2016). L'Europe méridionale depuis 20 ans: Dépeuplement, dépopulation et renouveau démographique. *Espace Populations Sociétés, 2015/3-2016/1*, 23. https://doi.org/10.4000/eps.6171

Fargues, P. (1990). Algérie, Maroc, Tunisie: vers la famille restreinte? *Population et Sociétés, 248*. https://www.ined.fr/fichier/s_rubrique/18984/pop_et_soc_francais_248.fr.pdf

Fargues, P. (1995). Les données démographiques de la paix au Proche-Orient. In L. Blin & P. Fargues (Eds.), *L'économie de la paix au Proche-Orient* (pp. 61–90). Maisonneuve et Larose, CEDEJ.

Fargues, P. (2000a). *Générations arabes: l'alchimie du nombre*. Fayard.

Fargues, P. (2000b). La démographie et la Méditerranée ou les faits contre les représentations. In E. Kienle (Ed.), *La reconstruction d'un espace d'échanges: la Méditerranée* (pp. 53–69). CEDEJ—Égypte/Soudan. https://doi.org/10.4000/books.cedej.758

Fargues, P., & Salinari, G. (2011). Flux migratoires et transition démographique. Evolution et scénarios pour l'avenir. In C. Jolly & "Mediterranean 2030" Consortium (Eds.), *Demain, la Méditerranée. Scénarios et projection à 2030* (pp. 71–113). Construire La Méditerranée. IPEMED—Institut de prospective économique du monde méditerranéen.

Herzfeld, M. (1987). *Anthropology through the looking-glass: Critical ethnography in the margins of Europe*. Cambridge University Press.

Horden, P., & Purcell, N. (2000). *The corrupting sea. A study of Mediterranean history*. Blackwell Publishers.

Huebner, S. (2016). A Mediterranean family? A comparative approach to the Ancient World. In S. Huebner & G. Nathan (Eds.), *Mediterranean families in antiquity: Households, extended families, and domestic space* (pp. 3–26). John Wiley & Sons.

Huntington, S. P. (1993). The clash of civilizations? *Foreign Affairs, 72*, 22–49. https://doi.org/10.2307/20045621

Ilbert, R. (2006). Questionner le concept "Méditerranée". Presentation presented at the Ateliers méditerranéens, MMSH. https://cinumed.mmsh.univ-aix.fr/collection/item/96810-questionner-le-concept-mediterranee?offset=2

ITAN. (2015). *Integrated territorial analysis of the neighbourhoods. main report*. European Union. ESPON Programme. https://www.espon.eu/sites/default/files/attachments/02_ITAN-FR-Main_report_FINAL_v15.pdf

Kayser, B. (1996). *Méditerranée. Une géographie de la fracture*. Encyclopédie de La Méditerranée 2. Edisud.

Lacoste, Y. (2001). La Méditerranée. *Hérodote, 103*, 3–39. https://doi.org/10.3917/her.103.0003

Laslett, P. (1983). Family and household as work group and kin group: Areas of traditional Europe compared. In R. Wall, J. Robin, & P. Laslett (Eds.), *Family forms in historic Europe* (pp. 513–563). Cambridge University Press.

Le Bris, A. (2021). Chapitre 5. Enfants nés hors mariage au Maghreb: l'influence du genre sur leurs trajectoires. In M. Jacquemin, M. Pilon, D. Bonnet, C. Deprez, & G. Pison (Eds.), *Être fille ou garçon : Regards croisés sur l'enfance et le genre* (pp. 127–149). Questions de Populations. Ined Éditions.

Lerch, M. (2018). Fertility and union formation during crisis and societal consolidation in the Western Balkans. *Population Studies, 72*, 217–234. https://doi.org/10.1080/00324728.2017.1412492

Matthijs, K., Neels, K., Timmerman, C., & Haers, J. (Ed.) (2016). *Population change in Europe, the Middle-East and North Africa. Beyond the demographic divide*. International population studies. Routledge. https://doi.org/10.4324/9781315601496

Oliveau, S., & Doignon, Y. (2014). Ever closer to the water: Recent developments in Mediterranean settlement patterns. *South-East European Journal of Political Science, II*, 22–30. https://halshs.archives-ouvertes.fr/halshs-01070622

Ouadah-Bedidi, Z., Vallin, J., & Bouchoucha, I. (2012). Unexpected developments in maghrebian fertility. *Population & Societies, 486*. https://doi.org/10.3917/popsoc.486.0001

Péguy, C.-P. (1986). L'univers géographique de Fernand Braudel. *Espaces Temps, 34*, 77–82. https://doi.org/10.3406/espat.1986.3355

Peristiany, J.-G. (1966). *Honour and shame: The values of Mediterranean society*. University of Chicago Press.

Peristiany, J. -G. (Ed.). (1968). *Contributions to Mediterranean sociology: Mediterranean rural communities and social change*. Mouton&Cie.

Peristiany, J.-G. (Ed.). (1976). *Mediterranean family structures*. Cambridge University Press.

Pfirsch, T. (2011). Une géographie de la famille en Europe du Sud. *Cybergeo: European Journal of Geography*. https://doi.org/10.4000/cybergeo.23669

Pina-Cabral, J. de. (1989). The Mediterranean as a category of regional comparison: A critical view. *Current Anthropology, 30*, 399–406. https://www.jstor.org/stable/2743537

Pitt-Rivers, J. (Ed.). (1963). *Mediterranean countrymen. Essays in the social anthropology of the Mediterranean*. Mouton.

Pyramus de Candolle, A. (1820). *Essai élémentaire de géographie botanique*. Imprimerie de F.G. Levrault.

Rashad, H. (2015). Demographic transition in Arab countries: A new perspective. *Journal of the Australian Population Association, 17*, 83–101. https://doi.org/10.1007/BF03029449

Reclus, E. (1876). *La Terre et les Hommes : l'Europe méridionale*. Nouvelle Géographie Universelle Tome 1. Hachette.

Roncayolo, M. (2002). Relire la Méditerranée de Fernand Braudel. In D. Borne & J. Scheibling (Eds.), *La Méditerranée* (pp. 216–231). Carré géographie 8. Hachette.

Sacchi, P., & Viazzo, P. P. (2014). Family and household. In P. Horden & S. Kinoshita (Eds.), *A companion to Mediterranean history* (pp. 234–249). Wiley Blackwell Companions to History. Wiley & Sons. https://doi.org/10.1002/9781118519356

Salvini, M. S. (2023). *Le popolazioni del Mediterraneo. Storia, cultura e demografia*. @racne.

Sardon, J. -P. (2001). Demographic change in the Balkans since the end of the 1980s. *Population, 13*, 49–70. https://www.jstor.org/stable/3030275

Sebti, M., Courbage, Y., Festy, P., & Kurzac-Souali, A.-C. (2009). Maghreb, Morocco, Marrakech: Demographic convergence, socioéconomic diversity. *Population & Societies, 459*. https://www.cairn-int.info/journal-population-and-societies-2009-8-page-1.htm

Smith, R. (1990). Monogamy, landed property and demographic regimes in pre-industrial Europe: Regional contrasts and temporal stabilities. In J. Landers & V. Reynolds (Eds.), *Fertility and resources* (pp. 164–188). Society for the Study of Human Biology Symposium Series 31. Cambridge University Press.

Sorre, M., & Sion, J. (1934). *Géographie Universelle, Tome VII. Méditerranée, péninsules méditerranéennes*. P. V. de la Blache & L. Gallois (Eds.). Armand Colin.

Tabutin, D., & Schoumaker, B. (2005). The demography of the Arab world and the middle East from the 1950s to the 2000s. *Population, 60*, 611–724. https://doi.org/10.3917/popu.505.0611

Tolosana, C. (2001). The ever-changing face of honour. In A. Blok, D. Albera, & C. Bromberger (Eds.), *L'anthropologie de la Méditerranée* (pp. 133–147). L'atelier méditerranéen. Maisonneuve et Larose, Maison Méditerranéenne des Sciences de l'Homme.

Troisi, J., & Von Kondratowitz, H.-J. (Eds.). (2013). *Ageing in the Mediterranean*. Policy Press.

Von Kondratowitz, H.-J. (2013). Squaring the circle: Demographic outlook and social development as determinants of ageing in the Mediterranean. In J. Troisi & H.-J. Von Kondratowitz (Eds.), *Ageing in the Mediterranean* (pp. 3–32). Policy Press.

References

Wihtol de Wenden, C. (2019). Migration flows in the Euro-Mediterranean region: The challenge of migration and asylum crisis in contemporary Europe and the global compact. In F. Francesca, A. Masi, C. Wihtol de Wenden, & D. Strangio (Eds.), *Migrations. Countries of immigrants, countries of migrants. Canada, Italy* (pp. 21–37). Migrazioni/Migrations. Edizioni Nuova Cultura.

Wilson, C. (2001). On the scale of global demographic convergence 1950–2000. *Population and Development Review, 27*, 155–171. https://doi.org/10.1111/j.1728-4457.2001.00155.x

Wilson, C. (2005). Transitions démographiques en Europe et dans le bassin méditerranéen. In P. S. Cassia & T. Fabre (Eds.), *Les défis et les peurs: entre Europe et Méditerranée* (pp. 21–48). Etudes Méditerranéennes. Actes Sud - Maison Méditerranéenne des Sciences de l'Homme.

Wilson, C. (2011). Understanding global demographic convergence since 1950. *Population and Development Review, 37*, 375–388. https://doi.org/10.1111/j.1728-4457.2011.00415.x

Zagaglia, B. (2013). Demographic transitions and social changes in the Mediterranean region. *IEMed Mediterranean yearbook*. European institute of the Mediterranean (IEMed). https://www.iemed.org/wp-content/uploads/2021/04/Anuari-2013-EN.pdf

Open Access This chapter is licensed under the terms of the Creative Commons Attribution 4.0 International License (http://creativecommons.org/licenses/by/4.0/), which permits use, sharing, adaptation, distribution and reproduction in any medium or format, as long as you give appropriate credit to the original author(s) and the source, provide a link to the Creative Commons license and indicate if changes were made.

The images or other third party material in this chapter are included in the chapter's Creative Commons license, unless indicated otherwise in a credit line to the material. If material is not included in the chapter's Creative Commons license and your intended use is not permitted by statutory regulation or exceeds the permitted use, you will need to obtain permission directly from the copyright holder.

Chapter 2
Spatial Distribution of Population and Urbanisation

Abstract Populations are not randomly distributed across the Earth's surface. Some regions are almost empty, while others concentrate with a large proportion of the human population. Analysing the spatial distribution of a population is an exercise involving geography and demography. It takes place on different scales, both global and local, as given the striking uneven distribution of populations in the Mediterranean and all over the world. This chapter will begin by describing the Mediterranean settlement, emphasising the contrasts that exist at different scales, and then identifying regularities and explanatory factors. We will end by looking at the phenomena structuring the contemporary distribution of the population: metropolisation and coastalisation.

Keywords Urbanisation · Settlement · Spatial distribution of the population · Coastline · Mediterranean

2.1 Introduction

Populations are not randomly distributed across the Earth's surface. Some regions are almost empty, while others concentrate with a large proportion of the human population. Analysing the spatial distribution of a population is an exercise involving geography and demography. It takes place on different scales, both global and local, as given the striking uneven distribution of populations in the Mediterranean and all over the world.

These spatial contrasts in population distribution are an important element in the functioning of societies, i.e. in their organisation and their future. While the spatial distribution of a population provides an image of societies at a given time, it is also the result of phenomena that characterise human time: the short-time duration of individuals and generations, population dynamics and the long-term duration of societies. It is also the consequence of populations adapting, more or less, to their environmental constraints (accessibility of places, available resources, quality, etc.), i.e. their capacity to take advantage of the latter to settle and live there.

© The Author(s) 2023
Y. Doignon et al., *Population Dynamics in the Mediterranean*,
SpringerBriefs in Population Studies,
https://doi.org/10.1007/978-3-031-37759-4_2

We will begin by describing the Mediterranean settlement, emphasising the contrasts that exist at different scales, and then identifying regularities and explanatory factors. We will end by looking at the phenomena structuring the contemporary distribution of the population: metropolisation and coastalisation.

2.2 Uneven Distribution of the Population

Spatial distribution of populations is quite heterogeneous throughout the world. Differences according to the chosen scale or the level of observation are always important. To describe this uneven distribution, it is customary to use population density, an interesting indicator since it relates a population to a given area.

The population density in the Mediterranean is 65 hbts/km^2 in 2020, which is slightly higher than at the world level (60 hbts/km^2). However, this average value hides great disparities (Oliveau & Doignon, 2014). There are marked inequalities between the two shores: the Southern Shore is much less populated than the Northern Shore (35 hbts/km^2 and 125 hbts/km^2 respectively), and if we look at the Eastern Shore, the population concentration is similar to that of the Northern Shore (125 hbts/km^2). Two out of three Mediterranean countries have a density between 60 and 130 inhabitants/km^2. However, Libya has only 4 hbts/km^2 and Algeria 15 hbts/km^2, as the extent of the desert regions is considerable in each of these countries. In contrast, the four most densely populated Mediterranean countries in 2020, apart from the city-states[1] (Monaco, Vatican, San Marino), are Israel (400 hbts/km^2), Lebanon (550 hbts/km^2), Palestine (830 hbts/km^2) and Malta (1640 hbts/km^2). This shows the extent to which the Near East, and especially its coastal strip, is one of the world's settlement centres.

If we look at the evolution of population densities since the middle of the twentieth century (Fig. 2.1), we see a general upward trend. The Mediterranean countries have seen their density multiply by an average of 2.5 between 1950 and 2020. The countries on the Northern Shore have generally experienced a weaker evolution: their density has been multiplied by less than 1.8, excluding Kosovo and Albania, where the multiplication coefficient is 2.2 and 2.3 respectively. On the other hand, the densities of the countries on the Southern and Eastern shores have been multiplied by at least 3, sometimes by more than 5 (Egypt, Palestine, Syria, Libya, Israel), and by 25 for Jordan. This sustained evolution is the result of later and faster demographic transitions than on the Northern shore, resulting in high rate of natural change (see Chap. 4). Migration can sometimes accentuate this population growth, as in Israel and Jordan (Chap. 9), but also occasionally, as in Lebanon in 2013–2015 with the arrival of Syrian refugees.

---

[1] In 2020, the population density is 24,780 hbts/km^2 in Monaco, 2,000 hbts/km^2 in the Vatican and 557 hbts/km^2 in San Marino.

2.2 Uneven Distribution of the Population

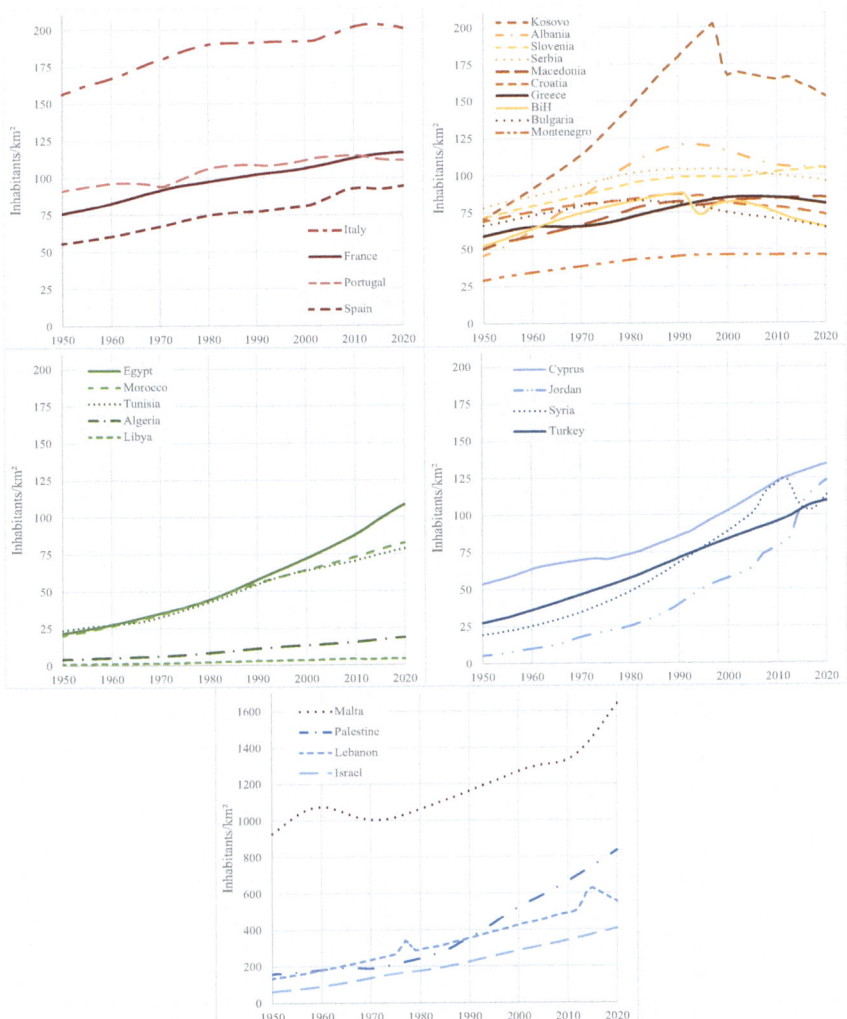

Fig. 2.1 Evolution of the population density in the Mediterranean (1950–2020) (*Source* World Population Prospects 2022. *Note* the most densely populated countries (Israel, Lebanon, Malta, Palestine) are placed in a separate graph so that the evolution of the other countries can be seen more clearly)

Although the general trend over the period 1950–2020 is towards an increase, we nevertheless observe decreases in population density in certain countries, as envisaged 20 years ago by Attané and Courbage (2004). This concerns a large part of the Balkan countries since the 1990s (Albania, Croatia, Serbia), or the 2000s (Bosnia-Herzegovina, Greece). These downward trends are mainly due to a declining demographic regime (Chap. 4). Kosovo and Bulgaria show interesting trajectories. The former saw a sharp drop in population density following the Kosovo war (1998–1999), from 200 hbts/km^2 in 1997 to 170 hbts/km^2 in 2000. The country then experienced significant emigration, leading to a continuous decrease in population density, which reached 150 hbts/km^2 in 2020, the level of the early 1980s. Bulgaria's population density has been decreasing since the early 1980s, and in 2020 it returned to the same level as in 1950, a unique case in the Mediterranean (Doignon, 2023). Very recently, some Southern European countries are starting to see their population density decrease as well, such as Portugal and Italy.

An analysis of population densities at the country level provides a general overview of the situation. Nevertheless, strong disparities in population density are generally visible at the sub-national level. France has an average density of 115 hbts/km^2, but this masks the wide variations that exist: the least dense communes have less than 5 hbts/km^2 and the densest ones exceed 20,000 hbts/km^2. Similarly, a country like Egypt has an average density comparable to France (of 110 inhabitants/km^2), but due to the size of the Saharan regions, it is actually mostly empty. In contrast, the Nile, and more particularly its delta, has very high densities. Rural areas can exceed 1,000 hbts/km^2, which is unusual outside monsoon South and East Asia, and Cairo reaches 40,000 hbts/km^2 (Oliveau et al., 2023).

Thus, the contrasts are reinforced when the Mediterranean settlement is mapped at a finer level (Fig. 2.2). Two main spatial structures can be observed. Firstly, there is the contrast between large, densely populated urban areas and less populated rural areas. This division is clearly visible in Spain with Madrid and Barcelona, in Turkey with Istanbul and Ankara, in Bulgaria with Sofia and in France with Paris. The second spatial structure is the contrast between the coast and inland. Of those living within 200 km of the Mediterranean,[2] about half are less than 50 km away, and 30% less than 10 km. This shows the extent to which the Mediterranean population is concentrated on the coast. On the Southern and Eastern shores, this difference is very marked between the large concentrations of populations on the urbanised coastlines and the much less dense desert inland region. This phenomenon is particularly striking in North Africa (from Morocco to Benghazi in Libya) and in the Near East (from the northern Sinai Peninsula to the Cilicia plain in Turkey). Egypt is a unique case in the Mediterranean. Indeed, unlike other regions, its settlement is not structured by the contrast between the coast and the inland region, but by a general contrast between the Nile and the rest of the country, even if some parts of its coastline are densely populated.

This coastal-inland spatial structure is also visible in Southern Europe, but with a less dense coastal strip. On the other hand, it is hardly found in the Balkans, where the densely populated areas are not located on the coast, but rather in the inland plains or valleys of the mountain ranges.

In general, and for several decades, the inland regions of the various shores of the Mediterranean have been marked by a population decline (Coudert, 2013; Liziard, 2013).

---

[2] Only the population of the countries we have defined as Mediterranean is included in this calculation (see introduction of this book).

2.2 Uneven Distribution of the Population

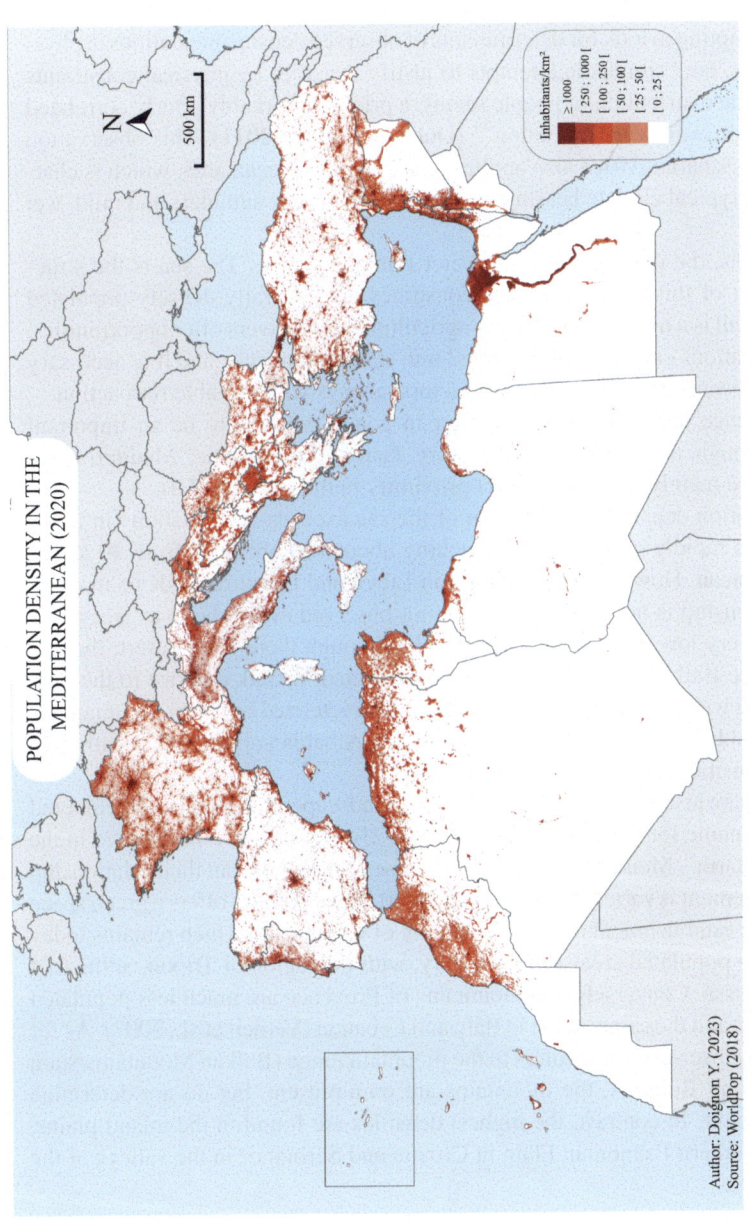

Fig. 2.2 Population density in the Mediterranean (2020) (*Source* WorldPop [2018] [Population Density, Unconstrained UN adjusted,[3] 1 km resolution])

---

[3] Only the population densities of Kosovo are not adjusted by those of the UN. Indeed, WorldPop used the World Population Prospects 2019 data, in which Kosovo's data were still aggregated with Serbia's.

2.3 Far from Determinism: Opportunities and Constraints of Mediterranean Areas

It is always tempting to look for determinants of observed density inequalities in physical conditions, but "simplistic attempts to justify densities by physical constraints have failed. The distribution of people seems, a priori, remarkably poorly correlated with climate, or even with vegetation"[4] (Dubresson et al., 2011). This observation made for Sub-Saharan Africa also applies to the Mediterranean area, which is characterised by a typical climate bearing its name, with hot, dry summers and mild, wet winters.

Nevertheless, the dominant role of water remains visible. The sea is the structuring element of this area, where the coastlines are generally densely populated regions. Rainfall is a major constraint on agriculture, while rivers offer opportunities. However, situations cannot easily be fitted into standard models, and it is necessary to consider the various combinations of factors, always with possible retroaction.

Thus, distance to the sea (and to water in general) seems to be an important element, although not the only explanatory factor. For instance, Mediterranean populations are mainly located in direct proximity to the sea (Fig. 2.3).

The population density within 10 km of the sea exceeds 400 hbts/km^2 in 2020, then decreases rapidly with distance, reaching about 100 hbts/km^2 from 40 km of the Mediterranean. However, the situation in Libya and Egypt reminds us that this general relationship is not so simple and is not observed everywhere, as areas near the sea have very low densities. Further north, although there is no desert, the low densities of the Balkan coast of the Adriatic Sea stand in stark contrast to the high densities of the western coast in Italy. The first is characterised by a very mountainous coastline, notably with the Dinaric Alps. Only the Albanian coastal plain with high population densities seems to be an exception.

Mountains are also part of the Mediterranean landscape. It should be remembered that the Latin name for the Mediterranean, *mare Mediterraneum*, means "sea in the middle of the earth". Mountains are present almost everywhere, but their relationship to human settlement is varied. In the Libyan desert, Jebel Akhdar offers a green space which saw the establishment of the ancient city of Cyrene and which remains today one of the rare populated areas of the country, with the region of Tripoli, at the foot of Jebel Nefoussa. Conversely, the mountains of Provence are much less populated than the plains, and the same is true in Italy and Lebanon (Verdeil et al., 2007). As for the Balkans, whose very name refers to the mountain range (Balkan Mountains/stara planina) crossing Bulgaria, the mountains are omnipresent, but do not determine human settlement. In contrast, the highest densities are found in the inland plains, such as the southern Pannonian Plain in Croatia and Serbia, or in the valleys of the mountain ranges.

---

[4] This text has been translated into English by the authors. The original text in French is as follows: "les tentatives simplistes de justification des densités par des contraintes physiques ont fait long feu. La répartition des hommes paraît, a priori, remarquablement mal corrélée au climat, voire à la végétation".

2.4 A Very Coastal and Increasing Urbanisation

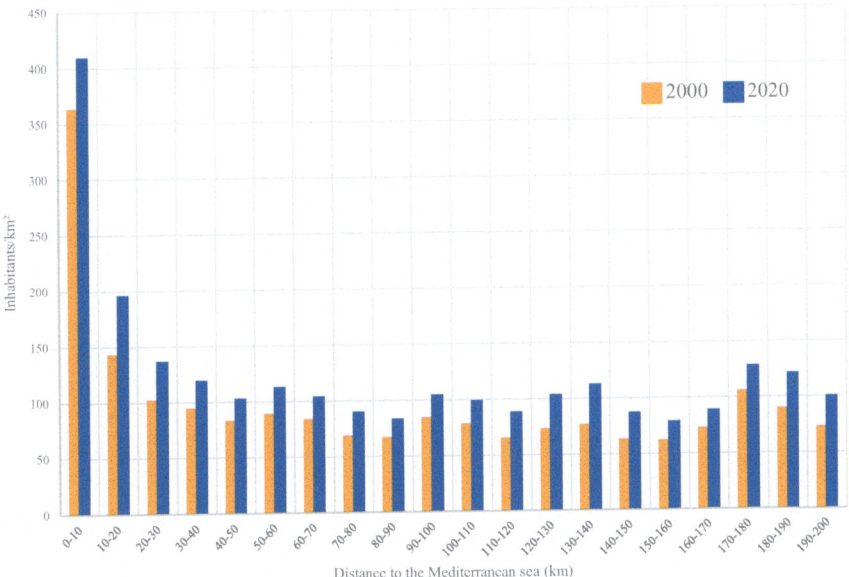

Fig. 2.3 Population density according to distance from the Mediterranean in 2000 and 2020 (*Source* WorldPop [2018] [Population counts, Unconstrained UN adjusted, 1 km resolution])

However, water is the only element that seems to play a dominant role everywhere. The sea coast, as we have already said, but more generally the rivers, strongly structure the Mediterranean settlement, more than any other environmental element. We could take the example of the Nile to convince ourselves of this, as it is the most visible. However, the structuring effects on the settlement of other rivers are just as obvious if we look at the Rhône, the Loire and the Seine (France), the Po and the Tiber (Italy), the Ebro and the Guadalquivir (Spain), the Jordan (Lebanon, Syria, Jordan, Israel, Palestine), the Euphrates and the Khabur (Syria) or the Tigris and the Gediz (Turkey). There are of course exceptions, the low densities of the Rhône Delta in France being a good counter-example to the concentrations observed in the Nile Delta.

2.4 A Very Coastal and Increasing Urbanisation

The Mediterranean is a place of ancient settlement and urbanisation. Mediterranean societies at the beginning of the modern era were characterised in particular by a peasant population settled in villages or small towns rather than in scattered settlements (Huebner, 2016), especially in North Africa (Tabutin et al., 2002). As an area of great circulation, the Mediterranean was very early on woven with cities and ports, the traces of which are still visible today, in a more or less visible way depending

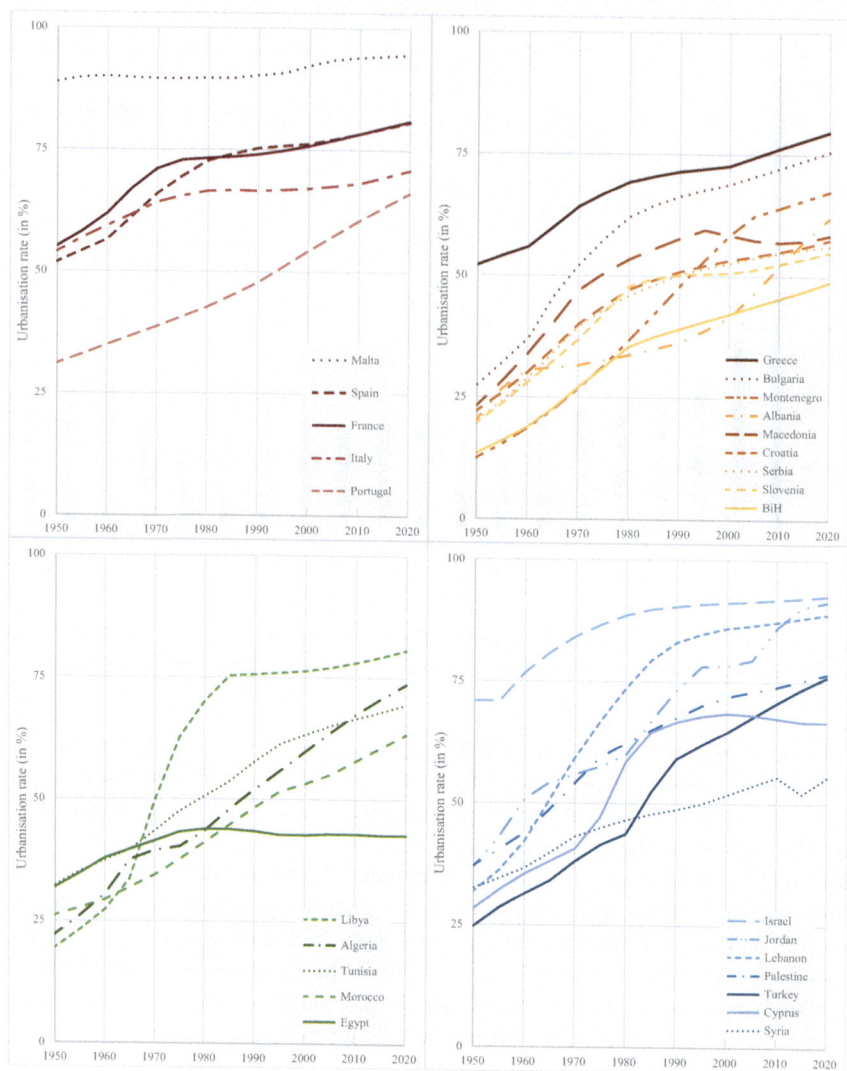

Fig. 2.4 Urbanisation rates in the Mediterranean (1950–2020) (*Source* World Urbanization Prospects 2018)

on the region. Nevertheless, the populations of the countries bordering it were still predominantly rural in the mid twentieth century (Fig. 2.4).

Indeed, 7 out of 10 Mediterranean countries had an urbanisation rate[5] below 50%. As a regional average, 34% of the Mediterranean population lived in a city in 1950. Some countries had very low levels, such as Montenegro, Bosnia-Herzegovina, Libya

---

[5] The urbanisation rate measures the proportion of the population living in cities. When it is below 50%, it means that a majority of the population lives in rural areas.

2.4 A Very Coastal and Increasing Urbanisation

and Slovenia, where less than 20% of the population lived in urban areas. Conversely, 6 countries had a predominantly urban population, mainly in Southern Europe (Spain, Italy, France, Malta), and also in Israel and Greece.

Since 1950, there has been an increase in urbanisation in all countries without exception. In 2020, 70% of the Mediterranean population was urban (regional average). All countries have an urbanisation rate above 50%, with the exception of Egypt (43%). The least urbanised countries are mainly found in the Balkans (Bosnia-Herzegovina, Slovenia, Serbia, Macedonia), and also in Syria. Egypt's trajectory is unique, as its urbanisation rate increases between 1950 and the mid-1970s, and then stagnates until the present day. Other countries have seen their urbanisation rates stagnate, such as Macedonia and Cyprus since the mid-1980s. Malta is the most urbanised country in the Mediterranean, with an urbanisation rate of almost 95% in 2020, and already 90% in 1950.

This general increase in urbanisation indicates a progressive concentration of the population in small areas (cities). In fact, the Mediterranean population is becoming increasingly concentrated in space. As we have already noted, the coastline concentrates populations, but these populations are also attracted to the cities, and the coastal villages are becoming urbanised.

According to the World Urbanization Prospects 2018 data, there were 163 urban agglomerations in the Mediterranean with more than 300,000 inhabitants in 2018 (Fig. 2.5). Of these cities, about 1 in 4 has more than one million inhabitants, and 60% of them are on the Southern and Eastern shores. In addition, there are 3 cities with more than 10 million inhabitants: Cairo (18.8 million), Istanbul (14.1 million), and Paris (10.7 million). The first two are among the 20 largest cities in the world. Since 1950, although almost all the cities in the Mediterranean countries have seen their populations increase, they have done so at different rates. The population growth of the cities on the Northern Shore has generally been more moderate. In fact, 80% of the cities on the Southern and Eastern shores saw their population multiply by at least 5 between 1950 and 2015, while the population of those on the Northern shore multiplied by 2 on average. In some cases, the increase has been particularly significant, such as Antalya (Turkey), which has gone from 27,000 inhabitants to 1.5 million today, a 40-fold increase in population. Amman, the Jordanian capital, has seen its population increase from 100,000 to over 1.7 million (a 20-fold increase). As a result of this very rapid urbanisation on the Southern and Eastern shores, partly due to a rural exodus and demographic transition, the large cities have seen the emergence of slums (Puschmann & Matthijs, 2016). These trends partly explain the significant increase in population density in coastal areas (Fig. 2.3).

The cities of the Mediterranean countries are characterised primarily by their coastal location. Indeed, 25% are located within 5 kms of the Mediterranean Sea, and 50% within 100 kms. Thus, many of the cities with more than one million inhabitants are ports: Barcelona, Marseille, Naples, Athens, Istanbul, Antalya, Izmir, Alexandria, Port Said, Tangiers, Haifa, Beirut, Tripoli, Tunis, Algiers, etc. 8 countries bordering the Mediterranean have a coastal capital, thus underlining the long-standing role of this sea in international trade. Some of these cities are also very old, generally dating back to antiquity, especially in the Middle East (Reba et al., 2018). This is particularly

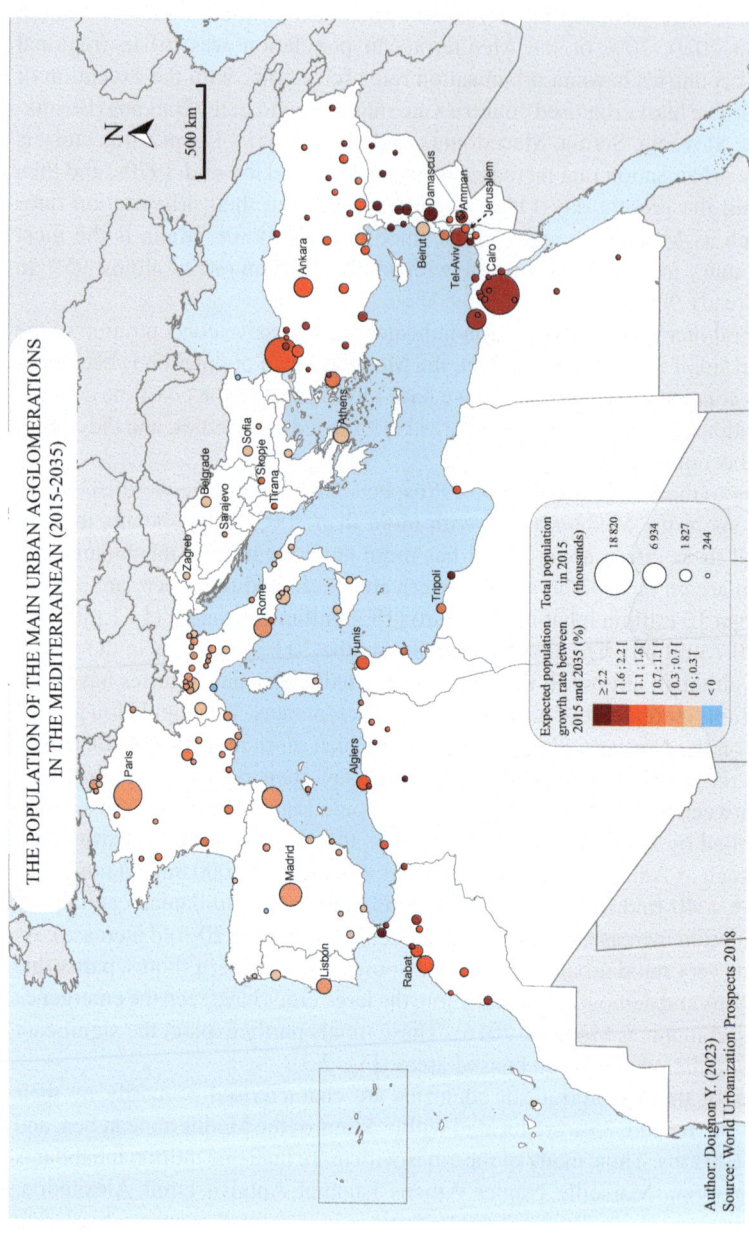

Fig. 2.5 Population of agglomerations with more than 300,000 inhabitants (2015), and projected population change between 2015 and 2035 (*Source* World Urbanization Prospects 2018)

evident between Istanbul and Alexandria, where there are many agglomerations with more than 300,000 inhabitants. The specific situation of the Balkans, where, with the exception of Greece, none of the countries has a coastal capital and where there are few large cities, should be recalled here.

Today, the settlement pattern is changing, and these cities are mainly taking advantage of longstanding benefits which they are converting to maintain their regional primacy. Urban settlement is spreading inland and the coastal location often becomes an asset for tourism or quality of life, rather than a necessity for the industrial or agricultural economy. From urbanisation, which concentrated inhabitants in cities, we have moved on to metropolisation, which agglomerates them in vast spaces comprising the central city, its suburbs and its outskirts sometimes over great distances. In France, for example, the urban fabric is now almost continuous along the Mediterranean coast and sometimes penetrates up to 50 km inland (Aix-Marseille metropolis). The same phenomenon can be observed in Spain, and to a lesser extent in many other countries, such as Libya, where the Tripoli conurbation now stretches almost 150 km from west to east (Moriconi-Ebrard & Pascal, 2020).

Tourism plays an important role in these settlement developments in several countries. In Western Europe, the shores of the Mediterranean attract a population of seasonal tourists, and also migrants who come to enjoy the living environment for their retirement (Doignon et al., 2017). In addition to these populations, there are also migrant populations who come to work from within the country or from abroad. These different populations can sometimes have a significant impact on the settlement. This is particularly the case in Spain, where the flow of retired foreign residents and the flow of workers to the Mediterranean coasts make it possible to maintain population growth in these regions (Oliveau et al., 2019).

Projections from the World Urbanization Prospects 2018 envisage that this urbanisation trend will continue to 2035, reinforcing both the urbanisation of all countries and the littoralisation of their population. For instance, the urbanisation rate in Mediterranean countries is expected to reach 80% by 2050. The population of agglomerations with more than 300,000 inhabitants in 2018 is expected to continue growing until 2035. This growth will again be greater in the cities of the Southern and Eastern shores, but at a lower rate than between 1950 and 2015 (Fig. 2.5).

2.5 Settlement Challenges in the Mediterranean

To conclude this chapter, we now turn to the settlement challenges that Mediterranean areas will face in the coming decades. Although the Mediterranean population is very heterogeneous and it is difficult to characterise it by a single trait, the populations share a common sea, a typical climate and fragile natural environments.

Although the degree to which the coasts are inhabited by humans is heterogeneous, the high level of coastal population poses real problems of pollution. The Mediterranean is one of the most polluted seas in the world, especially with plastics (Alessi & Di Carlo, 2018). Pollution of maritime waters is a real issue, too often left to the goodwill of States. This is significantly exacerbated by the poor management of waste generated by mass tourism, and the ever-increasing concentration of the population on the coastline. Pollution of maritime waters is also dependent on pollution, particularly industrial pollution, carried by the large rivers that flow into the Mediterranean, as is the case with the heavy metals discharged by the Rhône or the nitrates transported from agricultural areas. These various forms of pollution threaten one of the Mediterranean's major reservoirs of marine and coastal biodiversity.

Human pressure on the coasts is already very strong and is expected to increase, accentuating the constraints on nature and the human beings that occupy it. In the summer of 2021, fires were exceptionally widespread along the entire Mediterranean coastline (in Italy, Greece, Algeria, Turkey and the Balkans). Fires are one of the major threats facing the Mediterranean, as are tensions over water resources, coastal flooding, etc. Human pressure is therefore felt not only by nature, but by the settlement itself. It is true that climate change increase (also of human origin) is an aggravating factor; however it is primarily the presence of humans that is to blame. These fires are perhaps only the most dramatic part of the effects of climate change. Floods and flash floods are also increasing, due to the combined effect of land artificialisation on the one hand, and changes in rainfall patterns on the other.

Ultimately, the current settlement of the Mediterranean raises the question of its effects on ecosystems. Natural hazards are a real problem for societies (Laria, 2008). They will be accentuated by the densification of the population, the significant littoralisation of the population, urbanisation and climate change. The question is therefore that of the sustainability of the settlement in these conditions, and of the adaptation of societies, since the changes brought about will be inevitable (Borderon, 2023).

References

Alessi, E., & Di Carlo, G. (2018). *Pollution plastique en Méditerranée. Sortons du piège!* WWF. https://www.wwf.fr/sites/default/files/doc-2018-06/180608_rapport_plastiques_mediterranee.pdf

Attané, I., & Courbage, Y. (2004). *Demography in the Mediterranean region: Situation and projections*. Économica.

Borderon, M. (2023). Migrations, changements environnementaux et climatiques. In Y. Doignon & S. Oliveau (Eds.), *Dynamique du peuplement mondial. Comment la population habite le monde*. Encyclopédie Des Sciences. ISTE Editions.

Coudert, E. (2013). Une approche régionale de la population et de l'urbanisation en Méditerranée, rétrospective et projections à 2025. In J.-P. Carrière (Ed.), *Villes et projets urbains en Méditerranée* (pp. 21–31). Perspectives Villes et Territoires. Presses universitaires François-Rabelais.

Doignon, Y. (2023). Dépeuplement et dépopulation dans un monde en croissance. In Y. Doignon & S. Oliveau (Eds.), *Dynamique du peuplement mondial. Comment la population habite le monde*. Encyclopédie Des Sciences. ISTE Editions.

Doignon, Y., Blöss-Widmer, I., & Oliveau, S. (2017). Half a century of ageing in France: Dynamics and specificities of the Mediterranean coastline. In T. Blöss (Ed.), *Ageing, lifestyles and economic crises: The new people of the Mediterranean* (pp. 82–100). Routledge Studies in the European Economy. Routledge, Taylor & Francis Group.

References

Dubresson, A., Moreau, S., Raison, J.-P., & Steck, J.-F. (2011). *L'Afrique subsaharienne: Une géographie du changement* (3rd ed.). Armand Colin.

Huebner, S. (2016). A Mediterranean family? A comparative approach to the ancient World. In S. Huebner & G. Nathan (Eds.), *Mediterranean families in antiquity: Households, extended families, and domestic space* (pp. 3–26). John Wiley & Sons.

Laria, S. (2008). L'avenir en Méditerranée se jouera dans les villes. *Annales Des Mines - Responsabilité Et Environnement, 49*, 56–61. https://doi.org/10.3917/re.049.0056

Liziard, S. (2013). *Littoralisation de la façade nord-méditerranéenne: analyse spatiale et prospective dans le contexte du changement climatique*. Ph.D. Thesis in Geography, Nice, Nice Sophia Antipolis University. https://tel.archives-ouvertes.fr/tel-00927492/document

Moriconi-Ebrard, F., & Pascal, R. (2020). Peuplement et urbanisation de la Libye: construction d'une information cartographique. *Géoconfluences*. http://geoconfluences.ens-lyon.fr/informations-scientifiques/dossiers-regionaux/la-mediterranee-une-geographie-paradoxale/articles-scientifiques/demographie-libye

Oliveau, S., & Doignon, Y. (2014). Ever closer to the water: Recent developments in Mediterranean settlement patterns. *South-East European Journal of Political Science, II*, 22–30. https://halshs.archives-ouvertes.fr/halshs-01070622

Oliveau, S., Larue, Q., Doignon, Y., & Blöss-Widmer, I. (2019). Mapping foreign nationals in Spain: An exploratory approach at local level. *Genus, 75*, 5. https://doi.org/10.1186/s41118-018-0047-5

Oliveau, S., Doignon, Y., & Blöss-Widmer, I. (2023). Population distribution: Follow the Nile. In H. Bayoumi & K. Bennafla (Eds.), *An atlas of contemporary Egypt* (pp. 56–57). CNRS éditions. https://books.openedition.org/editionscnrs/58390

Puschmann, P., & Matthijs, K. (2016). The demographic transition in the Arab world: The dual role of marriage in family dynamics and population growth. In K. Matthijs, K. Neels, C. Timmerman, J. Haers, & S. Mels (Eds.), *Population change in Europe, the Middle-East and North Africa: Beyond the demographic divide* (pp. 119–165). International Population Studies. Routledge, Taylor & Francis Group. https://doi.org/10.4324/9781315601496

Reba, M., Reitsma, F., & Seto, K. C. (2018). *Historical urban population: 3700 BC-AD 2000*. NASA Socioeconomic Data and Applications Center (SEDAC). https://doi.org/10.7927/H4Z G6QBX

Tabutin, D., Vilquin, E., & Biraben, J.-N. (2002). *L'histoire de la population de l'Afrique du Nord pendant le deuxième millénaire*. Document de Travail 15. Centre de recherche en démographie.

Verdeil, E., Faour, G., & Velut, S. (2007). Population et peuplement. In *Atlas du Liban: Territoires et société* (pp. 64–90). Contemporain Co-Éditions. Presses de l'Ifpo, CNRS Liban. https://books.openedition.org/ifpo/402?lang=en

WorldPop. (2018). WorldPop (School of Geography and Environmental Science, University of Southampton; Department of Geography and Geosciences, University of Louisville; Departement de Geographie, Universite de Namur) and Center for International Earth Science Information Network (CIESIN), Columbia University. Global high resolution population denominators project—Funded by the Bill and Melinda Gates Foundation (OPP1134076). https://www.worldpop.org/

World Population Prospects. (2022). United Nations, Department of Economic and Social Affairs, Population Division. https://population.un.org/wpp/

World Urbanization Prospects. (2018). United Nations, Department of Economic and Social Affairs, Population Division. https://population.un.org/wup/

Open Access This chapter is licensed under the terms of the Creative Commons Attribution 4.0 International License (http://creativecommons.org/licenses/by/4.0/), which permits use, sharing, adaptation, distribution and reproduction in any medium or format, as long as you give appropriate credit to the original author(s) and the source, provide a link to the Creative Commons license and indicate if changes were made.

The images or other third party material in this chapter are included in the chapter's Creative Commons license, unless indicated otherwise in a credit line to the material. If material is not included in the chapter's Creative Commons license and your intended use is not permitted by statutory regulation or exceeds the permitted use, you will need to obtain permission directly from the copyright holder.

Chapter 3
Sex Ratio, Age Structure and Population Ageing

Abstract It is vital to examine the population composition, i.e. how the population being studied is structured. In demography, to understand the phenomena studied (firstly, births and deaths), it is common practice to examine the number of women in relation to the number of men and to distinguish the distribution of individuals by age. The most common representation of this gender and age composition is the "age pyramid". It is important to know the age and gender composition, as this largely determines a population's demographic dynamics. Elements relating to gender and age composition will enable better understanding of the dynamics outlined in the following chapters. In this chapter therefore, we will present the composition of the Mediterranean population from the perspective of sex ratios on the one hand, and the age distribution of populations on the other. We will also consider the implications of differences between countries at the sub-national level.

Keywords Age pyramid · Population ageing · Gender inequalities · Sex ratio · Mediterranean

3.1 Introduction

While studying the spatial distribution of a population is an important aspect to understanding it (see Chap. 2), it is also vital to examine its composition, i.e. how the population being studied is structured. There are several indicators to describe a population's composition. In demography, to understand the phenomena studied (firstly, births and deaths), it is common practice to examine the number of women in relation to the number of men and to distinguish the distribution of individuals by age. The most common representation of this gender and age composition is the "age pyramid".

It is important to know the age and gender composition, as this largely determines a population's demographic dynamics. For example, the birth rate is firstly the result of the number of women of childbearing age (between puberty and menopause), and secondly the intensity of fertility by age group (Chap. 5 examines to aspects of differentials fertility). Elements relating to gender and age composition will enable better understanding of the dynamics outlined in the following chapters. The birth rate, as we have said, but also mortality (Chap. 7), migration (Chap. 8) and population dynamics (Chap. 9).

In this chapter therefore, we will present the composition of the Mediterranean population from the perspective of sex ratios on the one hand, and the age distribution of populations on the other. We will also consider the implications of differences between countries at the sub-national level.

3.2 Gender Inequalities in the Mediterranean

The human species is characterised by an almost equal numerical balance between the sexes. On average, 105 boys are born for every 100 girls, but as the mortality rate for boys is slightly higher than for girls, the ratio between the two sexes reaches an equilibrium around the age of 20 and is maintained today until the age of 60. Secondly, the gap tends to widen between men who die earlier on average, and women (Chap. 7). Obviously, these orders of magnitude vary from one society to another, and have evolved over time. These inequalities in mortality can be explained by natural differences, but also by differences in personal behaviour and social constraints.

The male/female ratio, also known as the sex ratio, is the consequence of biological constants that cannot be explained, but also of differentiated cultural practices. Thus, in some countries there are imbalances in the sex ratio from birth. India and China are regularly cited in this regard, with a sex ratio that favours girls (Guilmoto & Oliveau, 2007). Around the Mediterranean, most countries have sex ratios at birth that follow the norm of 105 boys per 100 girls. In the 1970s and 1980s, excess female mortality was present in some countries on the Southern and Eastern shores (Locoh & Ouadah-Bedidi, 2014; Tabutin & Schoumaker, 2005), but this is no longer visible today (according to the *World Population Prospects* 2022 data at least). However, other countries did show sex ratio imbalances at birth: Albania, Montenegro, and Macedonia. All three countries show an unbalanced sex ratio at birth, indicating strong discrimination against girls (Fig. 3.1).[1]

These imbalances were particularly high in the past, and are now decreasing. Albania, for example, saw the sex ratio imbalance worsen in the mid-1990s, peaking at 113 boys for every 100 girls in the mid-1980s, and declining steadily since. The trends are different for these three countries, but they have all at some point had a sex ratio at birth that has exceeded 108 in the last 30 years. In 2020, they reached a level of around 107, higher than that observed in Southern Europe or the European Union.

This preference for boys is complex to explain, as it is based on cultural practices and lineage structures that are not explicit and are generally unconscious. Discriminatory practice, while there is no doubt, is not being claimed here. Nevertheless, for

---

[1] For at the sub-national level analysis of the sex ratio in former Yugoslavia, see Buisson (2016).

3.2 Gender Inequalities in the Mediterranean

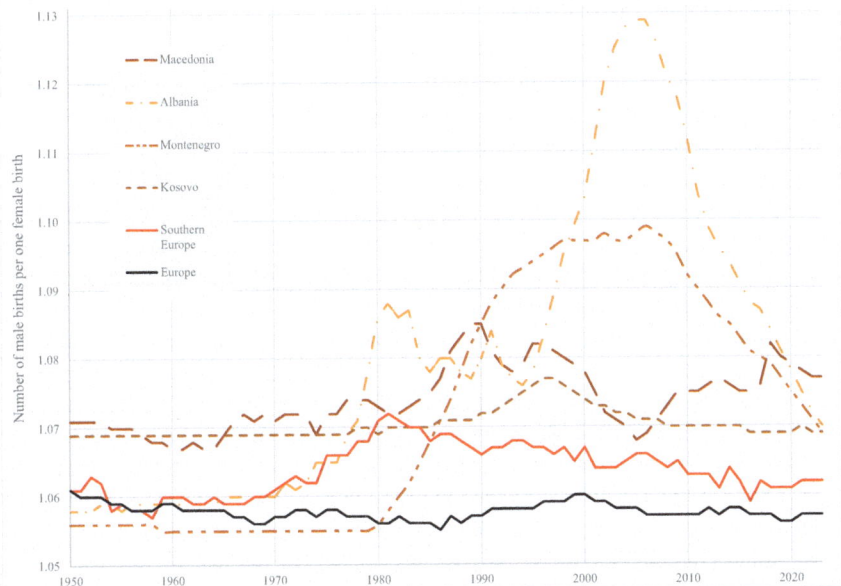

Fig. 3.1 Evolution of the sex ratio at birth in select South European countries (*Source* World Population Prospects 2022)

the preference for boys to be expressed by the disappearance of girls, there would have to be legal and medical contexts that allow for it. Thus, the development of ultrasound scans and abortion facilitated the use of prenatal selection. The development of these practices from the 1990s onwards is, for instance, visible in regions with a large Albanian population (Guilmoto & Duthé, 2013).

Nevertheless, traces of discrimination at birth may be erased over time in the composition of the general population, through a higher mortality of boys and then men, or through sex-differentiated migration, which can ultimately change the overall sex ratio. From this perspective, international migration can severely impact the overall sex ratio. This is the case for Albanian men who leave their country in greater numbers than women, thus rebalancing the overall sex ratio.

Finally, in general, men's mortality is higher than women's, and even more so at older ages (Chap. 7). As a result, countries with ageing populations generally have a sex ratio in favour of women. Delbès et al. (2006) summed it up well about Europe when they wrote that "women grow old alone, but men grow old with a partner".

3.3 An Ageing Population

Looking at a population in terms of its age structure enables understanding of the demographic potential in terms of replacement level, ageing, development opportunities, etc. The determinants of age structure are both the births and deaths rates (which are themselves the result of a cross between the fertility/age-specific mortality rates and the structure of the population by age and sex), and the effect of inward and outward migration. In 1950, the Mediterranean's age pyramid had a broad base and a rather thin top, which is a sign of a high average birth rate and an even higher mortality rate at advanced ages (Fig. 3.2).

The higher the birth rate, the greater the number of young people and the wider the base of the pyramid. This initially creates needs (in terms of educational infrastructure in particular), but also rapidly opportunities (through the influx of workers into the labour market). In 2020, the Mediterranean pyramid evolved. Its base was narrower, with a lower weight of young people in the population. In addition, there are more age groups above 30 than in 1950, and the top of the pyramid is much fuller. The weight of older people has increased, and the population has aged, generating many socio-demographic challenges (Blöss, 2018). This change in the age pyramid between 1950 and 2020 is the result of the demographic transition (Chap. 4), with a sharp drop in fertility, which fell below the generation replacement level in several countries (Chap. 5), a significant drop in mortality and improved survival to old age (Chap. 7).

In societies in transition from a demographic regime of high births and high deaths to a demographic regime of low births and low deaths (Chap. 4), there comes a time when there are still few old people and few young people. This leaves plenty of room

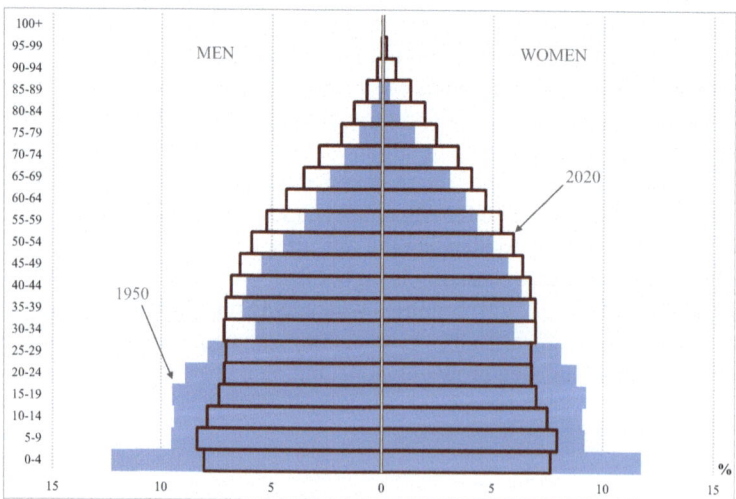

Fig. 3.2 Age pyramid of the Mediterranean in 1950 and 2020 (*Source* World Population Prospects 2022)

for people of working age, creating what is known as a demographic window of opportunity for the economy: the number of working people is greater than the number of people who depend on them (children and the elderly). A summary measure of this situation is the "dependency ratio", which relates the population aged under 20 and those aged 65 or over to the population aged 20–64. If the ratio is above 100, then there are more inactive than active people, and if it is below 100, then the number of active people is higher than the number of inactive people, suggesting a greater possibility of productivity in society.

This dependency ratio in the Mediterranean decreases significantly between 1950 and 2020, from 105 to less than 75 (Fig. 3.3). This decrease indicates a lower amount of young and old people in the population. This trend is primarily related to the falling birth rate (Chap. 4), which narrows the base of the pyramid. As the number of young people decreases, the dependency ratio decreases. However, there has been a recent increase in the dependency ratio in Balkan countries, Southern European countries and also in Israel. This is due to the ageing of the population, where more people are surviving into old age, increasing the amount of the elderly in the population. Countries on the Southern and Eastern shores retain higher dependency ratios than countries on the Northern Shore (Ambrosetti, 2020), particularly in the Near East, which is mainly due to a higher birth rate and thus a higher presence of children in the population. Two countries stand out due to their ratio trajectories. First of all, Israel has maintained a high ratio (>80%) since 1950, combining an improvement in the longevity of its elderly with a relatively high fertility rate. The second country is France, whose ratio is currently the highest on the Northern shore, due to a combination of a birth rate that has not fallen to the same extent as elsewhere in Europe, immigration that provides a steady supply of workers, and an ageing population.

3.4 Ongoing Significant Differences in Age Structure Between Regions

Looking at ratios at the country level is interesting and already shows remarkable differences. It is nevertheless more pertinent to approach the subject at a finer level in order to offer a more precise understanding of the age composition of the Mediterranean area. We have therefore constructed age pyramids at a sub-national level for each country that is as comparable as possible from one country to another in terms of average area (Doignon, 2020; Doignon & Oliveau, 2015). In order to allow for cartographic analyses, we have established a typology for age pyramids, which consists of 7 profiles (from the youngest to the oldest) and uses a hierarchical ascending classification (Fig. 3.4).[2]

The first profile type is an age pyramid with a very broad base and a narrow top. It represents a very young population, with a high birth rate (characteristic of a fairly

---

[2] The period represented is 2010–2015 due to data availability.

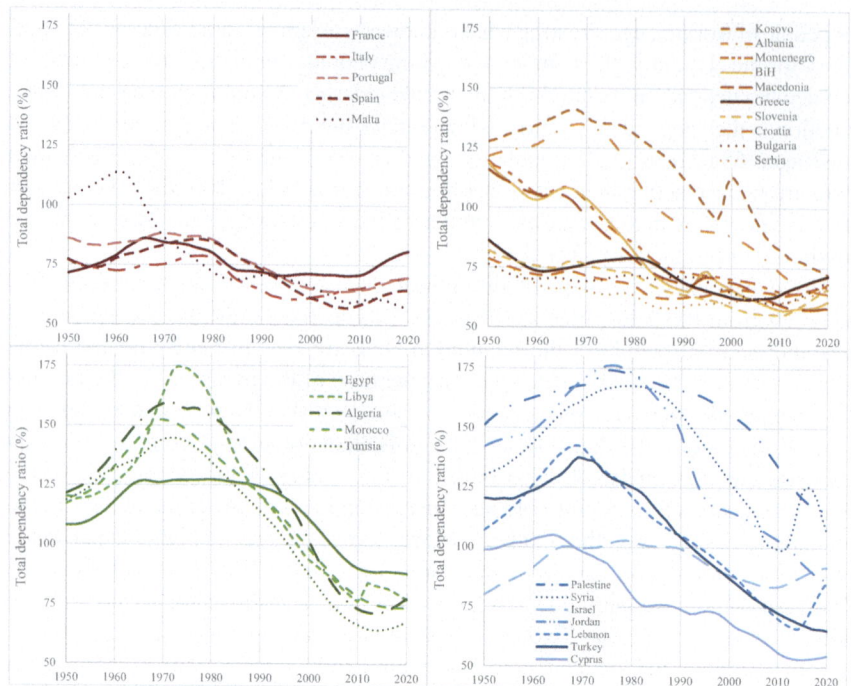

Fig. 3.3 Total dependency ratio in the Mediterranean (1950–2021). (*Source* World Population Prospects 2022. *Note* The total dependency ratio is the ratio of population aged 0–19 and 65 + per 100 population aged 20–64)

high fertility rate), and a low proportion of elderly people (on average less than 3% of the population is aged 65 or over). It includes part of the Nile Valley in Egypt, Palestine, Jordan, Syria, and also Turkish Kurdistan (with a higher fertility than the rest of the country) and some Saharan regions of Algeria.

The second type corresponds to a situation where the birth rate has started to decline, but is still high. People aged 65 and over still represent only 4.2% of the population. This type of age pyramid is essentially found in much of the Maghreb, and in the Nile delta in Egypt.

The third type is very similar to the second, but with the base of the pyramid showing the beginning of a recovery, indicating that a decline in fertility is taking place over time. It represents the situation in Libya, southern Morocco, the urban regions of the Maghreb (Casablanca, Rabat, Agadir, Oran, Algiers, Tunis, etc.), a large part of Tunisia, and Turkey, in the regions of Istanbul and Ankara, and on its southern border.

The fourth type represents the average characteristics of the Mediterranean area. The base of the pyramid is slightly sunken, indicating rather low fertility, and the top is fuller than the previous types. The share of elderly people in the population is about 9%. This type is found on all shores of the Mediterranean. It is characteristic

3.4 Ongoing Significant Differences in Age Structure Between Regions

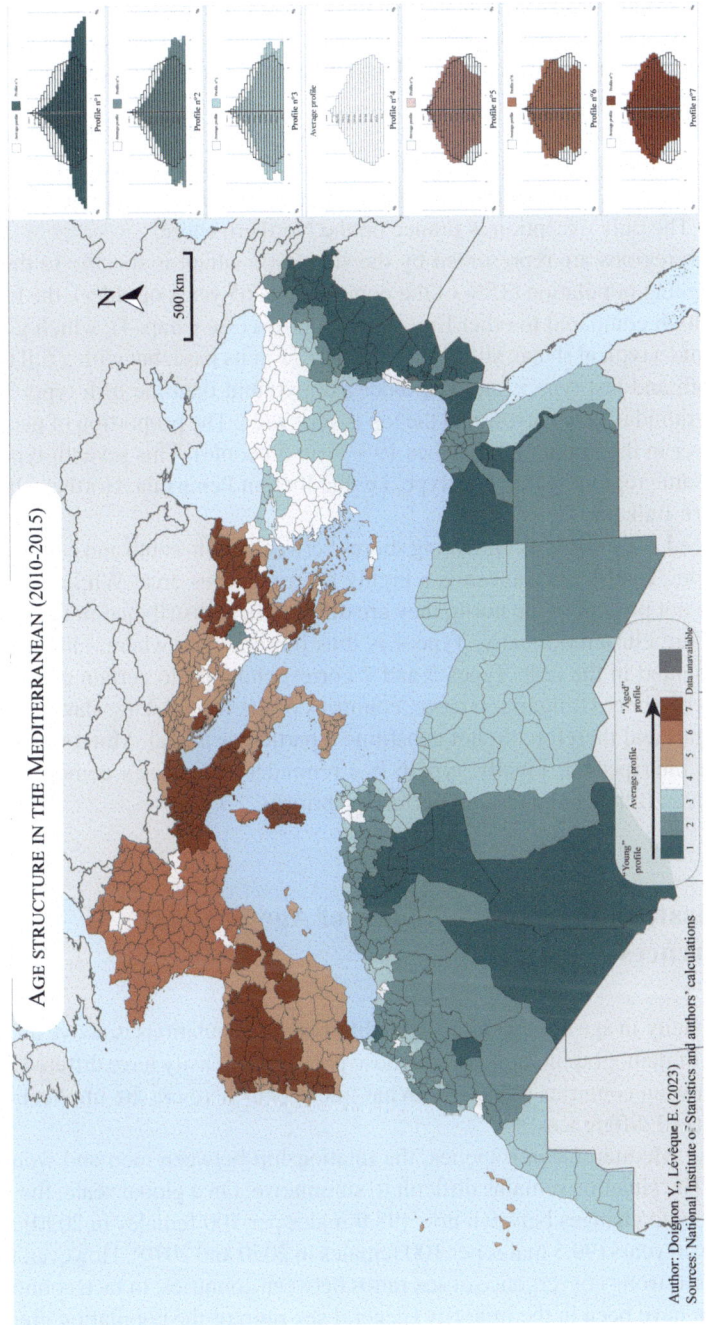

Fig. 3.4 Age structure in the Mediterranean (2010–15) (*Source* National Institutes of Statistics and authors' calculations)

of Albania, Montenegro, Macedonia, Lebanon and Cyprus, along with a large part of Turkey and certain localised rural areas of the Maghreb. Finally, some large urban centres have this profile, such as Paris, Lyon and Toulouse in France (as well as the departments bordering Switzerland, which attract many young workers), and Tel Aviv and Haifa in Israel.

The fifth type embodies European ageing, with a rather low birth rate. People aged 65 or over represent almost 15% of the population. This pattern is found in the Iberian Peninsula, southern Italy, and much of the Balkans, almost equal to the seventh type. The only exception is France on the Northern shore.

The French regions are represented by the sixth type which is specific to them. Despite the ageing population (15% of the population is 65 years or older), the birth rate remains high compared to other European countries (see Chap. 4), which gives the age pyramid a typical shape, still somewhat narrow at its base, but with a full top.

The seventh and last type is an even older age pyramid than the fifth type. The base of the pyramid is very narrow and the top is very wide. The proportion of people aged 65 or over in the population reaches 19% (1 in 5 people). This seventh type is found in the same regions as the fifth type, i.e. the Iberian Peninsula, Northern Italy and the eastern Balkans.

As evidenced, the model of contrasting shores between north, south and east needs to be rethought. The Mediterranean is a highly heterogeneous area. While profiles 1, 2 and 3 are not present in the north, they are differentially distributed in the south and east and are clustered locally. Type 4 is thus present everywhere, although it is over-represented in the east. Types 5 and 7 correspond only to certain countries on the Northern Shore (Bulgaria, Greece, countries of the former Yugoslavia, Italy, Spain, Portugal) and therefore do not constitute a particular model. Moreover, type 4 regions are interspersed. Finally, type 6 is a reminder of France's demographic uniqueness, even if the country is not perfectly uniform.

3.5 Implications and Consequences of Age Structure Differences

This heterogeneity in age composition of Mediterranean populations is above all the consequence of demographic transitions whose pace and intensity have differed and still differ between countries (Chap. 4). What interests us here are the implications of these observed differences.

Throughout Mediterranean societies, the relationship between men and women will change. The situation remains difficult to summarise. On a global scale, the sex ratio is unlikely to changes between now (98.9 males per 100 females in 2020) and the next 30 to 50 years (99.5 males per 100 females in 2050 and 2070). However, this stability hides a strong convergence of sex ratios between countries. In fact, countries where women have been in the minority (general sex ratio of the population greater than 100) are trending towards a better balance between the sexes. In fact, while in

1950 there were only 6 countries with a sex ratio greater than 105, in 2020 there was only 3 and in 50 years-time there will likely only be 2. At the same time, countries where women were in the majority (overall sex ratio of the population below 100) are also trending have been towards 100. 11 countries had a sex ratio below 95 in 1950 and 6 countries in 2020. However, in 50 years, only France is predicted to have a sex ratio below this value. The French case is once again different from the Mediterranean model, as its sex ratio will be even lower than 90! With this exception, the projections show a strong convergence of sex ratios towards a better numerical gender balance in all societies.

The reduction in the labour force could also lead to a greater demand for female labour, which, together with better education, could lead women to renegotiate their place, even within societies that some believe are still stuck in fairly traditional patriarchal forms of organisation.

References

Ambrosetti, E. (2020). Demographic challenges in the Mediterranean. *IEMed Mediterranean yearbook 2020*. European Institute of the Mediterranean (IEMed). https://www.iemed.org/wp-content/uploads/2021/01/Demographic-Challenges-in-the-Mediterranean.pdf

Blöss, T., (ed.) (2018). *Ageing, lifestyles and economic crises: The new people of the Mediterranean*. Routledge Studies in the European Economy. Routledge, Taylor & Francis.

Buisson, I. (2016). *Déséquilibre de sexes et conflits: une étude du territoire yougoslave entre 1981 et 2011*. Master's Thesis in Geography, Aix-en-Provence, Aix-Marseille University. https://dumas.ccsd.cnrs.fr/DEMOMED/dumas-01383003v1

Delbès, C., Gaymu, J., & Springer, S. (2006). Women grow old alone, but men grow old with a partner. A European Overview. *Population & Societies, 419*. https://doi.org/10.3917/popsoc.419.0001

Doignon, Y. (2020). Demographic ageing in the Mediterranean: The end of the spatial dichotomy between the shores? *Spatial Demography, 8*, 85–117. https://doi.org/10.1007/s40980-019-00054-2

Doignon, Y., & Oliveau, S. (2015). Territorial grids in the Mediterranean: Space versus population. *Bollettino dell'Associazione Italiana di Cartografia, 154*, 46–63. https://doi.org/10.13137/2282-472X/11827

Guilmoto, C. Z., & Duthé, G. (2013). Masculinization of births in Eastern Europe. *Population & Societies, 506*. https://doi.org/10.3917/popsoc.506.0001

Guilmoto, C. Z., & Oliveau, S. (2007). Sex ratio imbalances among children at micro-level: China and India compared. In *Population Association of America 2007*. http://paa2007.princeton.edu/papers/71096

Locoh, T., & Ouadah-Bedidi, Z. (2014). *Familles et rapports de genre au Maghreb, Evolutions ou révolutions*. Document de travail 213. Institut National d'Etudes Démographiques. https://www.ined.fr/fichier/s_rubrique/22779/document.travail.2014.213.magreb.genre.fr.pdf

Tabutin, D., & Schoumaker, B. (2005). The demography of the Arab world and the Middle East from the 1950s to the (2000s). *Population, 60*, 611–724. https://doi.org/10.3917/popu.505.0611

World Population Prospects. (2022). United Nations, Department of Economic and Social Affairs, Population Division. https://population.un.org/wpp/

Open Access This chapter is licensed under the terms of the Creative Commons Attribution 4.0 International License (http://creativecommons.org/licenses/by/4.0/), which permits use, sharing, adaptation, distribution and reproduction in any medium or format, as long as you give appropriate credit to the original author(s) and the source, provide a link to the Creative Commons license and indicate if changes were made.

The images or other third party material in this chapter are included in the chapter's Creative Commons license, unless indicated otherwise in a credit line to the material. If material is not included in the chapter's Creative Commons license and your intended use is not permitted by statutory regulation or exceeds the permitted use, you will need to obtain permission directly from the copyright holder.

Chapter 4
The Various of Demographic Transitions

Abstract Since the eighteenth century, and at different periods, the world's populations have been undergoing, or have undergone, a process of demographic transition. The Mediterranean countries present a great diversity of demographic transitions in terms of timing, pace, intensity, etc. The aim of this chapter is to take stock of demographic transitions in the Mediterranean by identifying the different types of demographic transition that have occurred since 1950. This typology makes it possible to place the national demographic transitions within a general model, while also highlighting the contrasting situations that exist in the Mediterranean.

Keywords Demographic transition · Demographic counter-transitions · Birth rate · Mortality rate · Natural change of population · Convergence · Mediterranean

4.1 Introduction

Since the eighteenth century, and at different periods, the world's populations have been undergoing, or have undergone, a process of demographic transition.[1] The Mediterranean countries present a great diversity of demographic transitions in terms of timing, pace, intensity, etc. (Doignon, 2020). The aim of this chapter is to take stock of demographic transitions in the Mediterranean by identifying the different types of demographic transition that have occurred since 1950. This typology makes it possible to place the national demographic transitions within a general model

---

[1] See Box 4.1 for an overview of the demographic transition.

© The Author(s) 2023
Y. Doignon et al., *Population Dynamics in the Mediterranean*,
SpringerBriefs in Population Studies,
https://doi.org/10.1007/978-3-031-37759-4_4

(Box 4.1), while also highlighting the contrasting situations that exist in the Mediterranean. Using data from the UN's *World Population Prospects, 2022*, we will construct a classification of demographic transitions according to four criteria:

- The status of the demographic transition in 1950, to indicate whether the transition has already begun, what step it is at, or whether it is already complete (pseudo-equilibrium[2] of mortality and fertility) (Fig. 4.1).
- The status of the demographic transition in the most recent period (2015–2019[3]).
- The type of post-transitional regime reached at the end of the transition: a zero natural change, a positive natural change or a negative natural change.
- The levels of mortality, birth rate and natural change.

By combining these four criteria, we will obtain 10 types of demographic transition, which we will then group into 6 broad types: demographic transitions that conform to the theoretical model (types 1, 2 and 3), transitions leading to a post-transitional regime of decline (types 4 and 5), the specific transition of Israel whose post-transitional regime retains strong population growth (type 6), recent and rapid transitions (types 7 and 8), cases of a sustained rise in birth rate (type 9), and recent and slow transitions (type 10).

> **Box 4.1: The demographic transition model**
>
> Demographic transition is the passage between two different demographic regimes, called "pre-transitional regime" and "post-transitional regime", corresponding to the demographic regimes in force before and after the transition respectively (Chesnais, 1992). This transition is usually formalised by a four-step process (Fig. 4.1).

---

[2] By pseudo-equilibrium we mean a situation where there are fluctuations in the mortality and birth rates, but where the overall trend is balanced.

[3] The graphs in this chapter will represent the period 1950–2022. However, the typology did not take into account the 2020–2022 period to avoid bias from cyclically differentiated effect of the Covid-19 pandemic.

4.1 Introduction

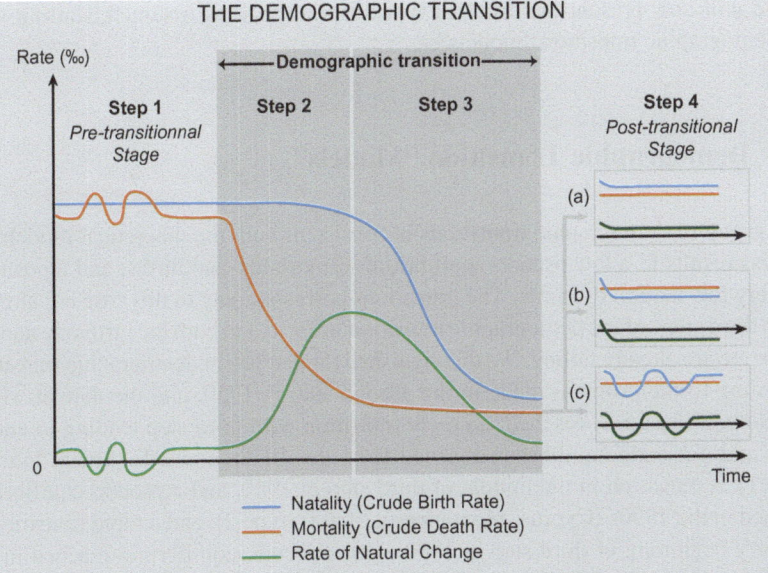

Fig. 4.1 Descriptive model of demographic transition (Figure created by Doignon Y.)

The first step is the pre-transitional regime, i.e. a demographic pseudo-equilibrium over the long term, resulting from a high birth rate (measured by the Crude Birth Rate[4] (CBR)) and a high death rate (measured by the Crude Death Rate[5] (CDR)). The second step is a reduction in mortality. This phase is initiated when a decline in mortality begins while the birth rate remains high. During this step, the natural balance (measured by the Rate of Natural Change (RNC[6])) increases. The third step is a decline in the birth rate. It begins when the birth rate starts to fall. The natural balance then also decreases. The second and third steps constitute a period of strong demographic imbalance caused by the difference in timing between the decrease in mortality and the decrease in birth rate. The last step, the post-transitional demographic regime, is characterised by a low birth rate, low mortality and consequently a low natural balance.

Through the specific characteristics of each transition, this descriptive model makes it possible to identify different forms of demographic transitions. We can observe variations in the duration of the transition as a function of the time lag between the two declines and their pace, original phasing, such as a birth rate that decreases before mortality, or different types of post-transitional regime. In this respect, three types of post-transitional regimes can be distinguished according to the RNC: a surplus regime (regime a in Fig. 4.1), a deficit regime (regime b) and a balanced regime (regime c). As this is a model, not all populations have the same demographic transition, but they all experience a convergence of their mortality and fertility towards lower levels than in the pre-transitional regime.

We will now present the different types of the typology obtained, starting with the demographic transition "models".

4.2 Demographic Transition "Models"

This group of demographic transitions is consistent with the theoretical model: the process results in a low pseudo-equilibrium of mortality and births, and a positive, but very low natural dynamic. The transitions corresponding to this case are already in the third step[7] of the demographic transition in 1950, i.e. both the birth rate and the death rate are already falling. We distinguished three types of demographic transition according to the progress made in the second step in 1950, and the date at which pseudo-equilibrium is reached: an early transition with third step tending to end in 1950 and a pseudo-equilibrium reached from the 1970s onwards (Spain, France) (type 1); a transition in the middle of third step in 1950, and a pseudo-equilibrium reached in the 1990s (Cyprus, Montenegro, Malta) (type 2); and a rapid transition at the very beginning of third step in 1950, with a pseudo-equilibrium reached in the middle of the 2000s (Macedonia, Albania, Kosovo) (type 3).

4.2.1 Type 1: Ancient Transition with Pseudo-Equilibrium in the 1970s (Spain, France)

This type is characterised by a demographic transition that is almost completed by 1950: mortality and birth rates are balanced, and the RNC is already around 10%. In 1950, the transition was clearly at the end of the third step of the process. A low pseudo-equilibrium has been observed since the mid-1970s for France and since the beginning of the 1990s for Spain (Fig. 4.2). The RNC tends to become very low. It has even become negative very recently in Spain. If the trend were to continue in the future, this country would have to be classified in another category of the typology, as the low pseudo-equilibrium would then be negative.

---

[4] The Crude Birth Rate (CBR) is calculated by dividing the number of live births in a year by the average population in that year.

[5] The Crude Death Rate (CDR) is calculated by dividing the number of deaths in a year by the average population in that year.

[6] The Rate of Natural Change (RNC) is calculated by subtracting the CDR from the CBR. For ease of reading, we use the annotations "CBR, "CDR" and "RNC" in this chapter instead of "Crude Birth Rate", "Crude Death Rate" and "Rate of Natural Change" respectively.

[7] In this chapter, the word "step" refers to the different stages of the demographic transition outlined in Fig. 4.1.

4.2 Demographic Transition "Models"

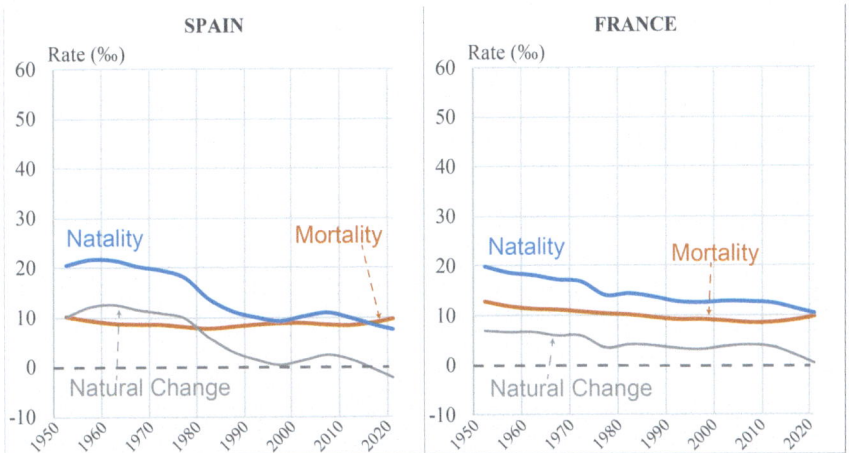

Fig. 4.2 Demographic transition in Spain and France (1950–2022) (*Source* World Population Prospects [2022] Calculations made by the authors. *Note* The time units used are five-year periods)

4.2.2 Type 2: Transition with Pseudo-Equilibrium in the Late 1990s (Cyprus, Montenegro, Malta)

In 1950, countries experiencing this type of transition were in the middle of the third step, with a relatively high CBR ($\approx$ 30‰) and a balanced mortality around 10‰ (Fig. 4.3). The RNC became quasi-stable and weak starting at the end of the 1990s: the process ends later than the previous type.

4.2.3 Type 3: Rapid Transition with Late Pseudo-Equilibrium from the 2000s Onwards (Macedonia, Albania, Kosovo)

In 1950, this type of transition occurred at the end of second step (Albania) or at the beginning of third step (Macedonia) (Fig. 4.4). This is a demographic transition that is in line with the theoretical model, one that is also occurring rapidly. The decline in mortality reached a pseudo-equilibrium in the late 1970s. The birth rate has been rapidly converging to very low rates ($\approx$ 10‰ in 2015–2019), The pseudo-equilibrium of these countries has been achieved late, from the 2000s onwards, except for Kosovo where the CBR has continued to decrease since the 2010s.

Out of 26 countries, 8 have experienced a transition in line with theoretical model. The other 18 countries have thus shown different transitions. We will begin with those with a post-transitional decline regime.

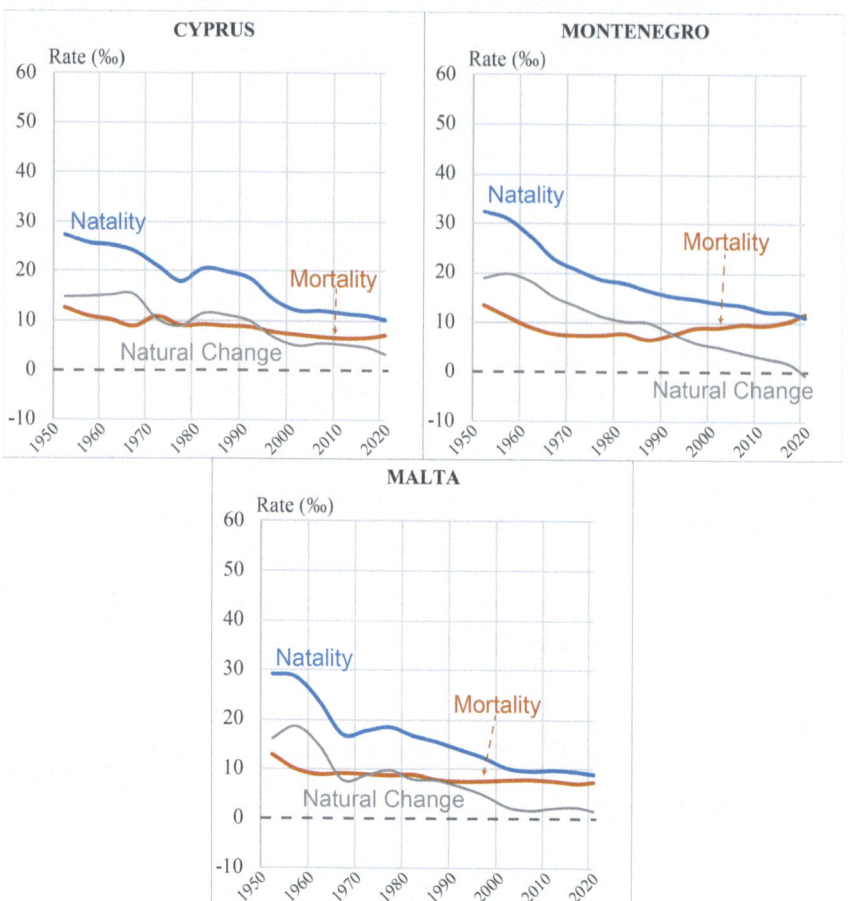

Fig. 4.3 Demographic transition of Cyprus, Montenegro, Malta (1950–2022) (*Source* World Population Prospects [2022] Calculations made by the authors. *Note* The time units used are five-year periods)

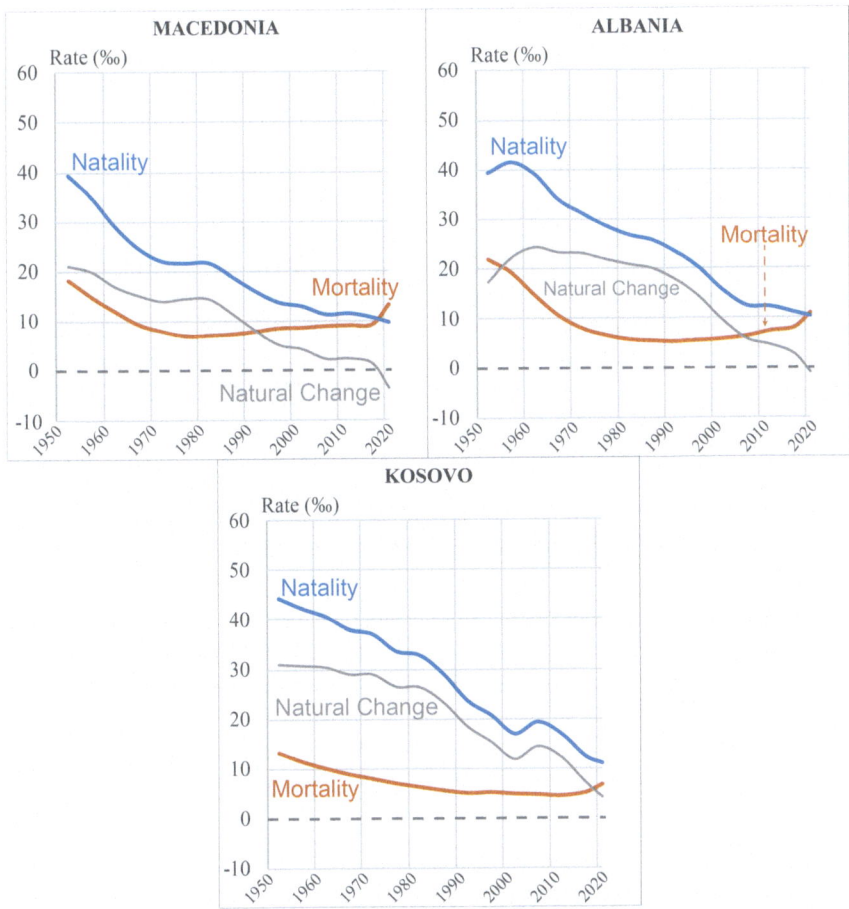

Fig. 4.4 Demographic transition in Macedonia, Albania and Kosovo (1950–2022) (*Source* World Population Prospects [2022] Calculations made by the authors. *Note* The time units used are five-year periods)

4.3 Completed Demographic Transition with a Post-Transitional Decline Regime

This group of transitions is distinguished from the previous one by a post-transitional demographic regime of slight decline, i.e. one with a slightly negative natural balance (number of deaths exceeding the number of births). We differentiate two types of transition: those occurring early, at the end of third step in 1950 with a pseudo-equilibrium reached in the 1980s–1990s (Italy, Portugal, Greece, Slovenia, Croatia, Bulgaria) (**type 4**); and those occurring later, in the middle of third step in 1950 and reaching a pseudo-equilibrium only in the 2000s (Serbia, Bosnia-Herzegovina) (**type 5**).

4.3.1 Type 4: Transition with Pseudo-Equilibrium in the 1980s–1990s (Italy, Portugal, Greece, Slovenia, Croatia, Bulgaria)

In 1950, demographic transitions of this type occurred at the end of third: mortality stabilised at 10% and fertility at around 20% (Fig. 4.5). Over the 1950–2019 period, the CBR gradually decreased to reach the CDR in the 1990s (1980s for Italy and Bulgaria), resulting in a near-zero RNC. Thereafter, the CDR exceeded the CBR, and the RNC became negative. In 2019, the demographic regime of these countries corresponds to Adolphe Landry's "contemporary regime" (1934) or Frank Notestein's "incipient decline" (1945), i.e. regimes characterised by a negative natural balance (regime b in Fig. 4.1).

4.3.2 Type 5: Transition with Pseudo-Equilibrium in the 2000s (Serbia, Bosnia-Herzegovina)

Such demographic transitions were in the middle of third step in 1950, with a still relatively high CBR (28–38‰). The inversion of the CDR and CBR and their pseudo-equilibrium can be observed in the 2000s (Fig. 4.6). These transitions differ from those of the previous type in two respects: a post-transitional regime of decline reached somewhat later, and a generally lower RNC. The temporary increase in the CDR in Bosnia-Herzegovina in the 1990s was due to the war in Yugoslavia.

4.4 Completed Demographic Transition with a Post-Transitional Regime with Sustained Population Growth (Type 6: Israel)

Israel's demographic transition is very specific. In 1950, the country was at the very end of third step, i.e. mortality was already low and the birth rate was about to stabilise (Fig. 4.7). The transition ended with an early pseudo-equilibrium in the early 1960s. However, the birth rate has been balanced at above 20% for 30 years now; mortality has also been stable at around 6% throughout this period. The post-transitional demographic regime is thus balanced, but with a high RNC (15–20%). This sustained birth rate is often explained by the implications of the Israeli-Palestinian conflict on the demographic patterns of these two territorial entities. Indeed, the preoccupation with being in the majority numerically has led to a "cradle war"[8] between the two populations. Youssef Courbage (2008) describes the very high fertility (more than 7

---

[8] This text has been translated into English by the authors. The original text in French is as follows: "guerre des berceaux".

4.4 Completed Demographic Transition with a Post-Transitional Regime …

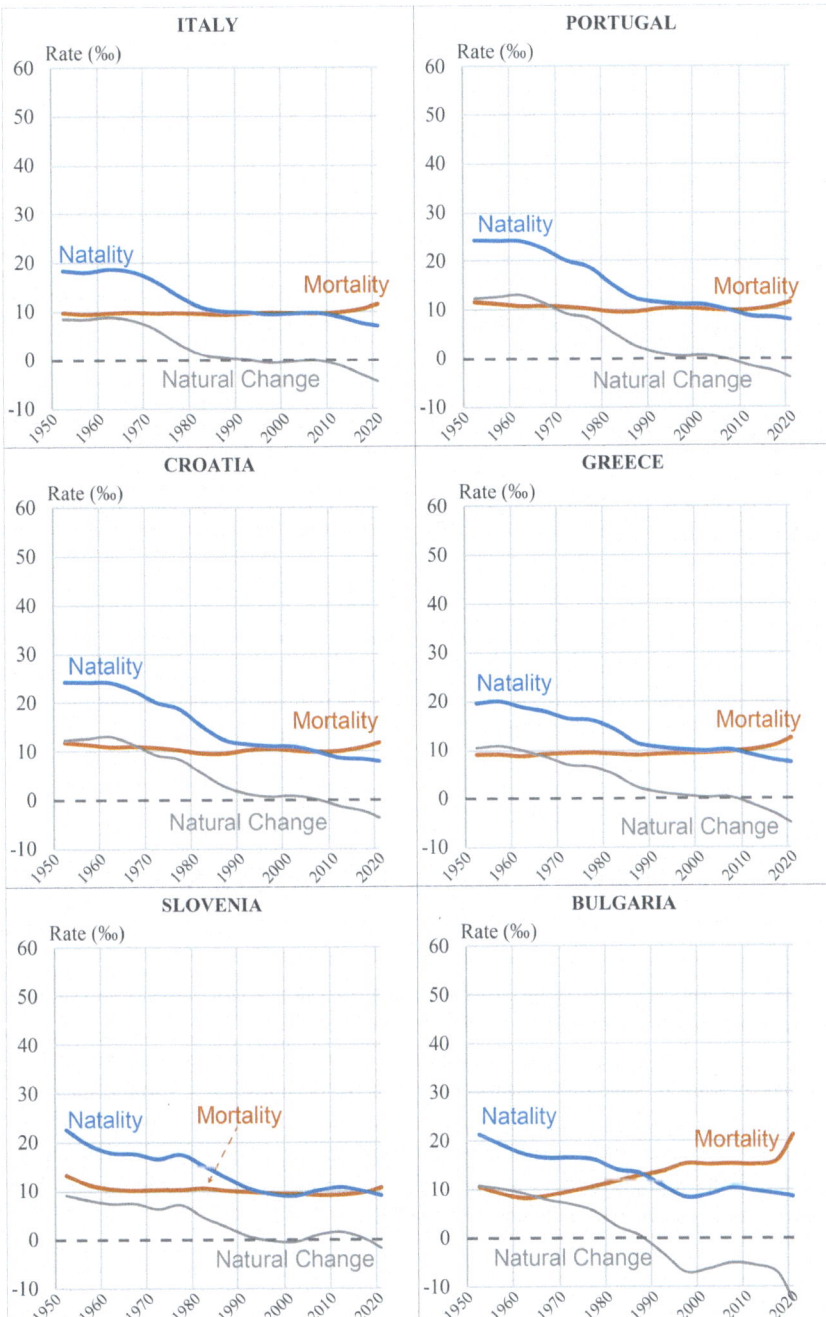

Fig. 4.5 Demographic transition in Italy, Portugal, Greece, Slovenia, Croatia and Bulgaria (1950–2022) (*Source* World Population Prospects [2022] Calculations made by the authors. *Note* The time units used are five-year periods)

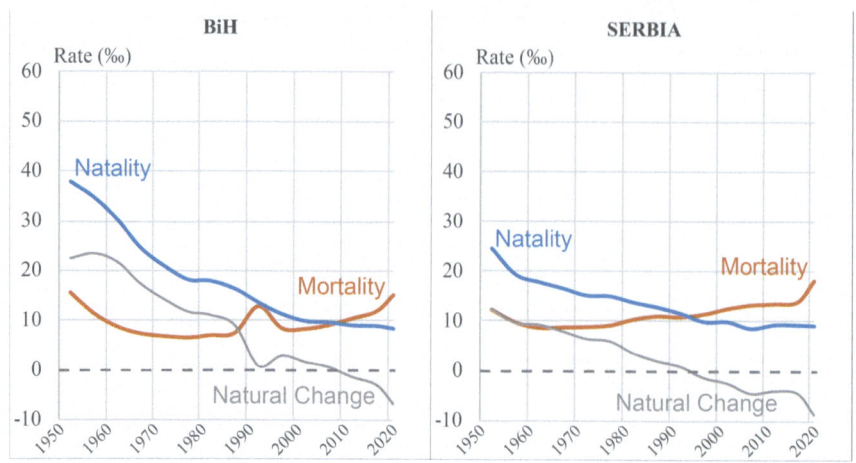

Fig. 4.6 Demographic transition in Serbia, Bosnia-Herzegovina (1950–2022) (*Source* World Population Prospects [2022] Calculations made by the authors. *Note* The time units used are five-year periods)

children per woman in the 2000s) of ultra-Orthodox Jews and religious nationalists as "combat fertility".[9] Palestinians also engaged in "militant natalism"[10] (more than 8 children per woman in the mid-1980s), during which time Yasser Arafat is said to have advocated that each family should have 12 children, 2 for the couple and 10 for the cause (Courbage, 2006).

4.5 Recent and Rapid Demographic Transition, Now Being Finalised

This group brings together demographic transitions that have started late but have been occurring at a faster pace than the European transitions. They are also currently being finalised. However, their post-transitional demographic regime could be characterised by a more sustained natural dynamic (RNC above 10%) than that of the Northern shore countries, whose RNC is below 5%. Among this group, we distinguish transitions according to timeframe: transitional processes with declines in the CBR and CDR already underway in 1950 (Lebanon, Turkey) (**type 7**) and later transitions (Libya, Morocco, Tunisia) (**type 8**).

---

[9] This text has been translated into English by the authors. The original text in French is as follows: "fécondité de combat".

[10] This text has been translated into English by the authors. The original text in French is as follows: "natalisme militant".

4.5 Recent and Rapid Demographic Transition, Now Being Finalised 53

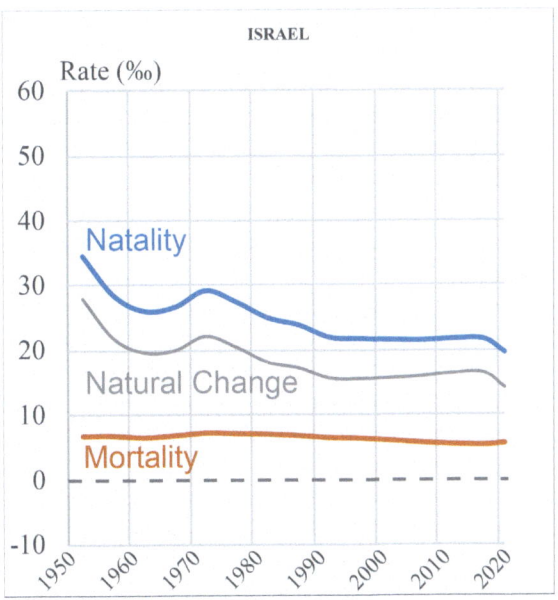

Fig. 4.7 Demographic transition in Israel (1950–2022) (*Source* World Population Prospects [2022] Calculations made by the authors. *Note* The time units used are five-year periods)

4.5.1 Type 7: Transition Already Underway in 1950 (Lebanon, Turkey)

In 1950, the demographic transition of these countries was at the beginning of third step, i.e. both births and deaths had started to decline (Fig. 4.8).

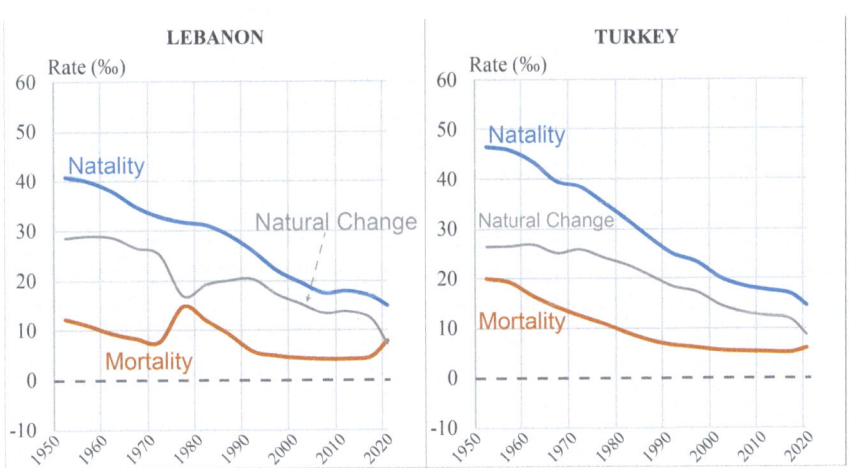

Fig. 4.8 Demographic transition in Lebanon and Turkey (1950–2022) (*Source* World Population Prospects [2022] Calculations made by the authors. *Note* The time units used are five-year periods)

The CBR however still remains high. The CDR balances out at around 4–5‰ in the 1990s in Lebanon,[11] and in the 2000s in Turkey. The rate of decline in the CBR has been slowing down since the 2000s, and seems to be levelling off in Lebanon, as in Turkey despite a downward trend. The demographic transition thus appears to be in the process of being finalised. On the other hand, the RNC is close to 10%, i.e. a higher level than in the Northern shore countries. The next 10–20 years will certainly reveal whether the post-transitional demographic regime of these countries will have almost no or low natural dynamics (like type 1 countries) or will be more sustained.

Note that the current level of mortality in these two countries ($\approx$ 4–5%) is lower than that of the countries on the Northern shore, whose CDR is generally above 8%. This may seem counter-intuitive, but it is not. This difference should not be interpreted as better sanitary conditions in Lebanon and Turkey compared to the countries on the Northern shore. This is because the CDR (and CBR) do not take into account the age structure of the population. These two indicators reflect both the health conditions and fertility of the populations, but also the age structure of countries. Thus, under equal health conditions, fewer deaths will occur in a younger population than in an older population. The fact that the countries on the Southern and Eastern shores are on average younger than those on the Northern shore partly explains their lower CDR.

4.5.2 Type 8: More Recent Transition (Libya, Morocco, Tunisia)

These are demographic transitions that have occurred relatively late. In 1950, the process seems to be in the middle of second step, i.e. the decline in mortality has started, but not yet for the birth rate (Fig. 4.9).

Libya is unique in that it is the only Mediterranean country where virtually all the step of the demographic transition can be observed over the period 1950–2019. The decline in the birth rate began in the 1960s, thus later than in most Mediterranean countries. The decline in the CBR was very rapid, from almost 50% to 20% in about 30 years in Tunisia and Libya, and in 45 years in Morocco. In the 2000s, the birth rate stabilised at around 20%, a level higher than those of the Northern shore countries. A pseudo-equilibrium of mortality and birth rate seems to have been found, and one could conclude that the transition was over. However, the birth rate has resumed its decline since the 2010s for all three countries, and it is difficult to say what kind of post-transitional demographic regime these countries are heading towards.

---

[11] The increase in the CDR in Lebanon in the mid-1970s was due to the war (1975–1982).

4.5 Recent and Rapid Demographic Transition, Now Being Finalised

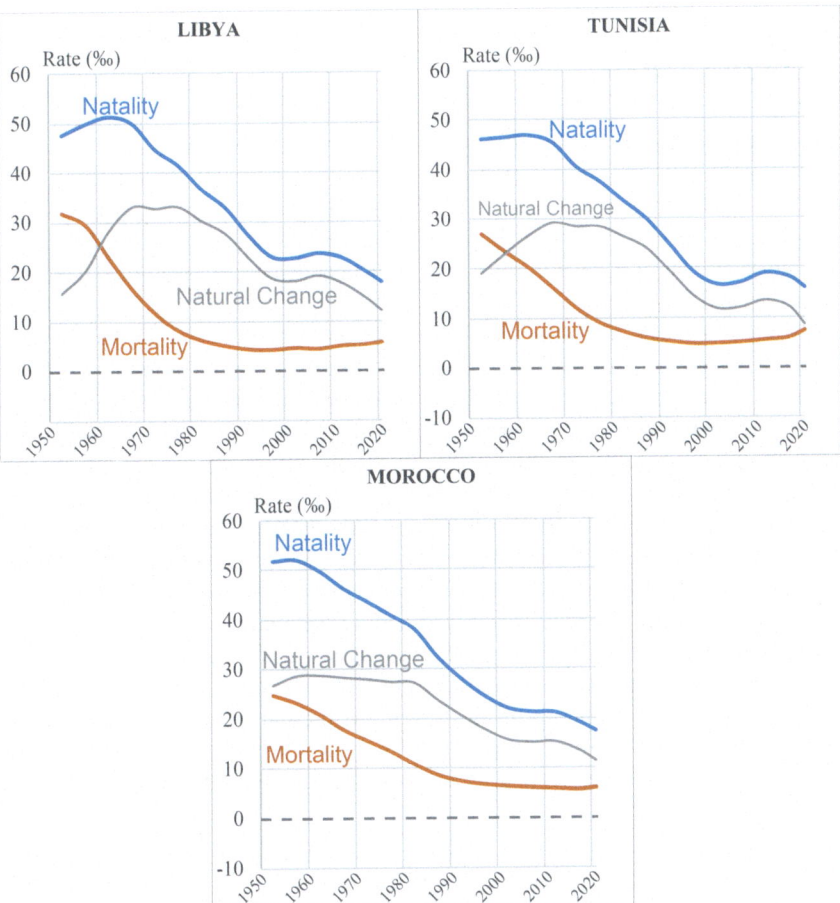

Fig. 4.9 Demographic transition in Libya, Morocco and Tunisia (1950–2022) (*Source* World Population Prospects [2022] Calculations made by the authors. *Note* The time units used are five-year periods)

Indeed, the RNC in the 2000s was quite high (between 10 and 20%), but it has been continuously decreasing to now around 10%.

4.6 Possible Demographic Counter-Transitions (Type 9: Egypt, Algeria)

This type of demographic transition is an exceptional case which, like the previous one, is found only in North Africa. Like the countries of type 8, the transition was late, since 1950 the transition was at the beginning of third step (Egypt) or in the middle of second step (Algeria) (Fig. 4.10). The demographic transition of Egypt and Algeria are singular, but currently share a sustained natural dynamic, as the RNC remains around 20‰.

Egypt is considered a "demographic exception" (Ambrosetti, 2011). The process seems rather slow and hesitant in the sense that the decline in the birth rate has been disjointed. The demographic transition was interrupted between 1970 and 1985, during which time the CBR even increased, before picking up again in the late 1980s (Doignon et al., 2021). By the end of the 1990s, the CBR stabilised at a high rate ($\approx$ 25‰) before increasing again from the late 2000s (Al Zalak & Goujon, 2017; Goujon & Al Zalak, 2018). During this period, the CDR remained at a low level. Between 1995 and 2010, a pseudo-equilibrium was reached for mortality and birth rates. This would seem to be a pause in the downward movement of the birth rate, and not a post-transitional equilibrium with a more sustained natural dynamic, since the birth rate had been falling again since the beginning of the 2010s.

Algeria shows a later, but less hesitant and more rapid decline in the birth rate. The CBR started to fall sharply in the 1970s. At present, there is no equilibrium in the birth rate, unlike for the death rate. The CBR reached the 20‰ threshold in 2000–2005, but then increases to 25‰ in 2010–2015, only to decrease again since the late 2010s.

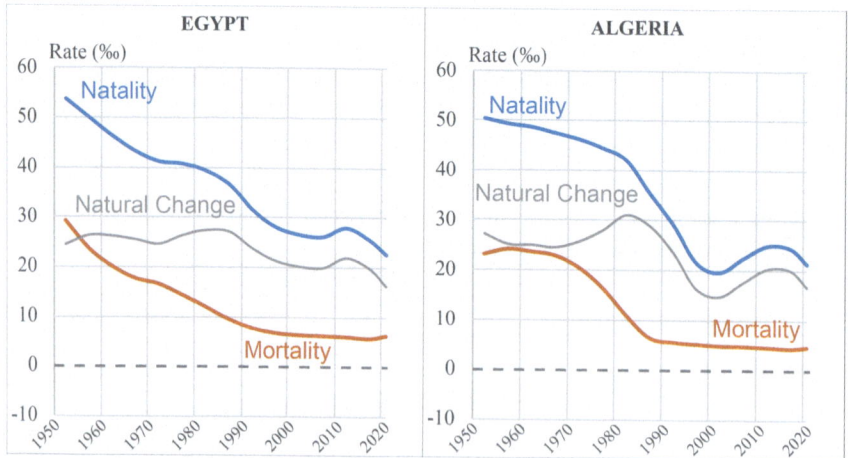

Fig. 4.10 Demographic transition in Egypt and Algeria (1950–2022) (*Source* World Population Prospects [2022] Calculations made by the authors. *Note* The time units used are five-year periods)

4.6 Possible Demographic Counter-Transitions (Type 9: Egypt, Algeria)

These particular trajectories, whether a hesitant decline or a significant increase in the birth rate,[12] raise questions about the process of demographic transition. Are these erratic trends, i.e. a temporary rise before a future fall, as was the case for Egypt in the 1970s? Or is it rather a real increase, where the post-transitional birth rate is stabilising at a higher level than theoretically expected? As this rise in the birth rate calls into question the possible equilibrium of the CBR, it is difficult to make a statement on the status of the demographic transition in Algeria, for example.

Moreover, this increase in the birth rate is not only explained by a greater proportion of women of childbearing age (structural effect), but also by an increase in fertility (see Chap. 5). Youssef Courbage (2015a, 2015b) calls it a "counter-transition".[13] Many recent increases in fertility have been observed in some European countries where fertility levels have fallen very low, for example Sweden in the 2000s. Nevertheless, it is atypical that fertility above 2 children per woman would rise significantly. From this point of view, Algeria and Egypt are not global exceptions. Let us not forget the *baby boom* in Europe, for example. In France, the total fertility rate rose from 1.85 (1941) to 3.03 (1947), before falling back to 1.82 in 1976. However, at the time, the *baby boom* was not seen as a 'counter-transition' because it calmed fears about the population's decline. For Egypt, it is difficult to conclude on the significance of the rise in birth rate, as it is very recent and only cover a relatively short period of time before falling again. In the case of Algeria, the trend has lasted longer. Is this increase in fertility comparable to the European *baby boom*, in a post- "Black Decade"[14] context? Could this be a data-related effect? Did the latter underestimate fertility until the early 2000s due to poor recording quality? The current increase would then be a consequence of improved civil registration. Zahia Ouadah-Bedidi et al. (2012) believe that a decrease in the age at marriage is partly responsible for the rise in fertility (see Chap. 6), that also suggest that couples may be moving towards a three-child model rather than the two-child model of Morocco and Tunisia. One could also envisage that Algerian fertility reached a minimum in 2000–2005. The rise would then constitute an adjustment towards the post-transitional level, in the same way as in Eastern Europe where some countries are currently seeing a rise in fertility.

---

[12] Increases in fertility are also observed in other Mediterranean countries, such as Kosovo and Tunisia in the 2000s. However, the intensity of the increase and its duration are not of the same order of magnitude as in Algeria.

[13] This text has been translated into English by the authors. The original text in French is as follows: "contre-transition".

[14] The "Black Decade" is a term used to describe the Algerian civil war (1991–2002).

4.7 Recent and Ongoing Transition, Slower Decline in Birth Rate (Type 10: Jordan, Palestine, Syria)

These demographic transitions have started late and have only occurred in the Near East (Fig. 4.11). In 1950, these transitions were at second step, i.e. falling mortality, but note for the birth rate. The latter was high ($\approx$ 50‰) and the decline was less rapid than the other late transitions (types 8 and 9). In fact, the CBR was still strong in 2015–2019 ($\approx$ 20–30‰), producing an even higher RNC (between 20 and 30‰) as the CDR is very low (4–5‰). Only mortality reached a balance in the 1990s. The demographic transition is therefore still underway, as the birth rate continues to fall. Palestine's demographic transition has been disrupted by the political situation and continued to be characterised by a high birth rate (although it has been declining since the early 1990s), despite a significant level of female education. The birth rate in Syria had slowed in the 1990s and stabilised at around 30‰ in the 2000s. This development is similar to that of Egypt or Libya in the same period. However, given the political situation in Syria, UN data after 2010 should be interpreted with great caution. The decline in birth rate, for example, from 30‰ to 20‰ in less than 10 years, should be attributed more to the Syrian conflict than to any possible rapid progress in the demographic transition.

4.8 A Diversity of Demographic Transitions Despite a General Convergence

This typology of demographic transitions in the Mediterranean highlights two essential characteristics. The first is a general convergence of births and deaths towards low rates. All Mediterranean countries are engaged in this transitional process. However, and this is the second characteristic revealed by the typology, this generalised convergence of mortality/birth rates towards low rates masks great diversity. The process does not take place in the same way in all countries: there is no single model of demographic transition in the Mediterranean, but several models. Finally, few countries have a "model" transition with almost zero population growth. The diversity of transitions is striking, whether in their form, pace, timing or the nature of the post-transitional regime.

The transitions of the Northern shore countries are those that best fit the theoretical descriptive model. Indeed, these transitions are different in terms of timing and pace, but their mortality and birth rates all stabilise at levels that result in low natural dynamics, whether positive or negative.

Countries on the Southern and Eastern shores, on the other hand, tend to have a higher RNC, due to a higher birth rate and lower mortality. This can partly be attributed to a younger age structure. With the inevitable ageing of the population, mortality is likely to increase, and the birth rate and RNC to decrease structurally. It is also possible that the countries on the Southern and Eastern shores will achieve

4.8 A Diversity of Demographic Transitions Despite a General Convergence

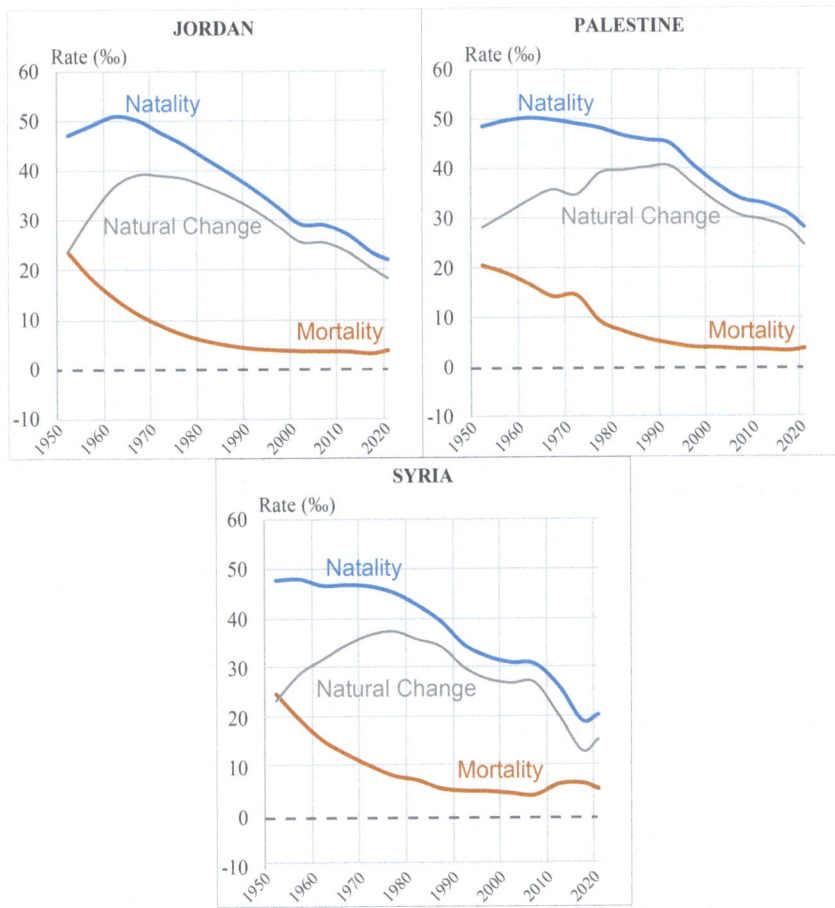

Fig. 4.11 Demographic transition in Jordan, Palestine and Syria (1950–2022) (*Source* World Population Prospects [2022] Calculations made by the authors. *Note* The time units used are five-year periods)

different post-transitional demographic regimes from those on the Northern shores, with, in particular, higher natural growth and an increasing population (without taking into account migration). Some of these countries, such as Israel and Tunisia, have achieved (or have nearly achieved) a pseudo-equilibrium in mortality and birth rates, but at levels that generate rather sustained natural growth. On the other hand, most of the countries on the Southern and Eastern shores have not reached a pseudo-equilibrium at present, either because the transition is ending or because the transition is still ongoing. On the other hand, there have been some rather unexpected trends, such as in Egypt or Algeria, with a recent and sometimes prolonged increase in the birth rate. It is therefore difficult to determine the type of post-transitional regime for most of the countries on the Southern and Eastern shores, i.e. whether it is a regime with weak but positive natural dynamics, or a regime characterised by more sustained natural growth than the Northern shore countries, as has been the case in Israel for more than 30 years.

Finally, it should be remembered that these broad trends observed at the country level also conceal a variety of local dynamics. Transitions can vary regionally in timing and intensity, and differences between urban and rural areas often exist (Coale & Watkins, 1986).

References

Al Zalak, Z., & Goujon A. (2017). Exploring the fertility trend in Egypt. *Demographic Research, 37*, 995–1030. https://doi.org/10.4054/DemRes.2017.37.32

Ambrosetti, E. (2011). *Égypte, l'exception démographique.* Les cahiers de l'INED 166. Institut National d'Études Démographiques. https://books.openedition.org/ined/1778?lang=en

Chesnais, J. (1992). *The demographic transition: Stages, patterns, and economic implications.* Clarendon Press; Oxford University Press.

Coale, A. J., & Watkins, S. C. (1986). *The decline of fertility in Europe.* Princeton University Press.

Courbage, Y. (2006). Les enjeux démographiques en Palestine après le retrait de Gaza. *Critique Internationale, 31*, 23–38. https://doi.org/10.3917/crii.031.0023

Courbage, Y. (2008). La guerre des berceaux. *Les collections de l'Histoire.* https://www.lhistoire.fr/%C2%AB-la-guerre-des-berceaux-%C2%BB

Courbage, Y. (2015a). Tunisie: la contre-transition démographique. Interview by Khadija Mohsen-Finan. *Orient XXI.* https://www.youtube.com/watch?v=FBxRclm8wnA

Courbage, Y. (2015b). Egypte, une transition démographique en marche arrière. *Orient XXI.* http://orientxxi.info/magazine/egypte-une-transition-demographique-en-marche-arriere,0956

Doignon, Y. (2020). Les transitions démographiques des pays méditerranéens depuis 1950. *Géoconfluences.* http://geoconfluences.ens-lyon.fr/informations-scientifiques/dossiers-region aux/la-mediterranee-une-geographie-paradoxale/articles-scientifiques/transitions-demograph iques

Doignon, Y., Ambrosetti, E., & Miccoli, S. (2021). The spatial diffusion of fertility decline in Egypt (1950–2006). *Genus, 77*, 23. https://doi.org/10.1186/s41118-021-00131-9

Goujon, A., & Zalak, Z. A. (2018). Why has fertility been increasing in Egypt? *Population & Societies, 551.* https://doi.org/10.3917/popsoc.551.0001

Landry, A. (1934). *La révolution démographique: études et essais sur les problèmes de la population.* Sirey.

Notestein, F. W. (1945). Population: The long view. In P. T. Schultz (Ed.), *Food for the world* (pp. 36–57). University of Chicago Press.

Ouadah-Bedidi, Z., Vallin, J., & Bouchoucha, I. (2012). Unexpected developments in Maghrebian fertility. *Population and Societies, 486.* https://doi.org/10.3917/popsoc.486.0001

World Population Prospects. (2022). United Nations, Department of Economic and Social Affairs, Population Division. https://population.un.org/wpp/

Open Access This chapter is licensed under the terms of the Creative Commons Attribution 4.0 International License (http://creativecommons.org/licenses/by/4.0/), which permits use, sharing, adaptation, distribution and reproduction in any medium or format, as long as you give appropriate credit to the original author(s) and the source, provide a link to the Creative Commons license and indicate if changes were made.

The images or other third party material in this chapter are included in the chapter's Creative Commons license, unless indicated otherwise in a credit line to the material. If material is not included in the chapter's Creative Commons license and your intended use is not permitted by statutory regulation or exceeds the permitted use, you will need to obtain permission directly from the copyright holder.

Chapter 5
Fertility Intensity and Timing

Abstract This chapter looks at the comparative evolution of fertility since 1950 through several synthetic indicators of fertility intensity (average number of children per woman) and timing (age at childbearing, all birth ranks combined). The Mediterranean area is still a fairly contrasted area in terms of fertility levels, but the reduction in the gaps between countries has been clear and rapid since the 1970s. Fertility is still relatively high in some Southern and Eastern Mediterranean countries and is decreasing noticeably, while very low levels can be observed on the Northern Shore (Spain, Portugal, Italy, Greece, etc.). The chapter also presents the most probable fertility trends in this region of the world by returning to the underlying hypotheses. Is the hypothesis of a sustainable convergence of fertility at the level of the replacement fertility rate between the shores foreseeable and, if so, over what time horizon?

Keywords Total fertility rate · Fertility intensity · Age-specific fertility rate · Fertility timing · Mean age at childbearing · Mediterranean

5.1 Introduction

This chapter looks at the comparative evolution of fertility since 1950 through several synthetic indicators of fertility intensity (average number of children per woman) and timing (age at childbearing, all birth ranks combined). The Mediterranean area is still a fairly contrasted area in terms of fertility levels, but the reduction in the gaps between countries has been clear and rapid since the 1970s. Fertility is still relatively high in some Southern and Eastern Mediterranean countries and is decreasing noticeably, while very low levels can be observed on the Northern Shore (Spain, Portugal, Italy, Greece, etc.). The chapter also presents the most probable fertility trends in this region of the world by returning to the underlying hypotheses. Is the hypothesis of a sustainable convergence of fertility at the level of the replacement fertility rate between the shores foreseeable and, if so, over what time horizon?

5.2 A Global Fertility Convergence

Through the process of demographic transition (see Chap. 4), the Mediterranean countries have seen their fertility decline according to different timing, currently reaching levels lower than in the past (Fig. 5.1).

The fertility gap between the most and least fertile countries has thus fallen from 5.5 children per woman in 1950 to only 2.6 children in 2020. The highest fertility

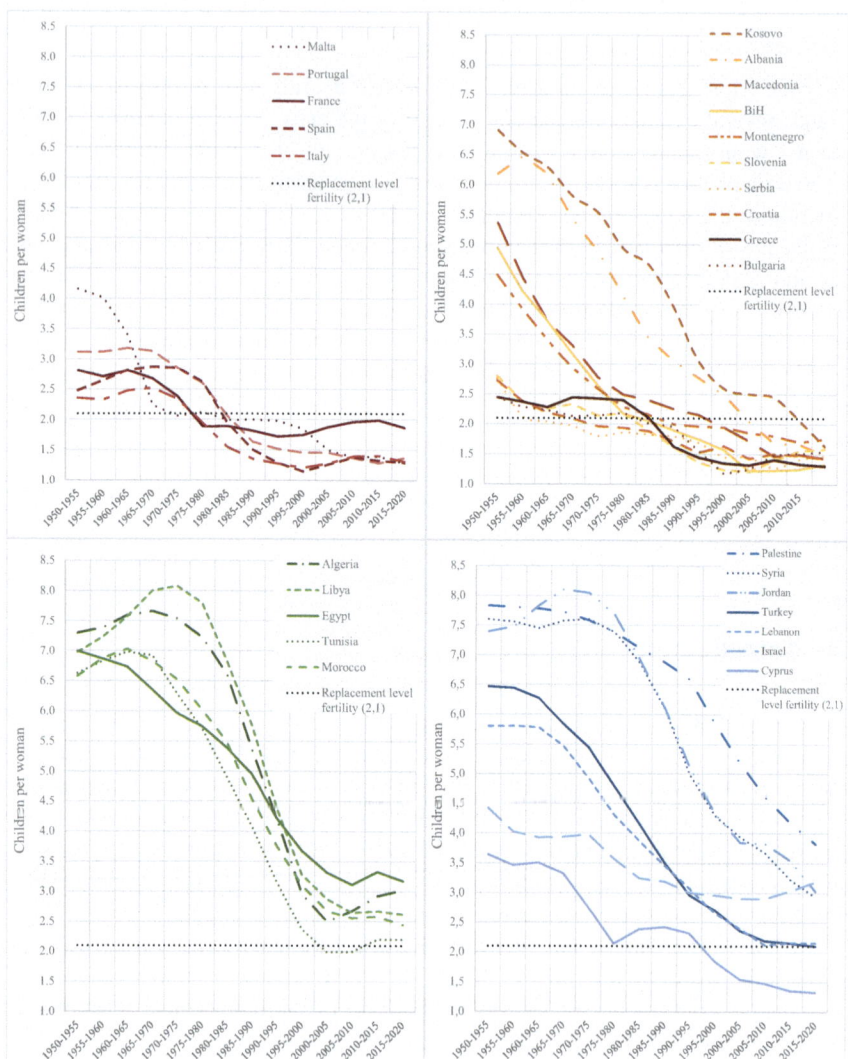

Fig. 5.1 Comparative fertility evolution in the Mediterranean (1950–2022) (*Source* World Population Prospects, 2022)

rates in the 1950s were over 7 children per woman, while the lowest were around 2.4 children per woman, compared to 3.8 and 1.3 children per woman respectively today. In the 1950s, none of the 27 Mediterranean countries had a fertility rate below 2.1 children per woman, a symbolic figure known as the population replacement level, whereas today there are 17. While the countries on the Northern shore were already well advanced in their transition in the 1950s, 1960s and 1970s (see Chap. 4), the countries on the Southern and Eastern shores did not experience a significant or very rapid decline in their fertility until the 1970s, with the exception of Cyprus and Israel, where the decline in fertility began before 1950.

This vast movement of convergence in the fertility between the countries of the Southern and Eastern shores and those of the Northern shore is, however, incomplete, and has occurred "albeit not always smoothly"[1] (Courbage, 1999). Figure 5.1 shows not only the different periods of decline, but also the fact that the majority of countries are now below the replacement level, in contrast to countries that still have relatively high fertility. This fertility rate of between 3 and 4 children per woman can be seen in highly populated countries such as Egypt and Algeria, along with more intermediate-sized states such as Palestine, Jordan and Israel.

While this decline in fertility in the countries of the Southern and Eastern shores had been cautiously envisaged (Seklani, 1960) or more so automatically been announced on account of the "universal" theory of demographic transition (see Chap. 4), other authors[2] did not think that it could be observed in the Arab-Muslim countries. However, with nuances depending on the region, the delay in the age of marriage[3] coupled with the spread of contraception has finally led to a decline in fertility in these countries (Fargues, 1989). At the same time, it was not rejected that this region of the world, plagued by a number of other "misidentified factors", could deviate from the expected course.[4] Although greatly attenuated today, differences between the behaviour of the populations of the Northern Shore (low fertility) compared to those of the Southern and Eastern shores (on average more fertile) are still clearly visible (Fig. 5.1) and subject to discussion. It should be noted, however, that the fertility of several countries on the Southern and Eastern shores (Cyprus, Lebanon, Turkey, Tunisia, and to a lesser extent Morocco and Libya) has reached levels close to or below the replacement level.

Will the higher fertility rates of Egypt, Morocco, Libya and Israel, which seem to have reached a pseudo-equilibrium, stabilise at a level above 2.1 children per

---

[1] This text has been translated into English by the authors. The original text in French is as follows: "non sans à-coups".

[2] "Dudley Kirk (1966) was one of the earliest demographers to note that Muslim populations tended to have high fertility, that there was no evidence of decline, and that in a given country, Muslims tended to have higher fertility than adherents of other religions" (Jones, 2006, 250).

[3] See Chap. 6 for an analysis of nuptiality rates and age at marriage.

[4] "The demography of this region escapes, in more than one case, the paradigm of transition which has been imposed as a scheme for explaining demographic change" (Courbage, 1999, 1).

This text has been translated into English by the authors. The original text in French is as follows: "La démographie de cette région échappe, dans plus d'un cas, au paradigme de la transition qui s'est imposé comme schéma d'explication des évolutions démographiques".

woman? Will fertility rates in the Palestinian Territories, Jordan and Syria fall significantly further? If so, to what level? Or will they remain above 2.1 children per woman? Are trend reversals or sustainable recoveries to be expected, as suggested by recent fertility trends in some countries (e.g. Egypt, Algeria) (Ouadah-Bedidi et al., 2012)? Is it possible to observe a homogenisation of fertility behaviour of all Mediterranean women, regardless of their nationality? Is a fertility rate of 1 or 2 children per woman a sustainable objective throughout the Mediterranean? The Euro-Mediterranean geopolitics (the Israeli-Palestinian conflict, the Syrian, Turkish and Greek situation, and the Balkans, etc.), and the different traditional and/or religious models of union formation (see Chap. 6) and of attachment to the family and to children in Mediterranean societies, lead us to reflect on these past evolutions and to formulate hypotheses on the future evolution of fertility in a singular Mediterranean context.

In an attempt to clarify this, an in-depth comparative analysis of indicators of fertility timing (the age at which women have children) and fertility intensity at different ages is carried out successively. It provides a clearer picture of the expected trends in women's fertility in this region of the world by pinpointing the common patterns and highlighting the exceptions.

5.3 The Intersection of Birth Timing and Fertility Intensity

5.3.1 Mean Age at Childbearing

For a given period, the mean childbearing age is an indicator of when a woman gives birth, through it mixes the behaviour of several different generations. Like any average, it needs to be interpreted carefully and be reconciled with fertility levels. If, however, we describe the evolution of the mean age at childbearing in the Mediterranean since 1950, we will be surprised to see that its value has changed only slightly, from 29.5 years on average in the region to 30 years at present. This overall situation can then be separated in several groups of countries (Fig. 5.2). While some countries show a virtually stable indicator throughout the period, others have experienced a V-shaped (sharp) or U-shaped (gentler) evolution: respectively, a rapid decline in the mean age at childbearing until the mid-1980s, followed by a rapid rise; or a slower decline until the 1990s, followed by a steady rise until the present.

The first group covers 7 countries (Algeria, Morocco, Tunisia, Jordan, Lebanon, Palestine, Syria), where the mean age at childbearing has never fallen significantly over the past 70 years. Two other countries can also be added to this group (Libya, Israel). The mean age in Libya has risen steadily from 30.8 years to 31.9 years today. Stable until the mid-1970s, the increase in age accelerated and stabilised at almost 33 years between 1995 and 2005, before decreasing to what it is now. The mean age in Israel has hardly ever fallen in the last 70 years, but has increased from 27.6 years in the 1950s-1970s to 30.6 years today. The mean childbearing age for this group of

5.3 The Intersection of Birth Timing and Fertility Intensity

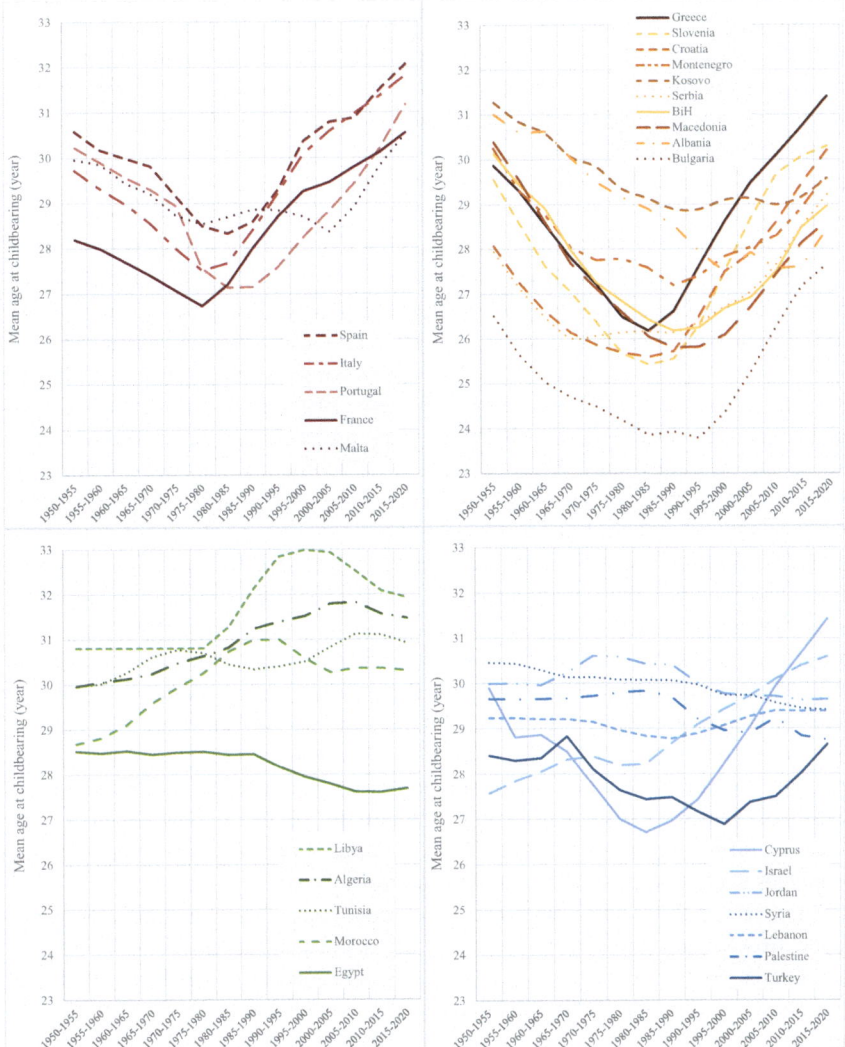

Fig. 5.2 Mean age at childbearing in the Mediterranean (1950–2019) (*Source* World Population Prospects, 2022)

countries has remained high (between 28 and 33 years) and fairly constant since 1950 (29.6 years in 1950, 30.3 years in the 1980s, 30.4 years today). They are all located in North Africa and the Near East. In these countries, the contraceptive discontinuation has not led to a reduction in the mean childbearing age, as it has been compensated for by the concomitant postponement of the age at marriage (see Chap. 6). This could mean that contraception is mainly used in these countries once the desired number of children has been reached, as already noted by Fargues (1989). Some of the countries in this group reach some of the highest levels in the Mediterranean, such as Algeria and Libya, where the mean age at childbearing is currently 31.5 and 31.9 years respectively. However, there is no convergence for these countries towards a single mean age. There is a clear dispersion of the childbearing ages.

The 9 other countries (Greece, France, Spain, Portugal, Slovenia, Montenegro, Italy, Cyprus, Malta) that make up the second group, shows a much earlier and more marked change in the average fertility age (V-shaped curve[5]). These countries are those in which contraceptive discontinuation has led to a reduction in the mean age at childbearing, as fewer unplanned births have been occurring at earlier ages. In a second phase, women in these countries have been postponing and spacing out the birth of their first (rank 1) and second (rank 2) child at increasingly advanced ages, leading to a rise in the mean age of mothers. Following this mechanism, there was a sharp fall in the mean age between the 1950s and 1980s, followed by a spectacular rise to very high levels in 2015–2019: 32 years for Spain and Italy, 31.4 years for Greece and 30.6 for France. These countries, unlike the previous ones, seem to be converging towards a similar mean childbearing age. What these countries have in common is that they have low fertility rates.

The third group consists of Bulgaria, closely followed by Croatia and Serbia. These countries had the lowest mean age at childbearing over most of the study period, never exceeding 28 years until recently. Since the early 1990s, however, the birth timing in these countries has been on the rise, reaching 28–29 years in 2020. They seem to be following suit of the previous group. Turkey can also be included in this group, as the age at childbearing has always been low, through notwithstanding its higher fertility relative to other countries in this group. Bosnia-Herzegovina and Macedonia, which started out with a childbearing age two years older than their Serbian and Croatian neighbours in the 1950s, now have the same U-shaped profile and have thus caught up to them. A convergence towards higher mean ages at childbearing in this group is underway.

We conclude this section with the three countries with atypical developments: Egypt, Kosovo and Albania. In the latter, the decline in the childbearing age has been almost continuous since 1950, from 31 to 27.5 years. It has hovered around this value since the mid-1990s, but appears to be rising again in 2015–2019. Kosovo follows a similar trajectory, but its age at childbearing stagnated at a higher level (29 years) between the 1980s and the late 2000s. As for Egypt, whose demography has been defined by Ambrosetti (2011) as exceptional, it has a rather stable age which mothers give birth, with a recent slightly downward trend (28.5 in 1950, 27.7 years 2020). Unlike the other Mediterranean countries, the mean age at childbearing is not increasing, but has been decreasing since the end of the 1980s, a sign of a specific fertility regime.

These mean ages at childbearing summarise a variable fertility according to women's age group. We will therefore analyse age-specific fertility rates in order to identify different age-specific fertility profiles, which will help highlight the different

---

[5] With the exception of Malta, which has a more U-shaped curve.

5.3 The Intersection of Birth Timing and Fertility Intensity

ways in which age groups contribute to fertility intensity and timing in different countries.

5.3.2 Fertility by Age Group

A typology of fertility rates by age group for the 27 countries in 2015–2019 shows more precise age-specific fertility profiles (Fig. 5.3). The higher the curves, the higher the fertility intensity, i.e. the higher the number of children per woman. The more they are shifted to the right, the higher the mean age at childbearing.

Two countries, Egypt and Palestine, have more or less the same profile with high fertility in the younger age groups. This distinguishes them from Israel, Jordan and Syria, who have a later fertility. At the other end of the spectrum, it is striking that about one in two Mediterranean countries now belongs to the category of countries with very low fertility. So far, this very low fertility is only found on the Northern Shore (Southern Europe and the Balkans). These very low fertility Mediterranean countries have an average fertility of 1.4 children per woman in 2015–2019. These are Cyprus, Bosnia-Herzegovina, Croatia, Greece, Italy, Malta, Montenegro, Macedonia, Portugal, Serbia, Slovenia and Spain. A third group, Bulgaria and Albania, has very low fertility like the countries in the previous group, but high fertility among young women, bringing their age-group fertility profile closer to that of Egypt and Palestine.

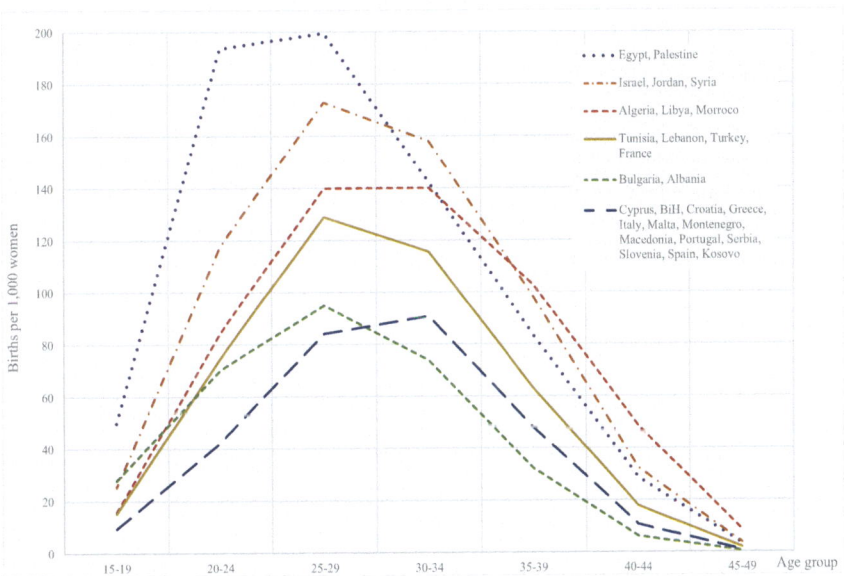

Fig. 5.3 Typology of fertility rates in the Mediterranean (2015–2019) (*Source* World Population Prospects, 2022)

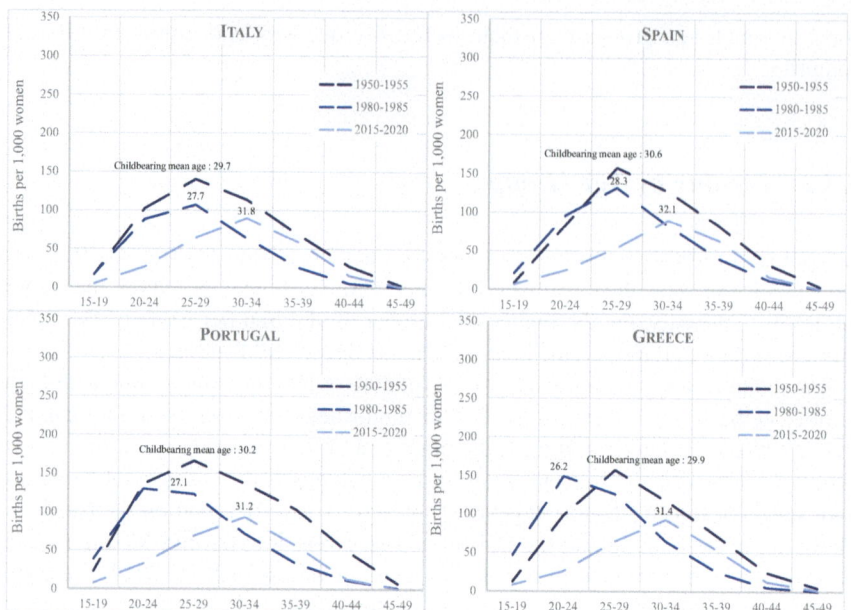

Fig. 5.4 Evolution of mean age at childbearing and fertility rates in Italy, Greece, Portugal, Spain (1950–2019) (*Source* World Population Prospects, 2022)

Among these countries that are below the replacement level fertility, four are emblematic of a very low fertility rate that has been in place for several decades. These are Italy, Portugal, Greece and Spain (Fig. 5.4).

These countries have low fertility at all ages (less than 100 births per 1000 women), as well as a mean age at childbearing of around 32 years (which is the same as the age at birth of the only child) which will continue to increase.[6] These ageing countries have been affected by various economic crises and have been slow to introduce genuine birth policies. This prolonged low fertility explains the negative natural balances of these countries (Chap. 4). It also creates a depopulation mechanism, which at the sub-national level can be accentuated by internal migration and an increasing number of elderly people (Doignon et al., 2016).

---

[6] It is possible to calculate for each age group how many women have already given birth to a child and to assess the evolution of this age-specific fertility from one period to the next. When the curves fall from one period to the next, it means that the number of children born to women of a given age group has decreased over time: girls have fewer children than their sisters, let alone their mothers at the same age. The fertility timeline reflects the mean age at which women have children. A postponement of the age at which women have their children is observed concomitantly with a decrease in fertility intensity (and vice versa). When the curves shift to the right, it means that births are occurring later on average. This decline in the age at which children are borne is a sign that the population has mastered modern contraception. This has spread throughout the population and is a sign of a transformation in the value and place of women in society. In order to analyse this evolution of the fertility timeline, in relation to intensity, it is useful to observe them simultaneously.

5.3 The Intersection of Birth Timing and Fertility Intensity

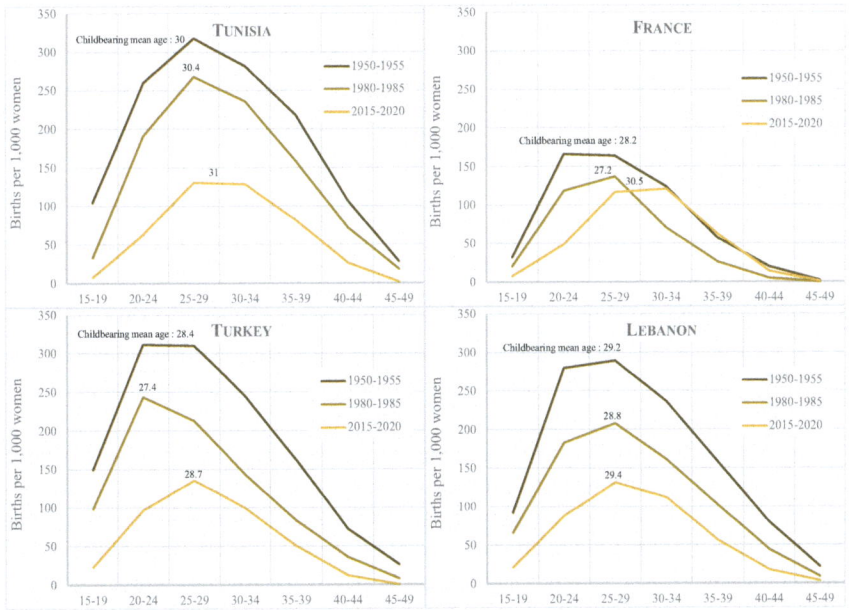

Fig. 5.5 Evolution of mean age at childbearing and fertility rates in France, Tunisia, Turkey, Lebanon (1950–2019) (*Source* World Population Prospects, 2022)

Other populated Mediterranean countries (France, Turkey, Tunisia, Lebanon) are also in a situation of low fertility, but whose level makes it possible to maintain a positive natural balance. These countries, unlike the previous ones, belong to different Mediterranean shores. They have a fertility rate around the replacement level, thus well above the previous group. These countries are experiencing a postponement of the age at which women have children, but with a more sustained intensity, especially over the age of 30 (Fig. 5.5).

France, Lebanon and Tunisia now have relatively similar characteristics: fertility around the replacement level and shifting towards older ages, although the history of fertility decline in Tunisia is much more recent[7] and rapid than in France. Turkey is included in this group because its fertility is at the replacement level. However, it differs in that its fertility intensity among 20–24 year-olds is much higher (almost double that of France and Tunisia). Turkey could have been in the Algeria/Morocco group, but was distinguished from these countries because of its long-standing lower fertility and its much lower fertility intensity at older ages.

---

[7] The history of fertility decline in the Maghreb and Tunisia in particular, is well documented (Fargues, 1989; Gastineau, 2012). As soon as they became independent (1956 for Morocco and Tunisia, 1962 for Algeria), these countries adopted very different population policies. Tunisia resorted to a very firm policy of limiting births since the 1960s (Lévêque, 2017; Ouadah-Bedidi et al., 2012). As a result, it had the earliest and most pronounced fertility transition, which many explain by a change in the family code that recognises equal rights between men and women (Fargues, 1989).

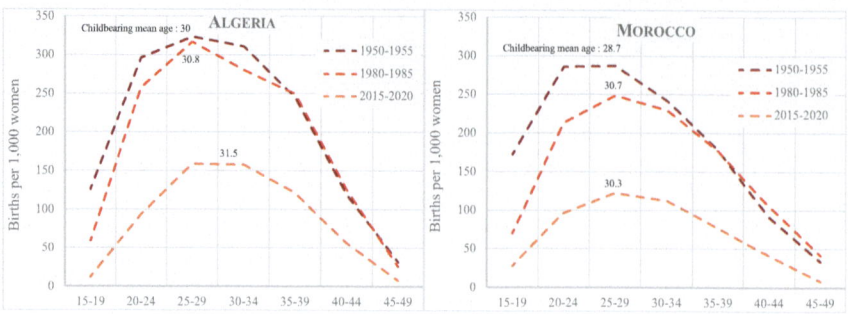

Fig. 5.6 Evolution of mean age at childbearing and fertility rates Algeria, Morocco (1950–2019) (*Source* World Population Prospects, 2022)

The other three groups identified in Fig. 5.3 cover intermediate to relatively high fertility situations.[8] The fertility profiles of Algeria and Morocco (Fig. 5.6), for example, differ from the previous group (Tunisia, France, Turkey, Lebanon) in that their fertility is more sustained after the age of 30. Births of rank 3 or 4 children are still very present in these societies, helping to boost fertility. Together with Libya, they are the only two countries[9] with such high mean ages, above 31 years, a characteristic more commonly found in the countries of the Northern shore.

5.4 Specific Contributions of Age Groups

By analysing the quantiles of fertility rate distributions by age group, we are able to the distinguish two large groups: one made up of 13 countries, the other of 14 (Fig. 5.7).

The first group's fertility is marked by a fairly early mean age at childbearing (below 30 years), whereas the second group's age is much older (above 30 years). Bulgaria, Egypt, Palestine, Syria, Turkey, Albania, Macedonia, Serbia, Jordan, Bosnia-Herzegovina, Lebanon, Montenegro and Kosovo are countries where births take place earlier on average (irrespective of their fertility levels, which may be very

---

[8] The difference in fertility behaviour between the Maghreb and the Near East can be explained in part by the colonial heritage and the strong influence of the diaspora, which is rather oriented towards Europe in the case of the Maghreb, and towards the Gulf countries in the case of the Near East (see Chap. 8). In the Maghreb, these factors constitute "the main and direct agent of European cultural influence" (This text has been translated into English by the authors. The original text in French is as follows: "l'agent principal et direct de l'influence culturelle européenne") (Courbage & Todd, 2014). Libya's behaviour is close to the Maghreb, as is Egypt's with Near Eastern countries (Lévêque, 2017).

[9] Unlike Tunisia, Algeria did not have the necessary means to control its population's fertility after independence. Nevertheless, fertility fell rapidly, particularly as a result of the lowering age of marriage, before the first birth control programme in 1983 was introduced and subsequently accelerating the phenomenon among all age groups (Ouadah-Bedidi et al., 2012).

5.4 Specific Contributions of Age Groups

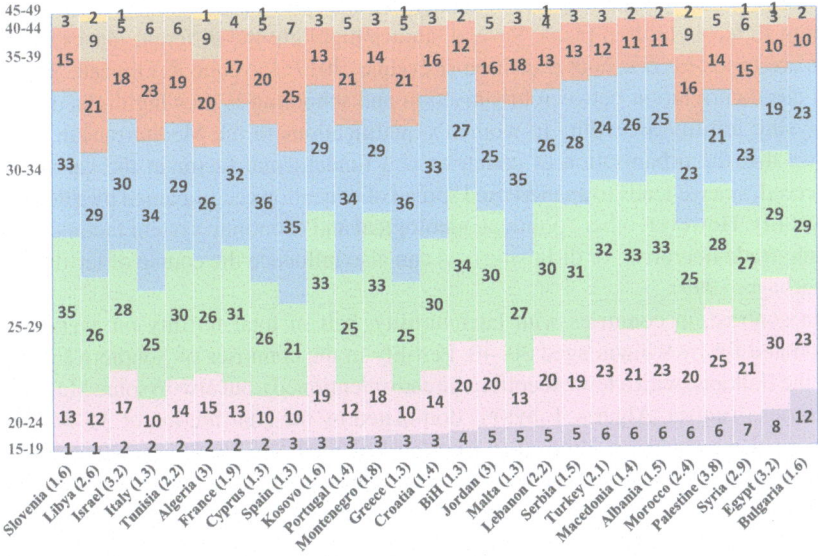

Fig. 5.7 Contribution of each age group to total fertility in % (2015–2019) (*Source* World Population Prospects, 2022. Calculations made by the authors)

different[10]). In contrast, births are more likely on average to be due to older women in the following countries: Malta, Portugal, Croatia, Spain, Greece, Italy, Tunisia, Algeria, Israel, Libya, France, Slovenia, Morocco and Cyprus.

In the first group with early fertility, 30% of total fertility is already reached at 25 years of age on average, and about 60% at 30 years. In the second group where births are occurring later in a woman's life, only 16% of total fertility is reached at age 25 on average and 43% at age 30.[11] In other words, 4 out of 10 births are to women over 30 in the first group compared to 6 out of 10 in the second.

Using this method, it is possible to identify a potential explanation for the decline in fertility in the first group with early fertility: it is due to the fertility behaviour of the youngest women. Will women aged 15–19, and especially aged 20–30, postpone the arrival of their first child and any subsequent children until later in life? Or will they continue to start their fertile life well before the age of 30? Increasing access to school and higher education, rising living standards, urbanisation and changing

---

[10] The higher fertility level of young women can therefore be found in countries where fertility is still high (Egypt, Morocco, Palestine, Turkey, Syria, Jordan), but also, though less intuitively, in countries on the northern shores (Bulgaria, Macedonia, Serbia, Albania), where the low total fertility level is largely due to the fertility of young women. For example, almost 12% of Bulgaria's total fertility is accounted for by 15–19 year olds, whereas in other countries with very low fertility (Italy, Portugal, Greece, Spain, etc.) this group contributes only 2 to 3%.

[11] From this point of view, Morocco is an exception, because despite an age at childbearing of over 30 years, the fertility level of young women (15–24 years) remains higher than that of the other countries in this group. Similarly, the fertility of women aged 30–39 is lower.

gender relations promote greater equality are likely to be determinants for postponing to have children plans. Several studies highlight the different places countries are in vis-à-vis school transition (Lévêque, 2017; Lévêque & Oliveau, 2019). The close correlation between urbanisation and schooling is thus highlighted after analysing fertility according to women's qualifications in the Mediterranean. This shows that the urbanisation of countries is a fundamental factor in the variations observed, since it leads to an increased spread of education accompanied by a decline in fertility. However, other "political, ideological and economic system factors, such as free-trade liberalism or dirigisme (…) can also influence the course of fertility"[12] (Courbage, 1999).

In contrast, in countries with later fertility, half of total fertility on average is accounted for by women aged 30–40. Fertility in the countries of Southern Europe and the Balkans (with a few exceptions already mentioned), but also in some Maghreb countries (Tunisia, Algeria, Libya) is dominated by the contribution of 30–34 year olds. In these countries, more than one third of total fertility is accounted for by women aged 30–34 alone. The fertility of these intermediate age groups in low total intensity countries is a sign of women's willingness to carry a pregnancy to term once a certain number of conditions are met (housing, professional situation, marital stability, etc.).

In a large number of Balkan countries (Bosnia, Albania, Slovenia, Montenegro, Macedonia, Serbia, Croatia), a notable contribution to fertility is made by 25–29 year olds. This contribution of the youngest is rather singular in that it only concerns countries with very low fertility. Thus, even among low fertility countries, it is still possible to introduce distinctions. The low fertility of the Balkans is still due to young or even very young women, while the low fertility of the largest countries in Southern Europe (Italy, Spain, Portugal) and Greece is due more to older women.

Fertility in the Maghreb countries remains marked. In addition to the contribution made by younger women who nevertheless postpone their first childbirth, a significant contribution is made by the older age groups, those aged 35–39 and 40–44. Spain, Italy, Portugal and even France, which have much lower fertility, also have fertility that has been driven by women over 35, but it does not resonate in the same way. In the Maghreb, it still represents a progression margin which may make it possible to imagine a drop in total fertility once these generations have disappeared.

The fertility of women over 45 contributes little to fertility (between 0.1 and 1.8% of the total). A hierarchy of countries according to their regional affiliation is however noted. More than 1.5% of total fertility in Morocco and Libya is still accounted for by women aged 45 or over. This was followed by Algeria (1.3%), Syria (1%), Lebanon (0.9%), Greece (0.6%), Egypt and Israel (0.5%). Despite this small contribution, the late fertility in North African or Near Eastern countries is a sign that stopping fertility may not be established in all strata of society and reveals

---

[12] This text has been translated into English by the authors. The original text in French is as follows: "facteurs politiques, idéologiques et sur les systèmes économiques: libéralisme libre-échangiste ou dirigisme, (…) peuvent également infléchir le cours de la fécondité".

potential differences between urban and rural areas. Higher order fertility (3 or more) has not completely disappeared and is probably due to older women.

The geographical distribution of these two groups is interesting. Indeed, it seems to extend the Hajnal line (Hajnal, 1965) into the Mediterranean. The latter divides the European continent along a north-east/south-west axis, from St Petersburg to Triest. It distinguishes two historically persistent European family patterns, with earlier fertility to the east of this demarcation than to the west. Thus, the countries in the first group are mainly found in the Eastern Mediterranean Basin, i.e. from Bosnia-Herzegovina to Egypt. In contrast, the countries in the second group are located in the western basin. This geographical demarcation also holds true for age at marriage and permanent celibacy (see Chap. 6).

In addition to the fact that these analyses make it possible to examine jointly the situation of all the Mediterranean countries with regard to the fertility timeline in 2015–2019, they make it possible to identify the age groups likely to modify their fertility behaviour from one generation to the next. By identifying the most fertile ages when it comes to fertility, it is possible to go beyond the United Nations projections and propose individualised scenarios on fertility changes.

5.5 (Un)certainties for the Future of Mediterranean Fertility

According to the median scenario of the *World Population Prospects* (2022), the fertility gap between the most and least fertile Mediterranean countries by 2060 will be less than 1 child per woman (0.8 children to be precise), whereas it is currently 2.5. This scenario highlights a significant reduction in fertility disparities in the Mediterranean (Fig. 5.8).

The estimated average fertility in the Mediterranean will fall from the current 2 children to 1.7 children per woman. This situation is unprecedented since this threshold, which does not allow for the level replacement of generations (one couple is replaced by less than one couple in adulthood), is foreseen in the median scenario. Figure 5.8 shows that in this median scenario,[13] only 3 countries remain above 2.1 children per woman (Israel, Palestine, Egypt) to which can be added Jordan,

---

[13] "Probabilistic projections are based on statistical models, mostly parametric. Uncertainty about certain components of the population can be captured by error terms, as in the case of time series, but it can also come from Bayesian inference of the model parameters. The whole point is to quantify the uncertainty about the future population. This can be done using the stochastic approach, the Bayesian approach, or even a combination of both" (Costemalle, 2021, 32).

This text has been translated into English by the authors. The original text in French is as follows: "Les projections probabilistes reposent sur des modèles statistiques, la plupart du temps paramétriques. L'incertitude sur certaines composantes de la population peut être captée par des termes d'erreurs, comme dans le cas des séries temporelles, mais elle peut aussi provenir d'une inférence bayésienne des paramètres du modèle. Tout l'objectif est de quantifier l'incertitude sur la population future. Pour cela, on peut utiliser l'approche stochastique, l'approche bayésienne, ou même une combinaison des deux".

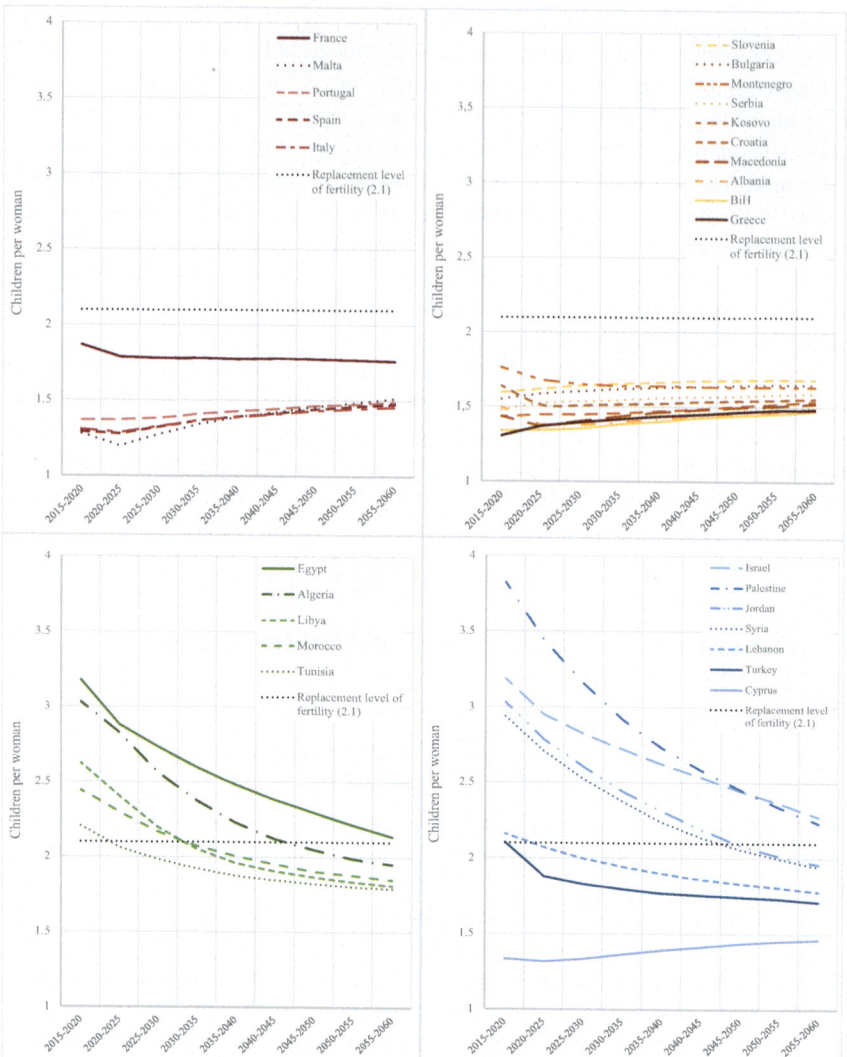

Fig. 5.8 Comparative fertility perspective for the Mediterranean, by country (2015–2055, median variant) (*Source* World Population Prospects, 2022)

Syria and Algeria (slightly below 2 children per woman). Of course, the fertility situation in the Mediterranean in 2060 varies according to the projection scenarios, and the confidence intervals considered for the probabilistic scenarios. For example, if we consider the upper bound of the 80% confidence interval (CI) of the median scenario, this would mean 10 countries would have a fertility rate above 2.1 children per woman instead of just 3 countries. Conversely, all countries would be below this threshold with the lower bound of the same CI. However, in all three cases, the projections demonstrate an overall fertility convergence in the Mediterranean (Fig. 5.8): convergence towards an average fertility rate of 1.35, 1.7 or 2.1 children for the lower limit of the 80% CI, the median scenario and the upper limit of the 80% CI respectively.

In view of the findings articulated in this chapter and based on the same observation made by other demographers specialising in the Mediterranean,[14] we wish to carry out a more individualised prospective reflection for the Mediterranean as a whole. Instead of a generalised convergence of the Mediterranean countries towards a single fertility level, it seems possible to envisage in the future a convergence by groups of countries (Doignon, 2020). The challenge would therefore be to take into account socio-political situations and territories on the basis of both their demographic history and recent developments so as to be able to anticipate reversals in the situation.

To contribute to this prospective exercise, we propose first of all to closely monitor the evolution of timing and fertility intensity in countries with very low fertility, in particular the countries of Southern Europe, the Balkan countries (Bosnia and Herzegovia, Croatia, Bulgaria, Albania), but also Cyprus. These countries are at the top of the list of countries with the lowest fertility in the world (along with Taiwan, Macao, Hong Kong, Singapore and Moldova), and ahead of or not far behind Japan, Germany and Italy. This very low fertility rate has been established over time and it is easy to imagine that it will remain stable or even continue to fall to historically low levels. This hypothesis is corroborated by the cumulative results of several surveys which show, despite the persistence of the two-child model, the rise in preferences for the one-child family model as well as for childless families (Sobotka & Beaujouan, 2014). In this way, the Balkans, Cyprus and Portugal could form a group in which a pattern of very low fertility (1.3–1.5 children per woman) would continue.

In Bulgaria and Albania too, surprises are to be expected from the younger generation. If the latter end up delaying their timing of fertility, the decline in fertility at younger ages will have a significant impact on overall fertility, allowing these countries to move into the group of countries with low fertility and late timing.

Israel's fertility is rather atypical in the sense that its fertility has been more or less stable since the mid-1980s at around 3 children per woman. This trend does not argue for a convergence to low levels within a 35-year time horizon. It is therefore likely that Israel's fertility will remain around 3 children per woman. It is more difficult to say for Palestine, as its fertility is still declining at present and the level at which it will stabilise is still uncertain.

Jordan and Syria are notable for the regularity and rapidity of their fertility decline, like Palestine. The latter, however, still has a fertility rate that is almost 1 child on average above Jordan and Syria. The future development of Jordan is still uncertain, as it is still decreasing at the moment, after a stagnation in the 2000s. For Syria, despite a pro-natalist policy, the political and economic crisis that affected the country from the 1980s onwards had a lasting effect on the population and led to a considerable

---

[14] We thus support the observation of the demographer Youssef Courbage, who already in 1999 insisted on the need to supplement these indispensable United Nations projections with methods that take into account specific situations.

drop in fertility (Lévêque, 2017), which is still ongoing. Fertility has certainly been affected by the conflict since 2011, although it is difficult to quantify this impact. When the conflict ends, fertility can follow several possible developments. Will there be catch-up fertility (and thus an increase in fertility) or will fertility rates during the Syrian conflict be maintained? There is therefore uncertainty about the future of Syrian fertility and the level at which it will stabilise.

Algeria, Libya, Morocco and Egypt are also countries whose fertility trends are uncertain given the situation observed in recent years. Their respective situations deserve to be studied separately. The Moroccan fertility rate is a source of concern since, after a sharp decline until the early 2000s, there have been periods of plateau and recovery (Ouadah-Bedidi et al., 2012). In Morocco, one interpretation given to the emergence of this resistance is the slowing down of the rate of progress of education as well as the geographical isolation of the country described as quite remote from the rest of the Arab world by Courbage and Todd (2014). Despite a very recent decline in fertility, one could imagine Morocco's fertility converging around 2.5 children. This is also true for Algeria and Egypt, which are showing signs of resistance to rejoining replacement level fertility due to early births, but which still extend into old age. It might be more likely that the threshold of 2.5 or even 3 children is a convergence threshold for the latter two countries. Turkish fertility, like Lebanese fertility, is likely to decline if younger women delay having children more. Otherwise, it could remain stable at around 2 children per woman.

The aspirations of a growing proportion of women of the new generations (see Chap. 6), which are very different from those of their sisters and mothers, will undoubtedly be factors that will weigh and argue in favour of lower fertility scenarios throughout the Mediterranean. However, different cultural models, changing gender relations and the geopolitics at work in this complex geographical area all work together to slow down these declines and reach thresholds. In the next few years, we could expect to see a decrease in the differences between countries where the fertility level amongst the most educated is already low. In countries where the fertility level of the most educated is still high, the trends will depend in part on the openness of local communities to globalisation and the openness of attitudes, as Fargues argues (2000).

References

Ambrosetti, E. (2011). *Égypte, l'exception démographique*. Les cahiers de l'INED 166. Institut National d'Études Démographiques. https://books.openedition.org/ined/1778?lang=en

Costemalle, V. (2021). Bayesian probabilistic population projections for France. *Economie et Statistique/Economics and Statistics*, 29–47. https://doi.org/10.24187/ecostat.2020.520d.2031

Courbage, Y. (1999). *New demographic scenarios in the Mediterranean region*. Travaux et documents 142. Institut National d'Etudes Démographiques-Presses Universitaires de France.

Courbage, Y., & Todd, E. (2014). *A convergence of civilizations: The transformation of Muslim societies around the world*. Columbia University Press.

References

Doignon, Y. (2020). Demographic ageing in the Mediterranean: The end of the spatial dichotomy between the shores? *Spatial Demography, 8*, 85–117. https://doi.org/10.1007/s40980-019-00054-2

Doignon, Y., Oliveau, S., & Blöss-Widmer, I. (2016). L'Europe méridionale depuis 20 ans: Dépeuplement, dépopulation et renouveau démographique. *Espace Populations Sociétés, 2015/3-2016/1*, 23. https://doi.org/10.4000/eps.6171

Fargues, P. (1989). The decline of Arab fertility. *Population, 44*, 147–175. http://www.jstor.org/stable/2949078

Fargues, P. (2000). *Générations arabes: l'alchimie du nombre*. Fayard.

Gastineau, B. (2012). Transition de la fécondité, développement et droits des femmes en Tunisie. *Les Cahiers d'EMAM, 21*, 75–94. https://doi.org/10.4000/emam.521

Hajnal, J. (1965). European marriage patterns in perspective. In D. V. Glass & D. E. C. Eversley (Eds.), *Population in history: Essays in historical demography, Volume I: General and Great Britain* (pp. 101–143). Edward Arnold; Aldine Publishing.

Jones, G. W. (2006). A demographic perspective on the Muslim world. *Journal of Population Research, 23*, 243–265. https://doi.org/10.1007/BF03031818

Kirk, D. (1966). Factors affecting moslem natality. In B. Berelson (Ed.), *Family planning and population programs* (pp. 149–154). University of Chicago Press.

Lévêque, É. (2017). *L'éducation efface-t-elle les frontières? L'exemple de la fécondité en Méditerranée*. Master's Thesis in Geography, Aix-Marseille University. https://dumas.ccsd.cnrs.fr/dumas-01612919

Lévêque, É., & Oliveau, S. (2019). La transition de la fécondité autour de la Méditerranée: convergence générale et hétérogénéités spatiales, un éclairage par l'éducation. *Espace Populations Sociétés, 2019/2*. https://doi.org/10.4000/eps.9025

Ouadah-Bedidi, Z., Vallin, J., & Bouchoucha, I. (2012). Unexpected developments in Maghrebian fertility. *Population & Societies, 486*. https://doi.org/10.3917/popsoc.486.0001

Seklani, M. (1960). La fécondité dans les pays arabes: données numériques, attitudes et comportements. *Population, 15*, 831–856. https://doi.org/10.2307/1526919

Sobotka, T., & Beaujouan, É. (2014). Two Is best? The persistence of a two-child family ideal in Europe. *Population and Development Review, 40*, 391–419. https://doi.org/10.1111/j.1728-4457.2014.00691.x

World Population Prospects 2022. (2022). United Nations, Department of Economic and Social Affairs, Population Division. https://population.un.org/wpp/

Open Access This chapter is licensed under the terms of the Creative Commons Attribution 4.0 International License (http://creativecommons.org/licenses/by/4.0/), which permits use, sharing, adaptation, distribution and reproduction in any medium or format, as long as you give appropriate credit to the original author(s) and the source, provide a link to the Creative Commons license and indicate if changes were made.

The images or other third party material in this chapter are included in the chapter's Creative Commons license, unless indicated otherwise in a credit line to the material. If material is not included in the chapter's Creative Commons license and your intended use is not permitted by statutory regulation or exceeds the permitted use, you will need to obtain permission directly from the copyright holder.

Chapter 6
Family Formation and Dissolution

Abstract The question of the unity of the family models in the Mediterranean has been the subject of much debate in the field of generations history. Some researchers have put forward the much disputed hypothesis of a past unity in the Mediterranean area in relation to marriage and the family. In modern times, however, we are dealing with very heterogeneous situations in this area. *A priori*, the populations on the different shores of the Mediterranean do not have much in common, with diversified Western family models on one side, and a very specific Arab-Muslim family model on the other. Although different on both sides of the Mediterranean, family models have nevertheless undergone profound changes over the last 70 years: some discuss a "marriage revolution" for the populations of the Southern and Eastern shores, others a second demographic transition in the European countries. In the same way that researchers envisage a convergence of family models in the world towards the Western family model could there be a convergence of Mediterranean family models due to these contemporary family changes? Without directly answering this question, this chapter will attempt to provide some food for thought. Therefore, among the many possible elements for analysing family models, we decided to focus on the formation and dissolution of marriages. We will present the evolution of demographic indicators relating to these two phenomena, starting with marriage and divorce rates, followed by indicators relating to age at marriage and the significance of permanent celibacy. Unlike, the other demographic phenomena, we were unable to use the large international databases to study all the Mediterranean countries since 1950 for these family formation and dissolution related topics. We had to instead collate data from different data providers to create long series.

Keywords Marriage · Divorce · Family formation · Family dissolution · Age at marriage · Permanent celibacy · Family model · Mediterranean

6.1 Introduction

The question of the unity of the family models in the Mediterranean has been the subject of much debate in the field of generations history (Sacchi and Viazzo, 2014). Some researchers have put forward the much disputed hypothesis of a past unity in the Mediterranean area in relation to marriage and the family (Goody, 1983). In modern times, however, we are dealing with very heterogeneous situations in this area. *A priori*, the populations on the different shores of the Mediterranean do not have much in common, with diversified Western family models on one side, and a very specific Arab-Muslim family model on the other.

Although different on both sides of the Mediterranean, family models have nevertheless undergone profound changes over the last 70 years: some discuss a "marriage revolution" for the populations of the Southern and Eastern shores (Tabutin and Schoumaker, 2005), others a second demographic transition in the European countries (Lesthaeghe, 2014). In the same way that researchers envisage a convergence of family models in the world towards the Western family model (Goode, 1963; Thornton, 2001) could there be a convergence of Mediterranean family models due to these contemporary family changes? Without directly answering this question, this chapter will attempt to provide some food for thought. Therefore, among the many possible elements for analysing family models, we decided to focus on the formation and dissolution of marriages. We will present the evolution of demographic indicators relating to these two phenomena, starting with marriage and divorce rates, followed by indicators relating to age at marriage and the significance of permanent celibacy. Unlike, the other demographic phenomena, we were unable to use the large international databases to study all the Mediterranean countries since 1950 for these family formation and dissolution related topics. We had to instead collate data from different data providers to create long series.

6.2 Major Marriage and Divorce Trends

6.2.1 *Marriage*

Historically, marriage is an important institution, but it does not necessarily occupy the same place in every society. It is therefore interesting to first analyse the frequency of marriages in Mediterranean countries, which has undergone major changes since 1950. We are using a nuptiality rate which relates the number of marriages in a time period to the population aged 15 years or older.[1]

---

[1] Usually, the crude nuptiality rate relates the number of marriages to the average total population in the same year. However, we prefer to relate it to the population of marriageable age (15 years or older). This makes it possible to control somewhat for the effect of the age structure and to compare more easily the nuptiality rate intensity in the Mediterranean countries.

6.2 Major Marriage and Divorce Trends

First, nuptiality rates are heterogeneous in the Mediterranean at the beginning of the observation period, no real difference between the Northern shore and the Southern and Eastern shores (Fig. 6.1). Indeed, they range from 9% (Malta) to 28% (Jordan) in the early 1960s. The lowest values (around 10%) are found in Southern Europe (Malta, France, Spain, Italy), and also in Cyprus and Libya. For higher values, countries from different shores are mixed. For example, the highest values (above 14%) are Jordan, Egypt, Bosnia-Herzegovina and Serbia. During this period, many European countries experienced a "golden age" of marriage. The nuptiality rate experienced a strong post-war increase, which lasted until the mid-1960s in Northern Europe and the 1970s for Southern Europe. In Spain, for example, in the 1956–1975 period, the nuptiality rate was almost at its highest for the twentieth century (Muñoz-Pérez & Recaño-Valverde, 2011). It is interesting to note that the vast majority of Mediterranean countries exceeded the nuptiality rate levels reached during the "golden age" of marriage by Southern European countries. This is because marriage is a religious duty in Islam, and it is universal (Locoh & Ouadah-Bedidi, 2014), meaning that the vast majority of adults are married.

The evolution of the nuptiality rate, up to the present day, has varied from region to region, but there has been a general downward trend. Southern Europe shows the simplest pattern, since from the 1970s onwards, the nuptiality rate has been decreasing continuously, until stabilising eventually at a low level (with the exception of Malta). In most cases, the nuptiality rate in Southern European countries has reduced by more than a factor of 2 and is now among the lowest in the European Union.

The Balkan countries generally follow the same trend, but with some exceptions. In terms of timing, the decline in the nuptiality rate does not begin in the 1970s everywhere: sometimes earlier (Slovenia as early as the 1950s) and sometimes later (Albania in the early 2000s). Moreover, the nuptiality rate achieved at present is highly variable from one country to another, with sometimes very low levels (Slovenia, Bulgaria) similar to those in Southern Europe, and sometimes rather high levels (>10%); such as in Albania and especially in Kosovo; the other Balkan countries showing intermediate levels (between 5 and 8%). Over the entire period, the nuptiality rate has strongly decreased, as it has been divided by 2 (or more) in the majority of Balkan countries, and by more than 3 in Slovenia.

In North Africa, the evolution of the nuptiality rate has generally taken place in three distinct phases. First, rates increased (except in Egypt and Algeria where they decreased) until the 1970s; then they decreased until reaching levels below 10%. In contrast to previous trajectories, however, there has been a significant increase in the nuptiality rate towards high levels during the 2000s. This last phase coincides with the recent increase in fertility in these countries (see Chap. 4). Egypt stands out, over the entire period, for having a higher nuptiality rate than the other North African countries.

Finally, the trajectories of the Near Eastern countries are on the decline over the period, with sometimes uneven developments (Jordan, Lebanon, Cyprus). However, the declines in these countries are generally smaller than those observed elsewhere

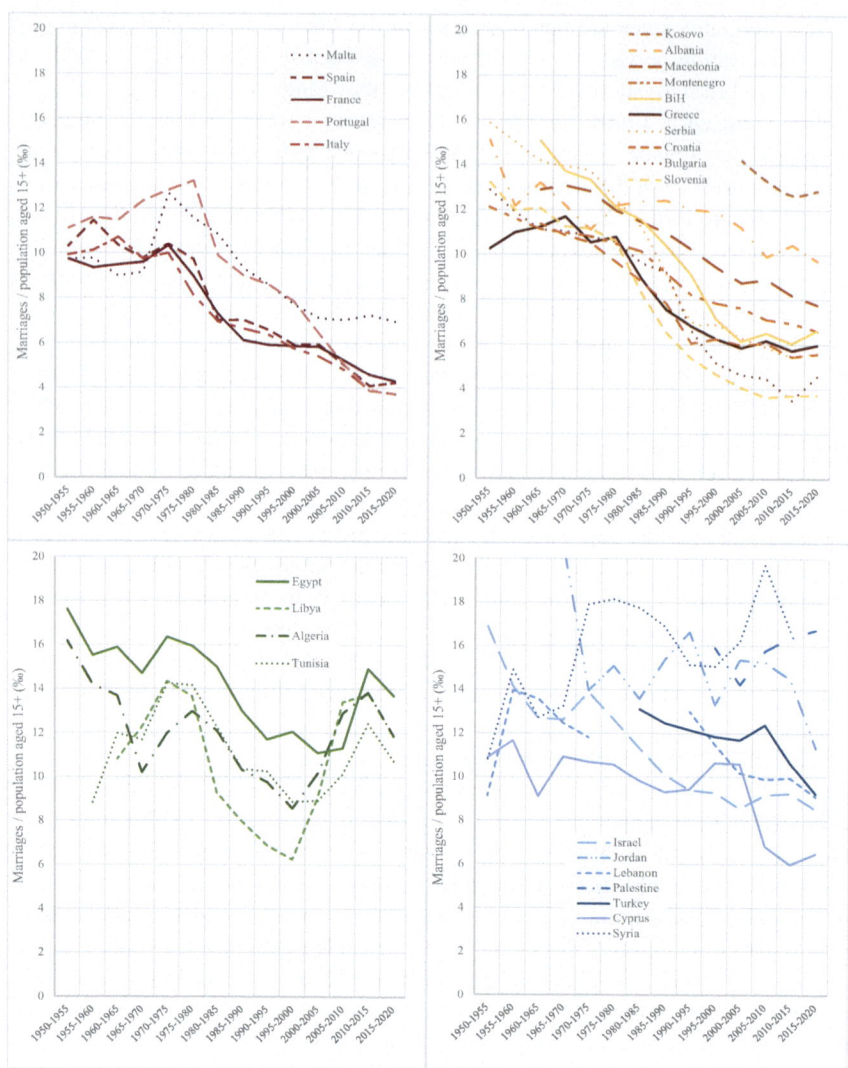

Fig. 6.1 Nuptiality rate in the Mediterranean (1950–2019) (*Sources* Demographic Statistics Database, National Office of Statistics, Eurostat, Demographic Yearbook [UN], World Population Prospect 2022. Calculations made by the authors. *N. B. 1* The number of marriages is related to the population aged 15 years and over [not to the total population]. *N.B. 2* Jordan's values between 1950 and 1970 are off graph. *N.B. 3* The evolution of the indicator is using averages calculated for 5-year periods)

in the Mediterranean. Only Palestine and Syria are exceptions, with the former experiencing an increase since the mid-2000s in line with North African countries, and the latter having a higher nuptiality rate today than in the 1950s.

These analyses show differentiated developments. They have finally led to a divergence since the 1980s, as the relative disparities are now higher. In 2015–2019, the nuptiality rate in the Mediterranean was spread over a wide range of values, from single to triple. This means that the frequency of marriages in societies is significantly different on either side of the Mediterranean. Moreover, unlike at the beginning of the period, the three Mediterranean shores are visibly different today. Indeed, the countries on the Northern Shore have the lowest values, and those on the Southern and Eastern shores the highest (despite the decrease in their nuptiality rate since the 1950s–1960s). There are some exceptions, with high values for Albania and Kosovo, and intermediate values for Israel and Cyprus.

This geographical contrast is partly explained by the age structure. For the same population, the age groups with the highest probability of marrying (20–40 years) will account for a larger share in the young population, resulting in a higher number of marriages, and thus a higher nuptiality rate than the older population. Thus, as the countries on the Southern and Eastern shores (but also Albania and Kosovo) are on average younger than the countries on the Northern Shore (including Israel and Cyprus) (see Chap. 2), it is not surprising that their nuptiality rates are higher. However, this difference in nuptiality rates between these two groups of countries can also be explained by other factors that we will discuss later in the chapter, such as the rate of remarriage.

6.2.2 Divorce

Divorce analysis measures the frequency of divorces in a population. We use divorce rates to conduct a comparison.[2]

The evolution of the divorce rate in the Mediterranean highlights several interesting elements (Fig. 6.2). The first is the higher level of divorce in Muslim-majority countries compared to Catholic-majority (or traditional) countries, especially before the 1980s. This is not surprising, as divorce/repudiation is a regulatory mechanism in the Arab-Muslim matrimonial system (Fargues, 1986). Unlike Catholicism, Islam allows a marriage to be broken via a mechanism other than by death. Divorce/repudiation is therefore a very common practice in Islam, although in reality it is an indicator of male dominance. Indeed, before the introduction of modern family law in some countries, divorce (repudiation) was initiated by the man (Locoh & Ouadah-Bedidi, 2014). However, this high divorce rate does not lead to an over-representation of divorced people in the population. On the contrary, there are few divorced people,

---

[2] As with marriage, we relate the number of divorces to the population aged 15 or over, and to the total population.

as remarriages are very common and quick. In Egypt, for example, divorcees represent less than 2% of the 15–59 year olds in 2017, for both men and women. By way of comparison, in France, in 2016, they represent about 6% for men and 8.5% for women, while the divorce rate is lower. This link between divorce and remarriage also helps to explain the higher nuptiality rate in the countries of the Southern and Eastern shores and is observed in the previous sub-section, a significant part of which is due to remarriage.

Despite this characteristic of the Arab-Muslim matrimonial system, disparities exist within the countries concerned from the beginning of the observation period. Even if divorce has been declining since the beginning of the twentieth century (Fargues, 1986), some countries still had very high levels (more than 4‰[3]) in the 1950s, for example Egypt and Jordan, or Libya in the early 1970s. Others have lower levels (less than 2%), such as Tunisia, Turkey, Syria and Lebanon. In general, these levels contrast with the divorce rates of the Northern shore countries, which generally did not exceed 1% in the 1950s, with the exception of Serbia and Albania.

In terms of divorce rate changes, what is important now is the heterogeneity of trajectories. In Southern Europe, the divorce rate was rather low in the 1950s. It then gradually increased, starting in the late 1960s in France, in the mid-1970s in Portugal, and in the early 2000s in Spain. A maximum of around 2.7% was reached by these three countries, before experiencing a decline in the 2010s. Italy has only recently experienced an increase in its divorce rate. Malta only allowed divorce in 2011, the last European country to do so, and has low levels at present. In the Balkans, the divorce rate is on the whole increasing over the whole period (though sometimes alternating between increasing and decreasing). However, the Balkan countries do not reach Southern European levels, as their divorce rates are generally between 1 and 2%. Serbia and Kosovo are the only countries to see a decrease in divortiality over the study period.

The trajectories are quite different on the Southern and Eastern shores. The evolution generally takes place in two stages, with varying timing: a decrease and then an increase in the divorce rate. Some of the declines are impressive: Egypt's divorce rate, for example, fell by a factor of 3 during a 50-year period before doubling in the 10 years that followed. Cyprus and Lebanon are exceptions to this general pattern, as their divorce rates only increase throughout the period, a trajectory similar to those in Southern Europe. Tunisia also shows a different trajectory, as its divorce rate has essentially stagnated since the 1960s. Today, the countries of the Southern and Eastern shores reach rather high levels of divorce since the vast majority exceed 2%. In other words, divorces are more frequent today in Egyptian, Palestinian or Jordanian societies than in France, Spain or Portugal, which have nevertheless experienced an unprecedented increase in their divorce rate since 1970.

---

[3] A level of 4‰ may seem low compared to other crude rates, such as crude birth or death rates. This is due to the choice of denominator for the indicator, in this case the population aged 15 years or over. If we had chosen 15–60 year olds, the indicator would have been even higher. In addition, the number of divorces, or marriages, is generally lower than the number of births or deaths.

6.2 Major Marriage and Divorce Trends

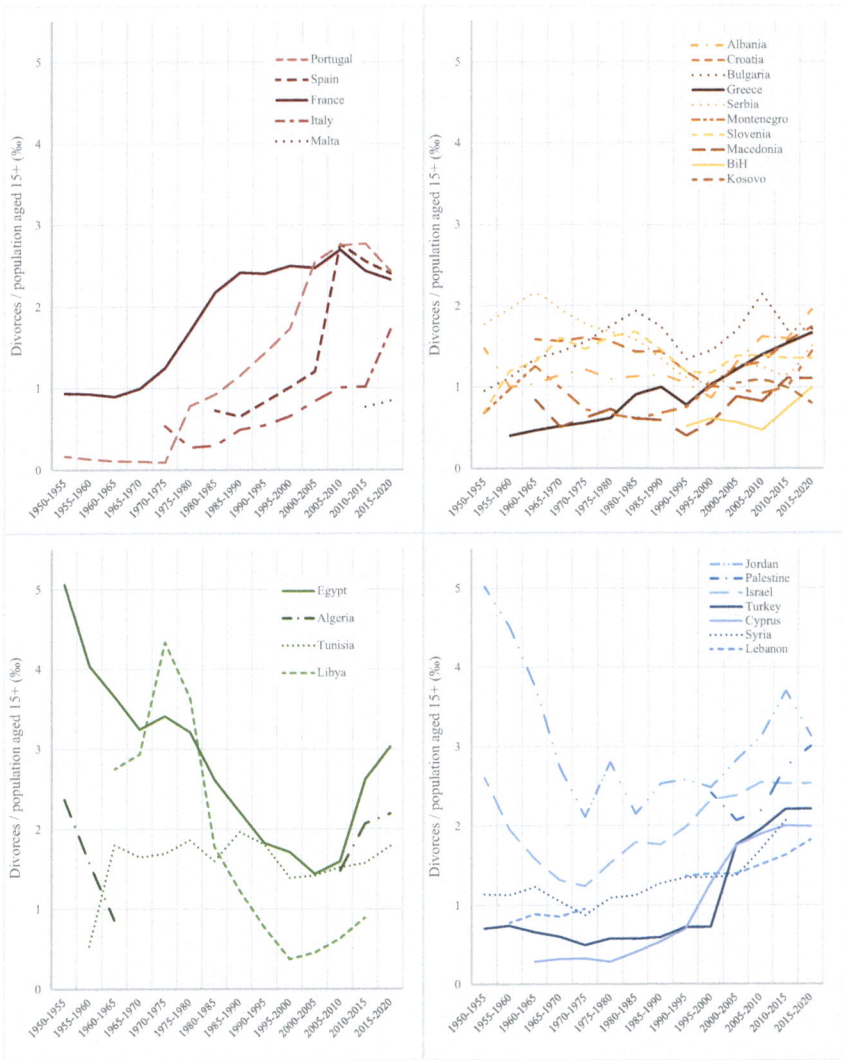

Fig. 6.2 Divorce rates in the Mediterranean (1950–2019) (*Sources* Demographic Statistics Database, National Office of Statistics, Eurostat, Demographic Yearbook [UN], World Population Prospect 2022. Calculations made by the authors. *N.B. 1* The number of divorces is related to the population aged 15 years or more (and not to the total population). *N.B. 2* The evolution of the indicator is based on averages calculated for periods of 5 years. *N.B. 3* The sharp increase in Turkey in the late 1990s is due to a break in the series)

These different trajectories lead to a convergence of the divorce rate in the Mediterranean, but in a different way from that observed for the total fertility rate (Chap. 4) or life expectancy at birth (in this chapter). For the latter, it is a convergence by catching up that is observed. Here, on the contrary, there is a convergence caused by the decline in high divortiality of the Southern and Eastern shores and the growing low divortiality of the Northern shore. Divorce rates in the Mediterranean today are mainly between 1 and 2.5%. The current relative disparities, although not negligible, are less significant than in the 1950s–1960s. Thus, at the end of the 2010s, there is still a contrast between the shores of the Mediterranean, even though some Southern European countries (France, Spain, Portugal), and to a lesser extent Albania, have similar (or even higher) levels of divorce than several Muslim countries.

These major trends point to far-reaching social changes in the Mediterranean. Generally speaking, and despite the variety of marriage trajectories, marriages are less frequent today than 60–70 years ago. In the 1960s, the vast majority of Mediterranean countries had a nuptiality rate of over 10%, today it is less than a third. At the same time, the frequency of divorce has increased in countries where it was low, and decreased in countries where it was high.

6.3 Changes in Marriage

In order to appreciate the changes in marriage in the Mediterranean, we will examine two important dimensions, namely the evolution of the age at marriage and permanent celibacy.

6.3.1 An Increase in Age at Marriage

One of the most dramatic changes is the increase in age upon first marriage for both men and women (Fig. 6.3). In this chapter, we use the singulate mean age at marriage (SMAM[4]) indicator to estimate the age upon first marriage.

In the 1950s–1960s, there were only four countries with an age upon first marriage for women[5] above 24. This age has increased everywhere in the Mediterranean, so much so that at present only Palestine and Egypt are below the age of 24.[6]

Before the 1970s, women could sometimes marry very young. This was particularly the case in North Africa where the age upon first marriage for women was

---

[4] The SMAM is an indirect method for estimating age upon first marriage from age-specific marital status.

[5] Only the age upon first marriage of women is shown here, as the age at first marriage of men shows a broadly similar trend.

[6] Turkey also has an age upon first marriage for women below 24 years, but following a recent decrease.

6.3 Changes in Marriage

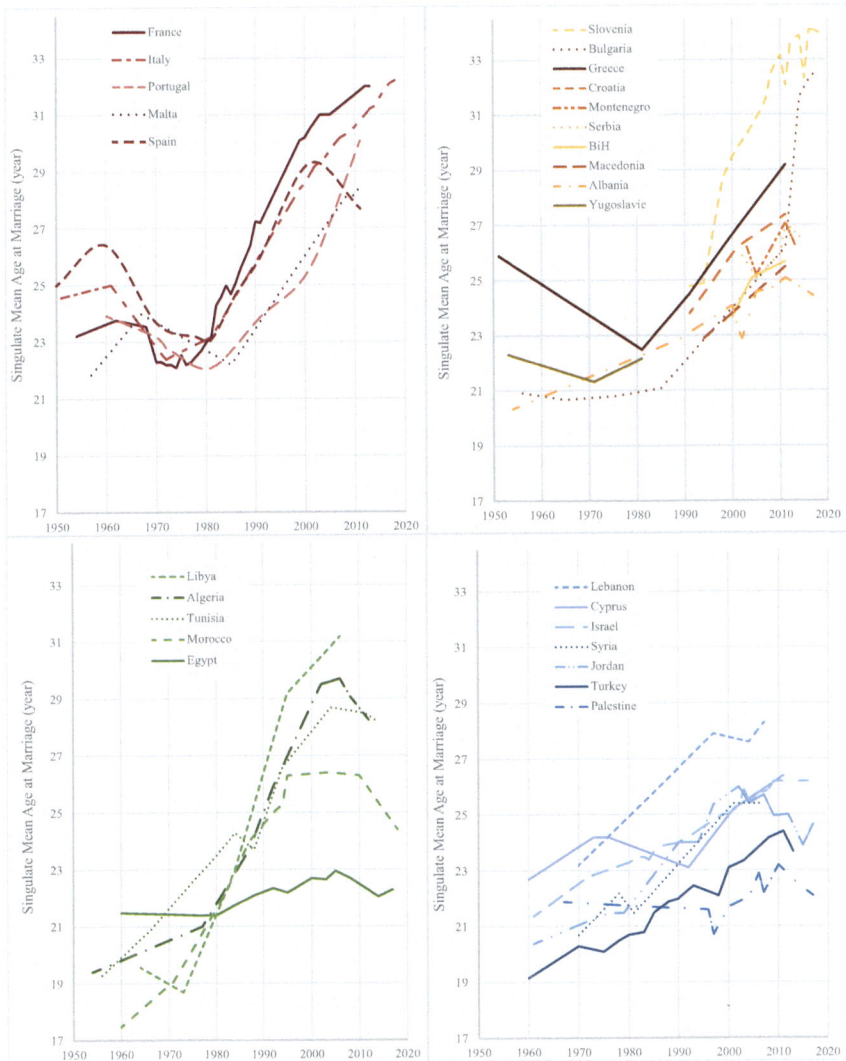

Fig. 6.3 Age upon first marriage of women in the Mediterranean (1950–2019) (*Sources* World Marriage Database [2019], Demographic Statistics Database, Demographic Yearbook [UN]. Calculations made by the authors. *N. B.* age upon first marriage is estimated with the singulate mean age at marriage [SMAM])

below 20 in the 1950s (except in Egypt), in the Near East (Turkey, Jordan), and in some Balkan countries (Albania, Bulgaria). Conversely, the countries where women married later (over the age of 22) were mainly in Southern Europe, but also in the Balkans (Yugoslavia, Greece) and the Near East (Cyprus, Palestine).

The age upon first marriage of women has therefore gradually increased to sometimes very high levels. In Southern Europe, there was first a decline in the age of marriage in the 1960s, which represented the "golden age" of marriage. It was not until the late 1970s or early 1980s that women's age at marriage began to increase; now, it is generally above 30 years. The trends are similar in the Balkans. The difference with Southern Europe lies in the levels reached in the 2010s. They are much lower in the Balkans, where they generally do not exceed the age of 27 years. The only exceptions are Slovenia, Bulgaria and Greece, the first two of which reach ages above 32.

In the Near East and North Africa, the age upon first marriage of women is increasing significantly, sometimes reaching very high levels today. This is the case, for example, in Algeria, Libya, Lebanon and Tunisia where the age is 28. Only Egypt and Palestine have had a moderate increase or even a stagnation in their age upon first marriage for women at around 22 years. From the 2000s onwards, the indicator starts to decrease in some countries (Algeria, Tunisia, Palestine, Jordan, Egypt, Morocco), generally those with a recent increase in fertility. Finally, the dichotomy between the Mediterranean shores of the 1950s and 1960s no longer exists today. In fact, it is now conceivable that the age upon first marriage for women is similar across different countries of the Mediterranean shores.

This increase in age at marriage can be explained by several factors. Firstly, the progression in education is decisive in this area, since by spending more time at school (primary, then secondary and increasingly university), individuals postpone the age at which they get married. Secondly, economic crises lead to uncertain and precarious living conditions, encouraging the postponement of marriage. In a neo-local system,[7] young couples form their own household upon marriage, and do not move in with the husband's parents. To do so, they must have sufficient resources to move out of the parental home and form a new household. Worsening socio-economic conditions (high youth unemployment, declining living standards, etc.) can hamper household formation for young couples, who have to wait longer to gather the necessary resources to establish their own household. Similarly, the rising cost of housing in large cities, and the increasing cost of marriage (dowry, festivities, etc.) in Arab-Muslim societies, also delay the union formation among young couples, and by extension the age at which they marry.

This increase in the age upon first marriage has two direct effects. The first is the decrease in the age gap between spouses, which is the result of a more rapid increase in the age upon first marriage for women than for men. In the 1950s, Arab-Muslim countries could have age gaps between spouses of more than 6 years,[8] while in other countries they were less than 4 years. However, despite this decrease, the age gaps

---

[7] A neo-local system implies that newlyweds form a new household, separate from of the husband's or wife's parents.

[8] The age gaps between spouses presented here are calculated from the singulate mean age at marriage (SMAM), which generally underestimates the actual gap compared to those calculated with micro-data (Ausubel et al., 2022).

6.3 Changes in Marriage

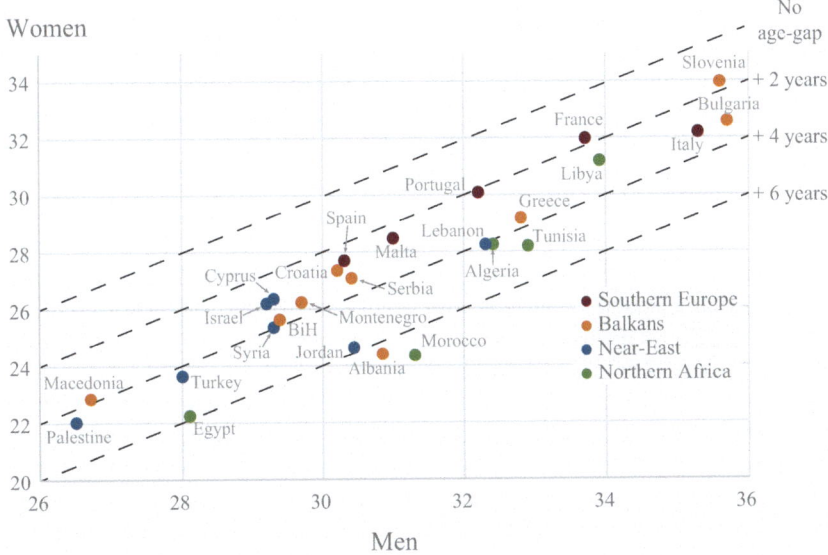

Fig. 6.4 Age difference of male and female singulate mean age at marriage (SMAM) in the Mediterranean in the 2010s (*Sources* World Marriage Database [2019], Demographic Statistics Database, Demographic Yearbook [UN]. Calculations made by the authors. *Reading tip*: the dotted lines represent an age gap between spouses. For example, the points on the line "+2 years" are countries where men are on average 2 years older than their spouses. The colour of a dot represents the regional area to which a country belongs)

between spouses in Arab-Muslim countries and in Albania, remain the largest in the Mediterranean (Fig. 6.4).

This is not surprising since the large age gap between spouses is one of the important characteristics of Arab-Muslim marriage, which has some of the highest levels in the world (Weeks, 2020). The age gap in the Mediterranean is on average just under 4 years, with a minimum of about 1.6 years in France and Slovenia. Surprisingly, this gap has been increasing recently in some countries, for example in Egypt, Algeria and Morocco, where it is again as high as 6 years (Ausubel et al., 2022).

The second consequence of the increase in the age upon first marriage concerns early marriage. An important feature of traditional Arab-Muslim marriage is the early marriage of girls (Rashad et al., 2005). In the 1960s in Morocco and Algeria, for example, more than half of all women were married before the age of 20. It was 40% in Tunisia, Egypt and Libya, and 30% in Turkey and Jordan. Early marriage also concerns countries on the Northern shore, as it was 30% in Albania and 20% in Bulgaria. With the increase in the age upon first marriage, and especially thanks to better education, fewer and fewer women are married before the age of 20. Early marriage has almost disappeared from the Mediterranean, since in the vast majority of countries the proportion of women married between the ages of 15 and 20 is less than 10%. The only notable exceptions are Egypt and Palestine, where the proportion has recently increased to 27 and 15% respectively. These situations show that trend reversals are possible even in cases where that seemed like a given.

6.3.2 Permanent Celibacy

In demography, the notion of celibacy is linked to the legal marital status of individuals. A single person is a person who is not married, but who may well be in a relationship. A permanent celibate is generally defined as a person aged 45–49 who has never married. They may, however, have already been in a relationship, or be in a legal union other than marriage (e.g. civil union). We have seen previously that the age upon first marriage has increased everywhere in the Mediterranean, this however implies that the population is marrying later on average, and not necessarily that it is marrying less. In this context, permanent celibacy makes it possible to estimate the proportion of a generation that has lived a large part of adult life without marrying, and in turn to assess the extent to which marriage remains an important institution for family formation.

Permanent female celibacy has generally increased in the Mediterranean (Fig. 6.5). In the 1950s, the vast majority of countries had levels below 5%. In contrast, high levels of permanent female celibacy could be found in Southern Europe, where levels reach 15% in Italy, Spain and Portugal, and even almost 25% in Malta. The evolution of permanent female celibacy in Southern Europe is singular in the Mediterranean, since it decreased until the 1990s, and then increased very rapidly to exceed the levels of the 1950s. At the end of the 2010s, permanent female celibacy reached 20% in Portugal and Italy, and over 30% in France. Only Malta has seen a continuous decline in proportion of permanent single women. Spain, on the other hand, has experienced a very moderate increase in comparison with other Southern European countries: permanent female celibacy barely exceeded 10% in the 2010s.

In the other Mediterranean countries, there is also a clear trend towards an increase in permanent female celibacy. This increase is often moderate, but sometimes significant. In the majority of countries, the current level of permanent female celibacy does not exceed 8%. However, several countries on both sides of the Mediterranean exceed 10%. In a number of countries, permanent celibacy is also at a high level: about 15% in Algeria, Morocco, Lebanon and Bulgaria, and even 28% in Slovenia. These levels should be compared with those reached by Western European countries at the beginning of the twentieth century. A characteristic of the family model in this region was late marriage and a high proportion of permanent celibacy. In 1900, it was generally above 10% for women, and reached 12% in France, 10% in Germany, 15% in Britain, and up to 20% in Portugal (Engelen & Puschmann, 2011). In this respect, the current levels reached by some Mediterranean countries are comparable and can be considered high, even unprecedented in the case of Arab-Muslim countries.

6.3 Changes in Marriage

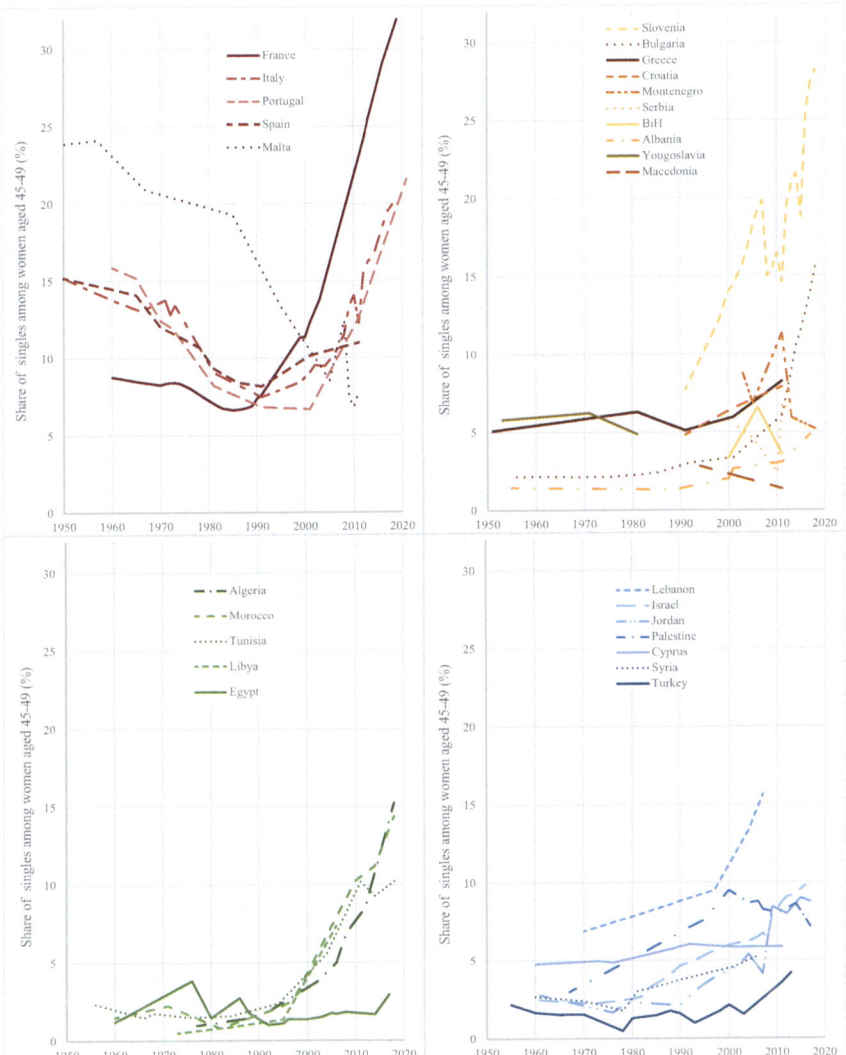

Fig. 6.5 Permanent female celibacy in the Mediterranean (1950–2019) (*Sources* World Marriage Database [2019], Demographic Statistics Database, Demographic Yearbook [UN], MICS. Calculations made by the authors)

We can see how there is no homogeneity within the Arab-Muslim countries, or even within each shore. Similar levels of permanent female celibacy can be found in countries on all shores.

With the increase in the age of marriage and the end of early marriage in most countries, we are witnessing the emergence of singlehood in society, and in particular among women. In many Mediterranean countries, people who have never married

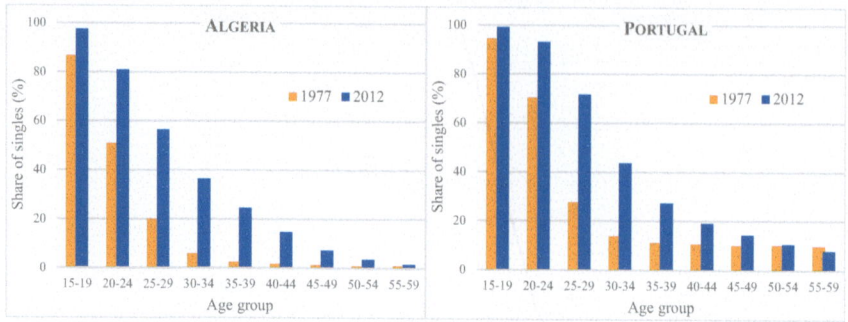

Fig. 6.6 Share of single people aged 15–59 (both sexes) in Portugal and Algeria (*Sources* World Marriage Database [2019], Demographic Statistics Database. Calculations made by the authors)

represent a larger share at each age group. The evolution is sometimes striking in some countries, for example in Algeria and Portugal (Fig. 6.6).

Whereas celibacy often only applied to a minority of age groups in the 1970s, it now concerns a much larger proportion, and sometimes a majority, of people in an age group. The 25–29 year olds in Algeria, for example, were only 20% single in 1977, but over 55% in 2012. We note that in this age group, but also in others, that the share of singles is higher in Algeria than in Portugal. These two countries illustrate how celibacy has become a mass phenomenon as it concerns a significant part of the population, in generally larger proportions than before.

6.3.3 Summary of Family Models

Finally, we propose a simple typology of current family models based on the following two characteristics: permanent female celibacy and female age at marriage (measured by the SMAM). Of course, a more complete typology of family models would take into account many other factors. The aim here however is to summarise the trends outlined above. The result is shown in Fig. 6.7.

There is a general difference between a matrimonial regime with rather low permanent female celibacy and where women marry relatively early, and a matrimonial regime with high permanent female celibacy and high age at marriage. Paradoxically, there is no distinction, either between the different shores of the Mediterranean, or between Arab-Muslim societies and Western societies. Rather, there is a difference between the Western Mediterranean and Eastern Mediterranean. On the Southern and Eastern shores, the "Petit Maghreb"[9] differs from the Near East; and on the Northern shore, Southern Europe and Slovenia stand out from the Balkan countries.

---

[9] This term refers to the western part of North Africa, i.e. Morocco, Algeria and Tunisia.

6.3 Changes in Marriage

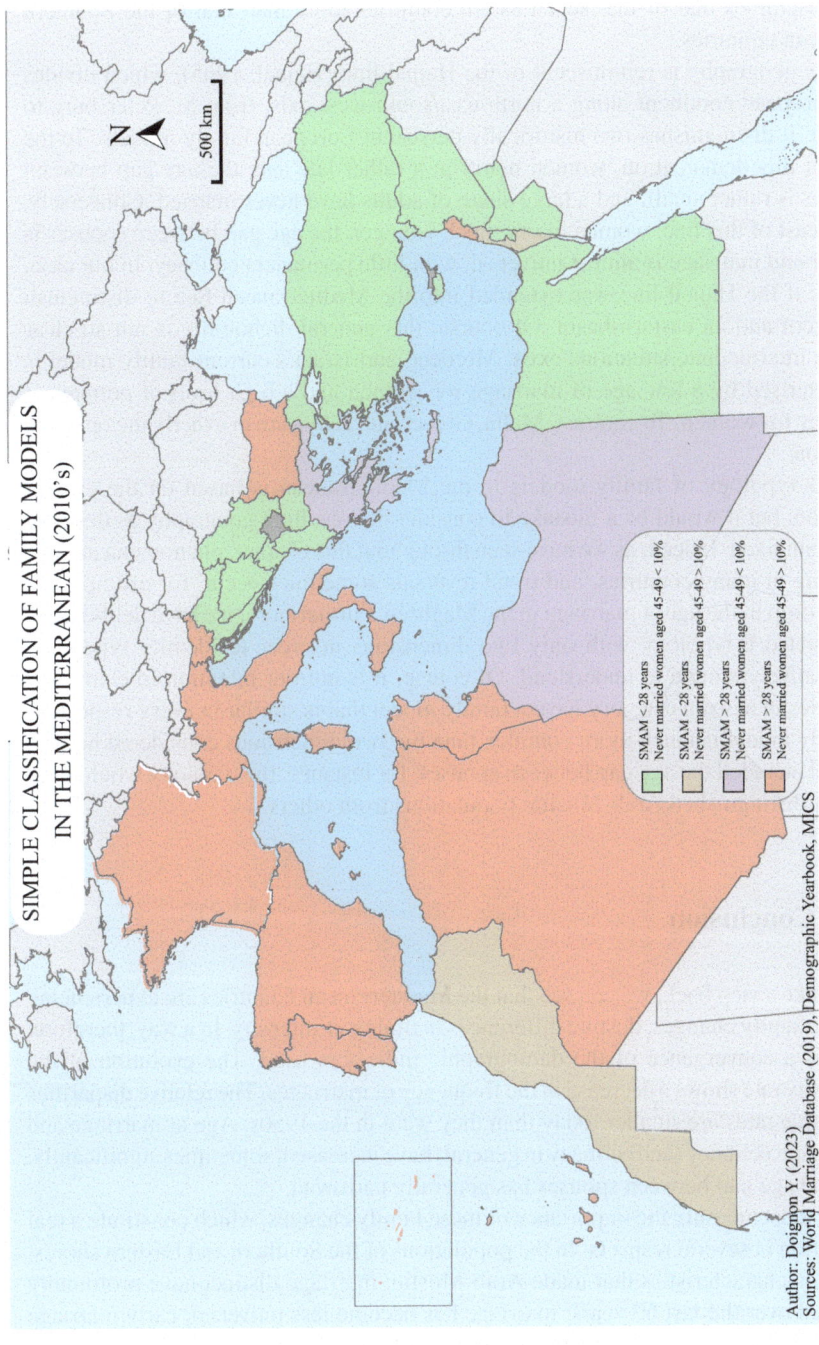

Fig. 6.7 Typology of current family models in the Mediterranean (*Sources* World Marriage Database [2019], Demographic Statistics Database, MICS. Calculations made by the authors. *N.B.* The dates used in each country are those most recently)

Thus defined by these two dimensions, the current family model in the Balkan countries resembles that of the Near Eastern countries more than that of the Southern European countries.

This geography is reminiscent of the Hajnal line (Hajnal, 1965), which divides the European continent along a north-east/south-west axis, from St. Petersburg to Trieste. It distinguishes two historically persistent European family models. To the west of this demarcation, women marry at a rather late age, the age gap between spouses is rather small, and a large share of adults have never married. Conversely, to the east of this line, women marry much younger, the age gap between spouses is greater and marriage is almost universal, with little permanent celibacy. In our case, it is as if the Hajnal line was extended into the Mediterranean Sea to distinguish a western and an eastern basin. Of course, this general dichotomy is not so clear cut, as intermediate situations exist. Morocco and Israel's current family model is characterised by a low age of marriage for women and a high level of permanent celibacy for women. To contrast, Malta, Greece and Libya are in exactly the opposite situation.

This typology of family models in the Mediterranean is based on the current situation, but it would be a mistake to consider the resulting geography as destined to remain fixed. Indeed, as we have seen throughout this chapter, phenomena are still evolving in many countries, and trend reversals sometimes occur, for example the recent drop in the age at marriage in the Maghreb. Furthermore, we have deliberately constructed a typology with only two dimensions in order to identify types that are relatively simple to understand. Of course, it is not our intention to claim that countries in a given category have a family model that is similar in every respect, as a family model is much more complex than the two dimensions considered here. If we had included the age gap between spouses, for instance, the typology would have further distinguished Arab-Muslim populations from others.

6.4 Conclusion

If we take a step back, we can see that the Mediterranean countries are experiencing similar family changes, despite differences in timing or intensity. In a way, therefore, there is a convergence of the demographic indicators used. The evolution of the nuptiality rate shows a decrease in the frequency of marriages. The relative disparities in divorce rates are smaller today than they were in the 1950s. Age at marriage and permanent celibacy (and celibacy in general) have increased, sometimes significantly. And the age gap between spouses has generally narrowed.

We must measure the importance of these family changes, which constitute a real revolution in several respects. In the populations of the Southern and Eastern shores, the main characteristics that made Arab-Muslim marriage distinct have profoundly changed over the last 60 years: marriage has become less universal, early marriage has disappeared in most countries, the divorce rate has been decreasing, and the age gap between spouses has been reduced. A similar observation can be found in the Balkan countries, which were traditionally characterised by universal and early marriage. With regard to the countries of Southern Europe, family changes since the 1970s are a break with the period of the "golden age" of marriage, which was ultimately a parenthesis in relation to past trends. These countries traditionally had a late marriage family model that was not universal.

References

Ausubel, J., Kramer, S., Shi, A. F., & Hackett, C. (2022). Measuring age differences among different-sex couples: Across religions and 130 countries, men are older than their female partners. *Population Studies, 76*, 465–476. https://doi.org/10.1080/00324728.2022.2094452

Demographic Statistics Database. United Nations Statistics Division. https://unstats.un.org/unsd/demographic-social/products/dyb/index.cshtml

Engelen, T., & Puschmann, P. (2011). How unique is the Western European marriage pattern? A comparison of nuptiality in historical Europe and the contemporary Arab world. *History of the Family, 16*, 387–400. https://doi.org/10.1016/j.hisfam.2011.07.004

Fargues, P. (1986). Traditions matrimoniales dans les sociétés arabes. *Population et Sociétés, 198*. https://www.ined.fr/fichier/s_rubrique/18983/pop_et_soc_francais_198.fr.pdf

Goode, W. J. (1963). *World revolution and family patterns*. Free Press.

Goody, J. (1983). *The development of the family and marriage in Europe*. Past and Present Publications. Cambridge University Press. https://doi.org/10.1017/CBO9780511607752

Hajnal, J. (1965). European marriage patterns in perspective. In D. V. Glass & D. E. C. Eversley (eds.), *Population in history: Essays in historical demography, volume I: General and great Britain* (pp. 101–143). Edward Arnold; Aldine Publishing.

Lesthaeghe, R. (2014). The second demographic transition: A concise overview of its development. *Proceedings of the National Academy of Sciences, 111*, 18112–18115. https://doi.org/10.1073/pnas.1420441111

Locoh, T., & Ouadah-Bedidi, Z. (2014). *Familles et rapports de genre au Maghreb, Evolutions ou révolutions*. Document de travail 213. Institut National d'Etudes Démographiques. https://www.ined.fr/fichier/s_rubrique/22779/document.travail.2014.213.magreb.genre.fr.pdf

Muñoz-Pérez, F., & Recaño-Valverde, J. (2011). A century of nuptiality in Spain, 1900–2007. *European Journal of Population, 27*, 487–515. https://doi.org/10.1007/s10680-011-9234-1

Rashad, H., Osman, M., & Roudi-Fahimi, F. (2005). Marriage in the Arab World. Population Reference Bureau, 8. https://u.demog.berkeley.edu/~jrw/Biblio/Eprints/PRB/files/MarriageInArabWorld_Eng.pdf

Sacchi, P., & Viazzo, P. P. (2014). Family and household. In P. Horden & S. Kinoshita (eds.), *A Companion to mediterranean history* (pp. 234–249). Wiley Blackwell Companions to History. Wiley & Sons. https://doi.org/10.1002/9781118519356

Tabutin, D., & Schoumaker, B. (2005). The demography of the Arab World and the middle East from the 1950s to the 2000s. *Population, 60*, 611–724. https://doi.org/10.3917/popu.505.0611

Thornton, A. (2001). The developmental paradigm, reading history sideways, and family change. *Demography, 38*, 449–465. https://doi.org/10.2307/3088311

Weeks, J. (2020). *Population: An introduction to concepts and issues* (13th ed.). Cengage.

World Marriage Data. (2019). United Nations, Department of Economic and Social Affairs, Population Division. https://population.un.org/MarriageData/Index.html

World Population Prospects. (2022). United Nations, Department of Economic and Social Affairs, Population Division. https://population.un.org/wpp/

Open Access This chapter is licensed under the terms of the Creative Commons Attribution 4.0 International License (http://creativecommons.org/licenses/by/4.0/), which permits use, sharing, adaptation, distribution and reproduction in any medium or format, as long as you give appropriate credit to the original author(s) and the source, provide a link to the Creative Commons license and indicate if changes were made.

The images or other third party material in this chapter are included in the chapter's Creative Commons license, unless indicated otherwise in a credit line to the material. If material is not included in the chapter's Creative Commons license and your intended use is not permitted by statutory regulation or exceeds the permitted use, you will need to obtain permission directly from the copyright holder.

Chapter 7
Mortality Profiles

Abstract The Mediterranean is currently characterised by rather low mortality. Indeed, life expectancy at birth exceeds the global average in almost all countries of the region. But this was not always the case. Mortality in the Mediterranean has fallen sharply since 1950: average life expectancy at birth was 78 years in 2019 compared to only 53 years in 1950. This dramatic increase in life expectancy at birth is a sign of great convergence between Mediterranean countries, but also of a profound shift in mortality patterns concerning both causes of mortality and ages at which people die. Despite these general trends of overall convergence in mortality, disparities persist between countries. This chapter takes a look at the evolution of mortality in the Mediterranean since 1950. We will start by describing trends in overall mortality by studying the indicator of life expectancy at birth. We will then analyse mortality by major age groups: child mortality (0–5 years), adult mortality (15–64 years) and mortality at advanced ages (65 years or older). Finally, to explain the identified mortality differences, we will take a look at the health transition in the Mediterranean in relation to the major causes of mortality.

Keywords Mortality · Mortality profiles · Infant and child mortality · Adult mortality · Mortality at advanced ages · Health transition · Mediterranean

7.1 Introduction

The Mediterranean is currently characterised by rather low mortality. Indeed, life expectancy at birth exceeds the global average in almost all countries of the region. But this was not always the case. Mortality in the Mediterranean has fallen sharply since 1950: average life expectancy at birth was 78 years in 2019 compared to only 53 years in 1950. This dramatic increase in life expectancy at birth is a sign of great convergence between Mediterranean countries, but also of a profound shift in

---

The original version of this chapter was revised: Figures 7.5 and 7.6 have been replaced. The erratum to this chapter can be found at
https://doi.org/10.1007/978-3-031-37759-4_11

© The Author(s) 2023, corrected publication 2023
Y. Doignon et al., *Population Dynamics in the Mediterranean*,
SpringerBriefs in Population Studies,
https://doi.org/10.1007/978-3-031-37759-4_7

mortality patterns concerning both causes of mortality and ages at which people die. Despite these general trends of overall convergence in mortality, disparities persist between countries. This chapter takes a look at the evolution of mortality in the Mediterranean since 1950.

We will start by describing trends in overall mortality by studying the indicator of life expectancy at birth. We will then analyse mortality by major age groups: child mortality (0–5 years), adult mortality (15–64 years) and mortality at advanced ages (65 years or older). Finally, to explain the identified mortality differences, we will take a look at the health transition in the Mediterranean in relation to the major causes of mortality.

7.2 Mortality at All Ages: Life Expectancy at Birth

7.2.1 A Very Heterogeneous Picture in 1950

In 1950, overall mortality levels were very disparate in the Mediterranean (Fig. 7.1). Life expectancies at birth (e_0)[1] ranged from 34 to 68 years. This meant that some countries were already progressing well in the transition from high to low mortality rate, while others still had a way to go. The former had e_0s above 60 years as seen in Southern Europe and in the majority of the Balkans, along with some countries in the Near East (Israel, Lebanon and Cyprus to a lesser extent). On the other hand, the latter were characterised by much higher mortality levels. Life expectancies at birth in North African countries were thus generally less than 40 years and those in the Near East between 45 and 50 years, corresponding respectively to the mortality trends of France at the beginning of the nineteenth century and Italy in the 1920s. Balkan countries (Albania, Bosnia-Herzegovina, and Macedonia) were in an intermediate situation with e_0s approaching 50 years of age.

Despite sometimes high mortality levels, the situation in 1950 would indicate that the Mediterranean populations were all nevertheless engaged in the process of mortality transition. Indeed, before mortality began to decrease with the Industrial Revolution in the late 18th to the early nineteenth century, the e_0 generally did not exceed 30–35 years in Europe (Weeks, 2020). However, all the Mediterranean countries more or less exceeded this threshold in 1950, showing that the mortality transition had potentially begun before the Second World War. For example, Egypt and Algeria saw their mortality gradually decrease from the beginning of the twentieth century (Fargues, 1986; Tabutin et al., 2002). This characteristic of the mortality transition in the Mediterranean is surely explained by the "Mediterranean hygienisation"[2] (Pouget, 2021). Indeed, rich exchanges of knowledge and medical practices have taken place between all the shores of the Mediterranean since the nineteenth

---

[1] For ease of reading, we use the annotation "e_0" in this chapter to mean "life expectancy at birth".

[2] This text has been translated into English by the authors. The original text in French is as follows: "hygiénisation méditerranéenne".

7.2 Mortality at All Ages: Life Expectancy at Birth

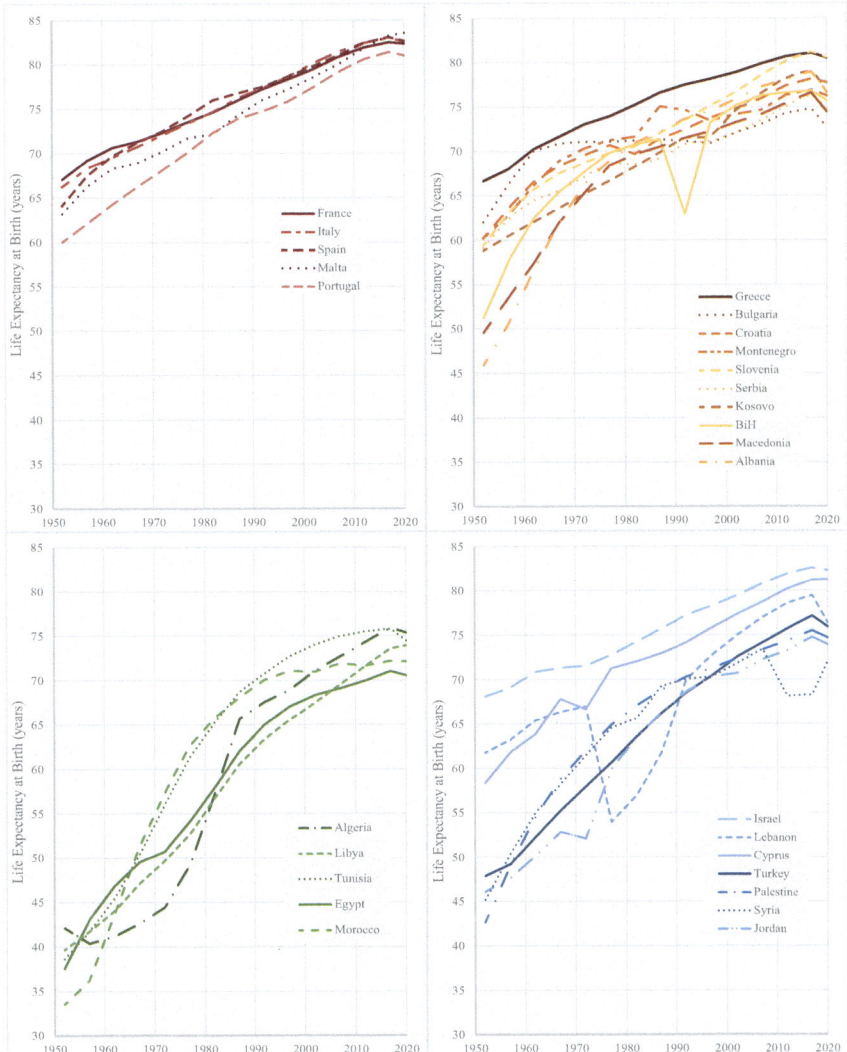

Fig. 7.1 Evolution of life expectancy at birth in the Mediterranean (1950–2021) (*Source* World Population Prospects 2022. Calculations made by the authors. *Note* The time units used are five-year periods)

century (Speziale, 2018). Doctors, nurses, sisters and missionaries were the vectors of the Pasteur revolution during the first half of the twentieth century.

Nevertheless, even though mortality declined relatively early in the Mediterranean, the health situation in many countries was still dire in 1950: child mortality was particularly high and few people reached old age. Indeed, a life expectancy at birth of 35 years, as in Egypt in 1950, meant that about one in four children died before one year and only 30% of a generation reached the age of 65. By way of comparison, during the same period, the proportions were respectively 2 children out of 10 and 50% in Macedonia (e_0 of 50 years), or 5 out of 100 and 68% in France (e_0 of 66 years). Thus, within the Mediterranean of the 1950s, there were very contrasting demographic realities, with populations located at an early stage of the mortality transition and others at an advanced stage.

7.2.2 General Convergence Since 1950[3]

Since 1950, mortality has declined significantly across the region, currently exceeding an e_0 of 70 years in all Mediterranean countries (Fig. 7.1). Mediterranean populations are all in a phase of low relative mortality: everywhere less than 2% of children die before the age of 1, and more than 75% of a generation reaches the age of 65. Great strides have been made to reduce mortality; previously, death was a serious threat to human society.

This decline in mortality has not occurred at the same rate everywhere though. It was particularly rapid for countries in a mortality transition that had just begun in 1950. France took almost 120 years to go from an e_0 of 40 to 70 years. Italy and Spain have done this in about 70 years, while Morocco and Egypt have done it in just under 60 years, Jordan in 40 years and Libya in 30 years. With this very rapid increase, the countries with the highest mortality in 1950 have bridged much of the gap that separated them from the populations most advanced in the mortality transition. It might be expected that some lagging countries would catch up with, or even overtake, the earlier countries and that the ranking of countries at the end of the period would be different from that at the beginning of the period. On the contrary, there is no upheaval in the hierarchy that prevailed in 1950. However, some trajectories are interesting to note, such as Lebanon and Turkey whose current e_0 equals (and exceeds) that of several Balkan countries, even though they experienced a more unfavourable situation in the 1950s. In 2019, Turkey's e_0 (77 years) was slightly higher than that of Serbia and Montenegro, whereas it was lower by more than 11 years in 1950. Also noteworthy is the particular situation of Bulgaria, which with an e_0 of 75 years is among the lowest life expectancies in the Mediterranean while it was among the highest in 1950.

A great convergence of mortality has therefore taken place and the current situation is much less heterogeneous than it was before. Mortality gaps in the Mediterranean have narrowed significantly since 1950. However, contrasts remain: 12 years separate the lowest e_0 (Egypt) and the highest (Italy) in 2019 and at least 5 years separate the

---

[3] In this chapter, even if some graphs represent the period 1950–2021, we will cover (unless otherwise stated) the period 1950–2019 in order to not take into account the mortality related to the Covid-19 pandemic (2020–2022). Indeed, the effects of this pandemic on life expectancy are not yet fully known. We would like to focus on the mortality situation of Mediterranean countries outside of any great shock (or almost).

e_0 of most North African countries ($e_0 < 76$ years) and that of Southern European countries ($e_0 > 81$ years).

7.2.3 Decreases in Life Expectancy at Birth

This tremendous victory over death must not make us forget that this progress can be reversed. If the e_0 increased in all the Mediterranean countries between 1950 and 2019, the evolution was not always steady and some setbacks were experienced. For example, the convergence of the e_0 observed in the Mediterranean has slowed down, and even came to a halt in the 1990s, a period from which the curves evolve almost in parallel. This is the effect of a slowdown in the rates of increase in the risk of death by age, particularly in the countries with the lowest e_0. While the relative disparities between countries reduced by a factor of four between 1950 and 1990, they have remained almost at the same level since then.

We also observe declines in e_0 in several Mediterranean countries during the study period. The most notable are attributable to wars and conflicts: the Algerian war (1954–1962), the Lebanese war (1975–1982), the Yugoslav war (1992–1995), wars and political destabilisation in Libya in the 2010s and the Syrian conflict since 2011. The increase in mortality over a short period of time is sometimes striking: annual data from the *World Population Prospects 2022* show that Bosnia-Herzegovina lost about 20 years of e_0 between 1990 and 1993 for example. In addition, post-conflict recovery time varies from country to country. Whereas Bosnia-Herzegovina seems to have taken 2 years to regain its pre-war e_0, Lebanon took about 10 years. Syria, meanwhile, still has not reached its 2010 e_0, despite being in recovery for several years.

The COVID-19 pandemic has also led to a more or less significant decrease in e_0 almost everywhere in the Mediterranean in 2020–2021. The impact of the virus varied by country: they were not affected at the same time and did not suffer the same number of waves of excess mortality. According to *World Population Prospects 2022* data, Mediterranean countries lost an average of 1.5 years of e_0, with large disparities within the region (Table 7.1). The countries with the greatest loss of e_0 (greater than 2 years) are located in the southern Balkans, along with North Africa and Lebanon.

7.2.4 Gender Inequalities

As elsewhere in the world, inequalities in mortality between men and women are significant in the Mediterranean. Mortality risks for men are generally higher than those for women. This difference in favour of women may be attributed to a biological advantage in the form of immune function, although it is difficult to measure this effect (Weeks, 2020). Thus, in the Mediterranean, the e_0 of men is lower by 5 years on average than that of women. However, the extent of the gender gap is not the same in all countries. It depends on social factors relating to the status of women in society. Thus, when a small gap is noted, it reflects an excess mortality of women, which reflects a rather deteriorated status. The gender gap in e_0 is also a function of progress in the mortality transition: the gaps between men and women, which are rather reduced at the beginning of the transition, are accentuated during the transition by the faster increase in women's e_0, and they finally decrease when men's e_0 progressively catches up with that of women. To illustrate this relationship, we use the evolution of the gender gap of e_0 of France since 1806 in comparison with that of other countries of Southern Europe (Fig. 7.2).

Before the transition, the gap in e_0 between men and women was generally quite small. In France, the gender gap was almost stable until the early 1860s and it was

Table 7.1 Loss of life expectancy at birth during the COVID-19 pandemic (2020–2021)

Scale of e_0 loss	Country
e_0 loss < 1 year	Cyprus, Syria, Morocco, France, Israel, Libya, Malta, Portugal, Montenegro
1 year < e_0 loss < 2 years	Egypt, Greece, Italy, Croatia, Slovenia, Spain, Palestine, Jordan, Bosnia-Herzegovina, Turkey
2 years < e_0 loss < 3 years	Algeria, Tunisia, Kosovo, Serbia, Albania
e_0 loss > 3 years	Bulgaria, Macedonia, Lebanon

Source World Population Prospects 2022. Calculations made by the authors

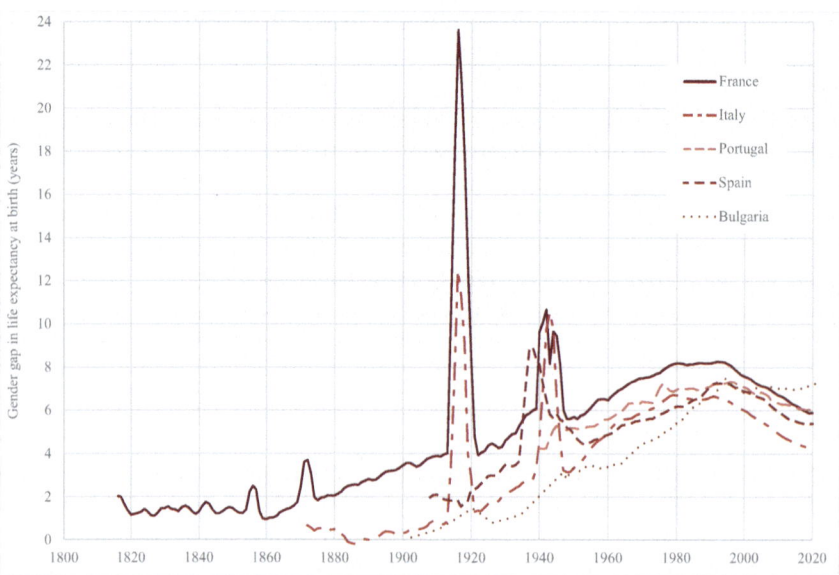

Fig. 7.2 Evolution of the gender gap in life expectancy at birth in some Southern European countries (*Source* Human Mortality Database, Human Life-Table Database. Calculations made by the authors)

less than 2 years (excluding exceptional periods). During the mortality transition, women's e_0 increased faster than men's, widening the gap. France has experienced a gradual increase in the gender gap since the 1860s. Apart from periods of war, it reached a maximum of slightly more than 8 years in the early 1990s, when it began to decrease until the present time (bell curve). This decrease in the gender gap can be explained both by a certain masculinisation of female behaviours (increase in tobacco and alcohol consumption, etc.), but also by changes in the epidemiological profile that we will discuss in the last part of this chapter. The other Southern European countries in Fig. 7.2 have the same evolution model, with some differences compared to that of the French. For Bulgaria, for example, once a maximum was reached, there was no decrease in the gender gap, but a stagnation for 30 years.

The evolution of the gender gap of e_0 in the Mediterranean since 1950 highlights a diversity of trajectories. We have classified them into 5 groups (Fig. 7.3).

The first brings together countries with the same bell-shaped trajectory presented previously, and whose gender gap has been decreasing for at least 20 years (or more). These are the countries of Southern Europe (except Malta), plus Croatia and Slovenia. Similar trajectories with stagnation (or a slight decrease) once the maximum has been reached make up the second group, which is almost exclusively comprised of Balkan countries. The third group concerns only countries on the Southern and Eastern shores, with gender gap trajectories increasing over the entire period. The fourth group includes Albania, Bosnia-Herzegovina and Cyprus, whose trajectories are downward over the entire period. Finally, the trajectories of the last group (Algeria, Kosovo, Lebanon and Palestine) do not have a clear evolution over the entire period. Across the board, the conflicts are clearly identifiable, showing how men's e_0 is more affected during these periods of instability.

The more rapid increase in the e_0 of women during the decline in mortality leads to sometimes considerable time lags between the two genders. In Bosnia-Herzegovina, for example, men in 2019 had an e_0 that women in the same country had reached almost 25 years before. There are considerable disparities, with a gap of about 10 years for Morocco and Algeria, and 30 years for Serbia, Tunisia and Croatia. The maximum was reached by Bulgaria with a lag of 60 years, meaning that in 2019 men reach an e_0 that women had in 1960.

7.3 The Different Mortality Profiles

Life expectancy at birth is a synthetic indicator of the mortality of a population. It gives indications of the health of a population at a given date, but potentially masks different age-specific mortality profiles for the same value (mean age at death). Different mortality patterns can correspond to the same life mean at birth. To better understand the mechanisms underlying the convergence of e_0 in the Mediterranean since 1950, as highlighted above, we will now analyse mortality broken down into 3 major age groups: infant and child mortality (under 5 years old), adult mortality (15–64 years) and mortality at advanced ages (65 years or more).

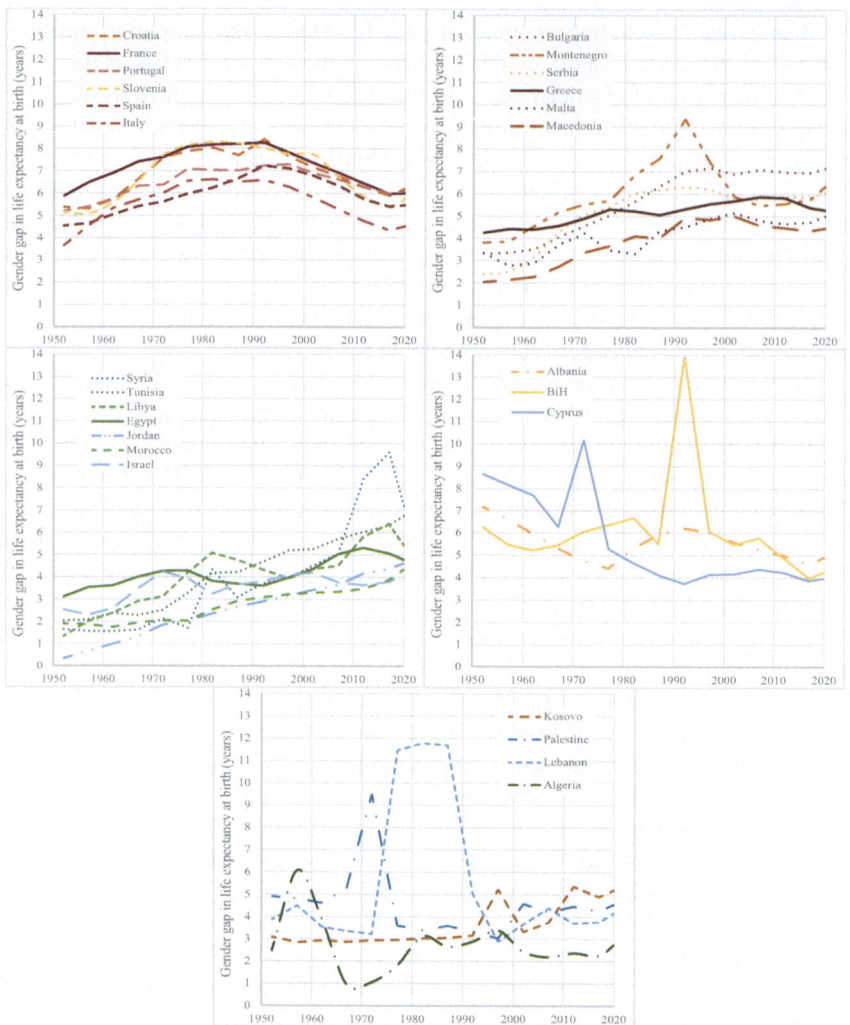

Fig. 7.3 Evolution of the gender gap in life expectancy at birth in the Mediterranean (1950–2021) (*Source* World Population Prospects 2022. Calculations made by the authors. *Note* The time units used are five-year periods)

7.3.1 Infant and Child Mortality (Under 5 Years Old)

For most of human history, infant and child mortality (i.e. children under 5 years old) remained at very high levels. It was not until the nineteenth century that it began to decline in European countries, then in other countries of the world according to

7.3 The Different Mortality Profiles

various timing. In 1950, the infant and child mortality rate (U5MR)[4] at the global level stood at 225‰; in 2019, it reached the low level of 38‰ in 2019, thus representing a drastic reduction in a short time on a historical scale. Over the same period, in the Mediterranean, the U5MR decreased on average from 180 to 20‰.

In 1950, U5MR values spread over a wide spectrum, ranging from about 40‰ to over 350‰ (Fig. 7.4). This disparity meant that more than 90% of children reached the age of 5 in some countries, and only 55% in others. However, this proportion exceeded 70% in the vast majority of Mediterranean countries. This infant and child mortality strongly converged towards lower levels throughout the Mediterranean, with sometimes very large reductions in some countries. In 2019, the values were concentrated in a narrower spectrum than in 1950: there were indeed 10 Mediterranean countries above the world average in 1950, while there were none in 2019. No country (except Syria[5]) has a U5MR above 25‰. More than 97% of children survive up to 5 years across the Mediterranean. Infant and child mortality is now low.

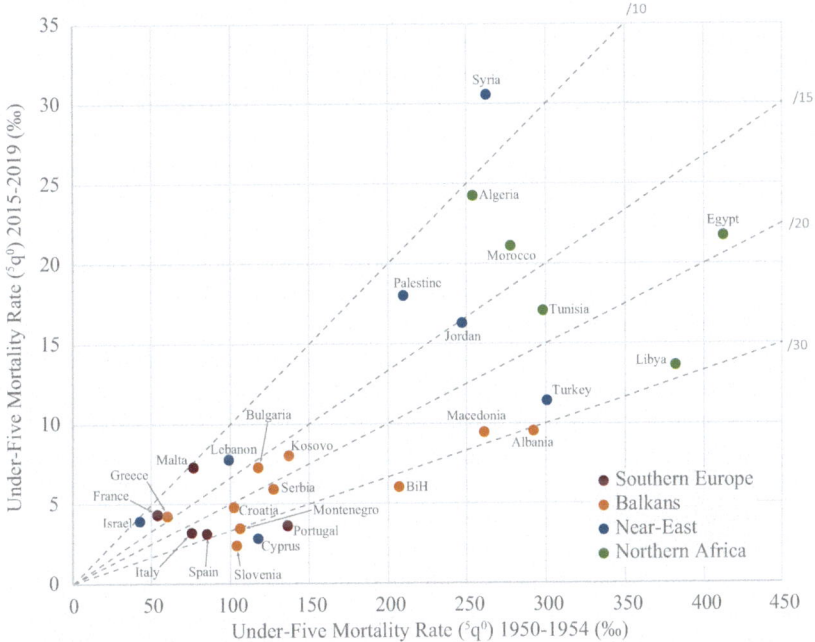

Fig. 7.4 Child mortality in the Mediterranean (1950–2019) (*Source* World Population Prospects 2022. Graphic developed by the authors. *Reading tip* the dotted lines represent the change between 1950–1954 and 2015–2019. For example, points on the "/30" line have child mortality that has been divided by 30 between the two periods. The colour of a dot represents the regional area to which a country belongs)

---

[4] For ease of reading, we use the expression "U5MR" (Under-five Mortality Rate) in this chapter to mean "infant and child mortality".

[5] This is mainly due to the war, as Syria's U5MR was below 20‰ at the end of the 2000s.

In 1950, there was a contrast between countries that were well underway in the health transition and those that were still at an early stage. The former had a U5MR of less than 150‰, and included the countries of the Northern shore plus the more advanced countries of the Southern and Eastern shores (Israel, Lebanon and Cyprus). The latter had a U5MR higher than 200‰, and were mainly on the Southern and Eastern shores, but also on the Northern Shore (Albania, Macedonia and Bosnia-Herzegovina). This dichotomy can still be seen in 2019, but with much smaller gaps between countries. Figure 7.4 thus shows that the most spectacular increases in the decline of the UM5R concerned countries such as Libya, Turkey and Albania (countries located below the right marked " /30", indicating a division by 30 of infant and child mortality).

7.3.2 Adult Mortality (15–64 Years Old)

Whilst the highest risks of death are concentrated at the younger and older age groups, adult mortality (considered here as mortality between 15 and 65 years) should not be underestimated. Indeed, the odds of dying before age 65 were not negligible in 1950, even after surviving to the age of 5; in fact, differences are still observed today. Adult mortality also contributes to inequalities in life expectancy between men and women due to excess mortality following childbearing and pregnancy.

In 1950, all Mediterranean countries saw at least 25% of people who reached the age of 5 die before the age of 65. This proportion reached more than 60% in some countries (Tunisia, Morocco, Jordan, Libya). Since 1950, adult mortality has declined throughout the Mediterranean (Fig. 7.5).

The intensity of this reduction is not commensurate with the reduction in infant and child mortality. While the latter has been divided by a factor of 10 in almost all countries, adult mortality has been divided by a ratio of "only" between 2 and 5, which is nevertheless far from negligible. The current situation is much more enviable than it was 70 years ago, because in all the Mediterranean countries, at least 75% of people who have reached the age of 5 can expect to reach the age of 65.

In 1950, there was clear opposition between the Northern Shore (with Turkey, Cyprus, Israel and Lebanon) with adult mortality levels below 400‰, and the Southern and Eastern shores (with Bosnia-Herzegovina) with levels above 400‰. In 2019, we no longer see this geographical contrast. The highest levels (>200‰) are mainly on the Southern and Eastern shores (Egypt, Syria, Libya, Bulgaria). In contrast, lower levels of adult mortality are routinely found in countries on all shores of the Mediterranean. For example, adult deaths between 120‰ and 175‰ concern countries in North Africa (Tunisia, Morocco, Algeria), the Near East (Palestine, Jordan, Turkey) and the Balkans (Montenegro, Serbia, Croatia, Bosnia-Herzegovina, Macedonia, Kosovo). This means that similar adult mortality conditions can be shared by countries on both sides of the Mediterranean.

7.3 The Different Mortality Profiles

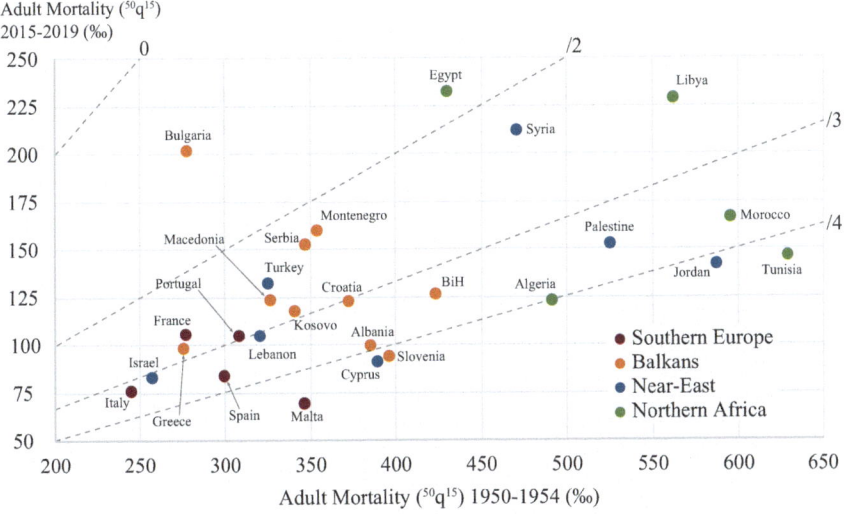

Fig. 7.5 Adult mortality in the Mediterranean (1950–2019) (*Source* World Population Prospects 2022. Graphic developed by the authors. *Reading tip* The dotted lines represent the change between 1950–1954 and 2015–2019. For example, points on the "/4" line have an adult mortality that has been divided by 4 between the two periods. The colour of a dot represents the regional area to which a country belongs)

7.3.3 Mortality at Advanced Ages (65 Years Old or Older)

In 1950, we saw that the high levels of infant, child and adult mortality in the Mediterranean meant that a significant part of a generation did not reach the age of 65 (with great variability between countries). Once this age is reached, how many more years can a person expect to live? To measure this, we use the life expectancy indicator at age 65 (e_{65}),[6] which is the number of years an individual will live on average if they have the same probabilities of death as previous generations at the same time.

All Mediterranean countries had an e_{65} between 10 and 14 years in 1950 (Fig. 7.6). It increased everywhere by 4.5 years on regional average from 12 to 16.8 years (in 2019). However, developments vary greatly from country to country. Over the study period, in contrast to infant and adult mortality, there is a trend over the period towards divergence in the e_{65}. Indeed, differences between countries increased, as many of the countries with the highest e_{65} in 1950 were also those that's experienced the highest increase (see Sect. 7.4 of this chapter). Southern European countries and Israel have all seen their e_{65} increase by more than 50%, even though their e_{65} was already among the highest in the region in 1950 (>13 years). They have thus widened the gap with the other Mediterranean countries, most of which have had a more moderate rate of growth.

---

[6] For ease of reading, we use the annotation "e_{65}" in this chapter to mean "life expectancy at 65 years".

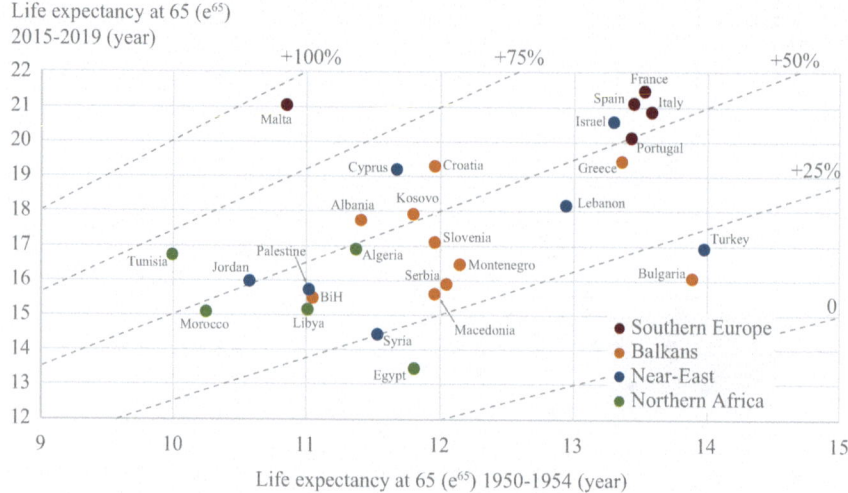

Fig. 7.6 Life expectancy at age 65 in the Mediterranean (1950–2019) (*Source* World Population Prospects 2022. Graphic developed by the authors. *Reading tip*: the dotted lines represent the change between 1950–1954 and 2015–2019. For example, points on the "+75%" line have a life expectancy at age 65 that was increased by 75% between the two periods. The colour of a dot represents the regional area to which a country belongs)

Unusual trajectories are also a noteworthy. Bulgaria had the second highest e_{65} in the Mediterranean in 1950, but it only increased by 2 years, thus arriving at 17th place in 2019. Malta, meanwhile, saw its e_{65} almost double over the study period, moving from 24th to 3rd place.

As a result, countries' e_{65}s are spread over a wider range of values in 2019 than in 1950. There were 9 Mediterranean countries with an e_{65} below the world average in 1950, and 15 in 2019. This situation illustrates the divergence in life expectancy at age 65 that has occurred in the Mediterranean between these two dates.

It is possible to distinguish 4 groups of countries in 2019, reflecting differences between the shores of the Mediterranean. The first group is made up of the countries of Southern Europe and Israel, with an e_{65} over 20 years; they clearly stand out from the other countries. Cyprus, Croatia and Greece form the second group. With an e_{65} between 19 and 20, they follow the previous group. The third group (Syria, Egypt, Morocco, Libya) has the lowest e_{65} (less than 15 years). The last group brings together all the other countries, from all sides, with an e_{65} between 15 and 18 years.

7.4 The Health Transition

This general convergence of the e_0 in the Mediterranean, linked to declines in mortality at different ages, actually reflects a profound change in the diseases causing mortality (epidemiological profile) in a population (Frenk et al., 1991; Omran, 1971).

Historically, the epidemiological profile has long been dominated by infectious diseases. In industrial countries, the increase in e_0 from the end of the eighteenth century until the 1960s was essentially due to the fight against infectious diseases (Vallin & Meslé, 2004). This progress can be attributed to various factors, both sociocultural and medical: the control of major epidemics, the disappearance of famines and food shortages due to food production and distribution improvement; the improvement of nutrition, health and hygiene policies; progress in the distribution of drinking water and sanitation systems; and finally vaccines and antibiotics. The main implication of the massive decline in infectious diseases was the drastic reduction in infant and child mortality, and more generally the decline in mortality under the age of 50. This is why the e_0 was able to increase beyond the ancestral level of 30–35 years.

In the Mediterranean, the general convergence of the e_0 is explained by the timing lags in this victory over infectious diseases. Countries with high e_{0s} in 1950 had been fighting these diseases for a long time and had virtually eliminated them. On the other hand, this was not the case for countries with low e_0s whose infectious diseases still kept infant and child mortality at high levels. These countries benefited from the transfer of public health knowledge and medical technologies developed in Europe and North America. By making them available to all their populations, their e_0 increased very rapidly and these countries have made up some of the ground lost to the pioneer countries. In 2019, infectious diseases also accounted for only 2% of deaths in the Mediterranean, with the prevalence of AIDS being low in this region. Current differences in infant and child mortality between countries are mainly explained by the management of neonatal conditions (prematurity, etc.).

The historic triumph over infectious diseases does not mean that they are definitely a thing of the past, as the COVID-19 pandemic has reminded us. We have seen the emergence of new infectious diseases since 1950, such as AIDS, Ebola, Zika, SARS, West Nile virus, H1N1, H5N1 and so on. They still pose major threats to populations, especially when air travel allows diseases to be spread around the world within hours.

With the control of infectious diseases, societies now face other causes of mortality: chronic diseases (cardiovascular, tumours/cancers, diabetes, etc.) and society diseases (smoking, alcoholism, suicide, homicides, road accidents, etc.). The inability to fight against these various diseases leads to a stagnation of the e_0 or at least a much more moderate increase in it. The e_0 of Western countries, for example, reached similar levels at the end of the 1950s thanks to their control of infectious diseases. On the other hand, there was a stagnation in their e_0 in the 1960s, as the main causes of mortality were more chronic diseases and societal diseases (Vallin & Meslé, 2014). It was not until the 1970s that effective ways of combating cardiovascular diseases were discovered. This "cardiovascular revolution" thus allowed a new progression of the e_0.

However, it is more difficult to reduce mortality from cardiovascular disease than it is for infectious diseases (Meslé & Vallin, 2006). Firstly, medical prevention is more complicated, as the population needs to be made aware of the important risk factors related to diet and lifestyle, in order to change their individual behaviours. This objective is hence more difficult to implement than the prevention of infectious diseases, which relies mainly on vaccination and antibiotics. Secondly, treatment technologies are much more expensive and are not attainable for all countries, which is especially the case for cardiovascular diseases and cancers.

In Europe, Western countries managed to fight against cardiovascular diseases and saw their e_0 increase. It is these countries that also saw increased life expectancy at advanced ages. Conversely, the countries of Eastern Europe were unable to take advantage of the new means of combating this type of disease, and thus had an e_0 which stagnated or even decreased (Vallin & Meslé, 2014). This may be due to economic difficulties, which have not allowed for the dissemination of treatment technologies, but also to the highly centralised political system which has proven to be less effective when individual responsibility was needed. Thus, from the 1970s onwards, there was a divergence in e_0 between the countries of Eastern and Western Europe, even though the former had closed most of their e_0 gap.

Similarly, the Mediterranean countries have not been equal in the face of cardiovascular diseases (Fig. 7.7).

The richer ones were able to take advantage of the new control methods and see their e_0 continue to increase (and now exceed 80 years). In contrast, for the other

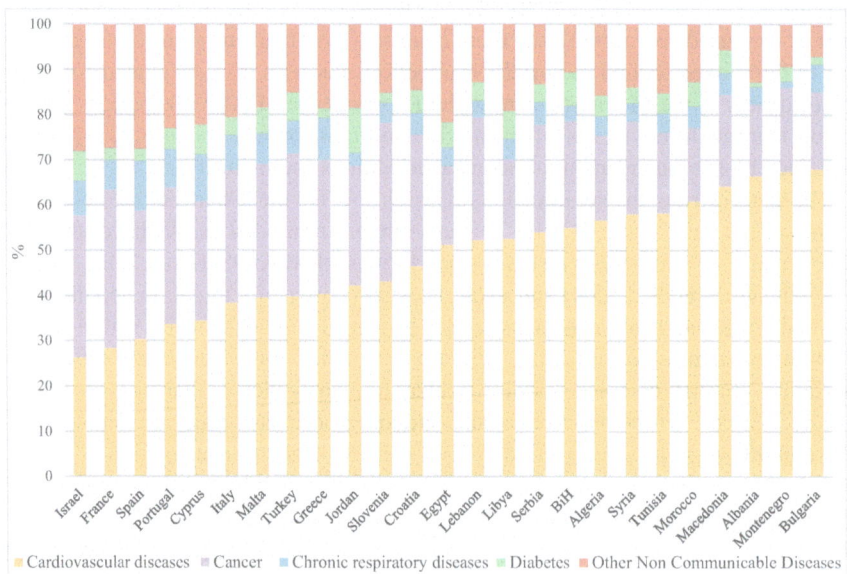

Fig. 7.7 Distribution of causes of death among non-communicable diseases (2019) (*Source* NCD Data [WHO])

countries, economic difficulties and a certain political centralism may have been an obstacle and the increase in e_0 was more moderate. This inequality in the fight against cardiovascular diseases is reflected in the burden of these diseases in the Mediterranean (Fig. 7.7). In half the countries, these diseases account for more than 50% of deaths from non-communicable diseases.[7] In contrast, they represent less than 30% in the most advanced countries in the fight against these diseases (e.g. Israel, France and Spain).

This inequality in mortality from cardiovascular diseases gives rise to different epidemiological profiles in the Mediterranean countries. In general, countries that manage to control cardiovascular diseases are more likely to face cancers and neurodegenerative diseases (Fig. 7.7). Cancers account for 25% of deaths from noncommunicable diseases on average in the region. They exceed 30% in countries such as France, Slovenia, Israel, Turkey or Portugal (although cancer mortality has been decreasing for some decades now) and represent less than 20% in all North African countries and in Albania, Bulgaria and Montenegro.

This unequal situation with regard to cardiovascular diseases and cancers is partly responsible for the divergence in e_{65} observed between 1950 and 2019, and also for the current disparities in adult mortality. The progression of e_{65} is correlated with the ability to manage chronic diseases that occur with age, cancers, neurodegenerative diseases and accidents.

Moreover, not all Mediterranean populations are affected with the same intensity by societal diseases. Arab-Muslim countries are generally much less affected by alcohol-related deaths (three times less than in other Mediterranean countries) and, to a lesser extent, by smoking-related deaths. In contrast, road traffic deaths are higher, particularly in Algeria, Libya and Jordan, which may explain some of the current disparities in adult mortality.

Finally, the Mediterranean countries are very unevenly affected by obesity, which is a risk factor for cardiovascular diseases and diabetes in particular. It is particularly high in countries on the Southern and Eastern shores, which affected one in three adults over the age of 18 on average in 2015, compared with one in five in other countries.

7.5 Conclusion

In 1950, Mediterranean societies experienced very different mortality conditions. Since then, there has been a great convergence of life expectancy at birth, driven by the decline in infant, child and adult mortality with the control of infectious diseases. All countries are now in a low mortality phase. However, the convergence of life expectancy at birth stopped about 30 years ago and the analysis of the data even

---

[7] The WHO classifies deaths into three main categories: communicable, maternal, perinatal and nutritional diseases; noncommunicable diseases; and accidents. We focus on non-communicable diseases, as they comprise the bulk of chronic and societal diseases.

reveals a divergence of mortality after 65 years. These trends can be attributed at least in part to the uneven capacities of Mediterranean countries to combat cardiovascular disease, neurodegenerative diseases and cancer. There is no doubt, however, that an improvement in these capacities could lead to a resumption of the convergence of mortality after age 65, and thus of life expectancy at birth. This is an important issue because the number of older people will continue to increase by 2060 (see Chap. 2).

References

Fargues, P. (1986). Un siècle de transition démographique en Afrique méditerranéenne 1885–1985. *Population, 41*, 205–232. https://doi.org/10.2307/1533059

Frenk, J., Bobadilla, J. L., Stern, C., Frejka, T., & Lozano, R. (1991). Elements for a theory of the health transition. *Health Transition Review, 1*, 21–38. http://www.jstor.org/stable/40608615

Human Life-Table Database (HLD). Max Planck Institute, University of California at Berkeley (USA), French Institute for Demographic Studies (France). http://www.lifetable.de/

Human Mortality Database (HMD). Max Planck Institute, University of California at Berkeley (USA), French Institute for Demographic Studies (France). www.mortality.org/

Meslé, F., & Vallin, J. (2006). The health transition: Trends and prospects. In G. Caselli, J. Vallin, & G. J. Wunsch (Eds.), *Demography: Analysis and synthesis* (Vol. II, pp. 247–260). Elsevier.

Omran, A. R. (1971). The epidemiologic transition: A theory of the epidemiology of population change. *The Milbank Memorial Fund Quarterly, 49*, 509–538. https://doi.org/10.1111/j.1468-0009.2005.00398.x

Pouget, B. (2021). La Méditerranée et les grandes épidémies. Retour sur un demi-siècle de travaux historiques. *Cahiers de la Méditerranée, 103*, 173–189. https://doi.org/10.4000/cdlm.15133

Speziale, S. (2018). Les médecins européens, médiateurs scientifiques et culturels en Afrique méditerranéenne entre le XVIIIe et le XIXe siècle. *Cahiers De La Méditerranée, 96*, 231–248. https://doi.org/10.4000/cdlm.10953

Tabutin, D., Vilquin, E., & Biraben, J.-N. (2002). *L'histoire de la population de l'Afrique du Nord pendant le deuxième millénaire.* Document de Travail 15. Centre de recherche en démographie.

Vallin, J., & Meslé, F. (2004). Convergences and divergences in mortality. A new approach to health transition. *Demographic Research, 2*, 10–43. https://doi.org/10.4054/DemRes.2004.S2.2

Vallin, J., & Meslé, F. (2014). De la transition épidémiologique à la transition sanitaire: l'improbable convergence générale. In D. Tabutin & B. Masquelier (eds.), *Ralentissements, résistances et ruptures dans les transitions démographiques* (pp. 257–290). Actes de La Chaire Quetelet [2010]. Presses Universitaires de Louvain.

Weeks, J. (2020). *Population: An introduction to concepts and issues* (13th ed.). Cengage.

WHO Mortality Database. World Health Organization. https://platform.who.int/mortality

World Population Prospects. (2022). United Nations, Department of Economic and Social Affairs, Population Division. https://population.un.org/wpp/

Open Access This chapter is licensed under the terms of the Creative Commons Attribution 4.0 International License (http://creativecommons.org/licenses/by/4.0/), which permits use, sharing, adaptation, distribution and reproduction in any medium or format, as long as you give appropriate credit to the original author(s) and the source, provide a link to the Creative Commons license and indicate if changes were made.

The images or other third party material in this chapter are included in the chapter's Creative Commons license, unless indicated otherwise in a credit line to the material. If material is not included in the chapter's Creative Commons license and your intended use is not permitted by statutory regulation or exceeds the permitted use, you will need to obtain permission directly from the copyright holder.

Chapter 8
The Mediterranean Migration System

Abstract Together with the border between the US and Mexico, the Mediterranean is the largest migration area in the world. The stock of migrants resident in the Mediterranean countries was 42.6 million in 2020. About 2/3 of these international migrants are found in 4 countries (France, Spain, Italy, Turkey) and 20% in the rest of the Near East (Jordan, Lebanon, Israel, Syria, Palestine). The absolute number of these international migrants can vary greatly from one country to another; the migrants can thus represent a significant share of the overall population. The Mediterranean Basin has been historically characterised by a regular circulation of people within the region. The period after World War II till today (1948–2022) has been characterised by several changes in the Mediterranean migration system, which were largely driven by economic and political factors. Through a chronological approach, we can identify five periods that synthetise the evolution of migration in the Mediterranean region during this period.

Keywords International migrations · Migration system · High skilled migration · Irregular migration · Mediterranean

8.1 Introduction

Together with the border between the US and Mexico, the Mediterranean is the largest migration area in the world (Venier & Oliveau, 2023). The stock of migrants resident in the Mediterranean countries was 42.6 million (Fig. 8.1) in 2020. About 2/3 of these international migrants are found in 4 countries (France, Spain, Italy, Turkey) and 20% in the rest of the Near East (Jordan, Lebanon, Israel, Syria, Palestine). The absolute number of these international migrants can vary greatly from one country to another; the migrants can thus represent a significant share of the overall population. For example, they represent more than 20% of the population in Malta, Jordan, Lebanon and Israel.

46.1 million people (representing 16.4% of all international migrants) is the stock of emigrants whose country of origin is one of the Mediterranean countries and

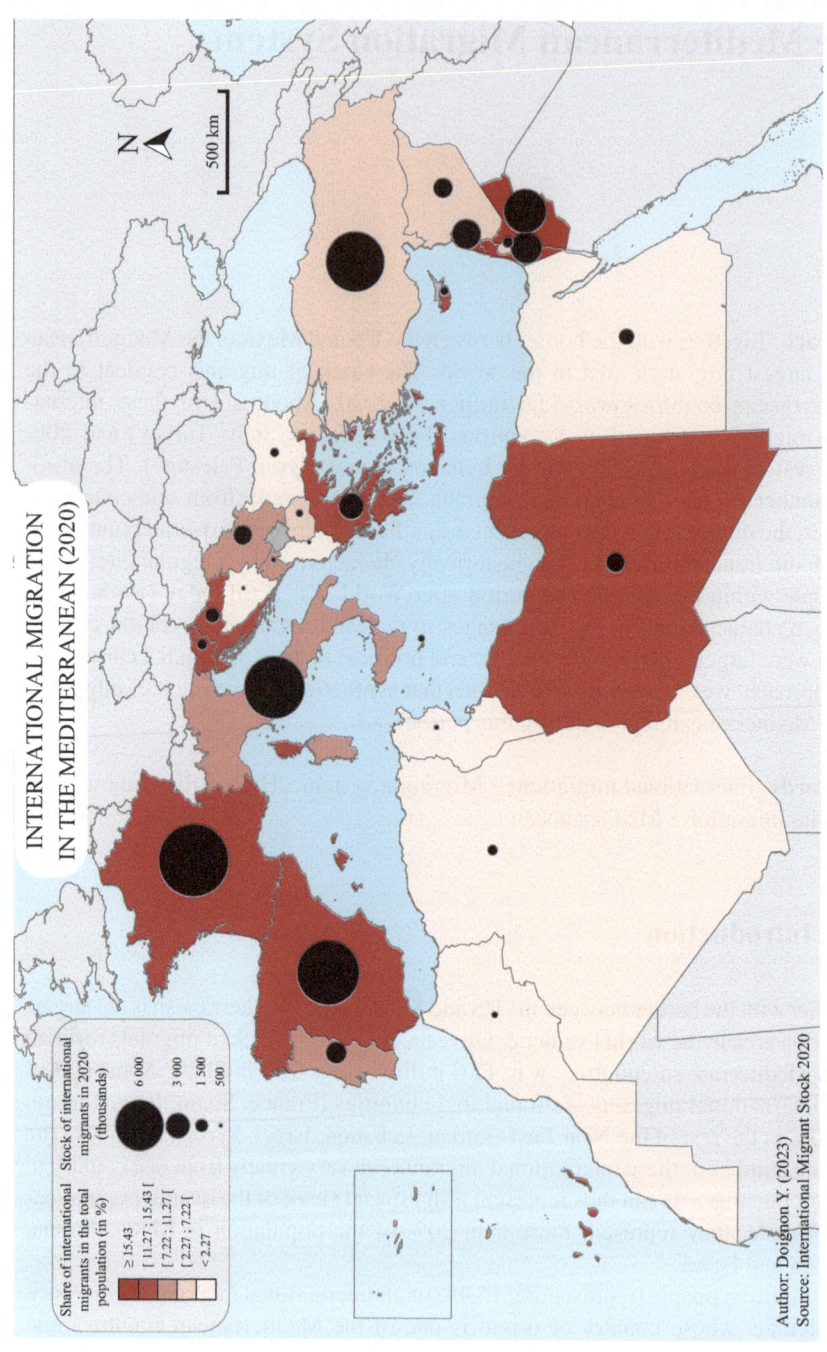

Fig. 8.1 Stock of migrants and share of total population (in %) in the Mediterranean (2020) (*Source* International Migrant Stock [2020] [United Nations])

who have emigrated all over the world (including other Mediterranean countries) from their country of origin. Indeed, a significant proportion of these Mediterranean emigrants moved within the Mediterranean region: 22.6 million emigrants moved from their home to another country belonging to the Mediterranean Basin.

The migration in the Mediterranean region is largely influenced by the unequal age structure of the resident population which is a consequence of the so-called demographic transition. As discussed elsewhere in this book (see Chaps. 3 and 4), the countries of the Mediterranean Basin are at a different transition stage. As a consequence, while the median age in most of the ageing countries of the North Mediterranean is over 40 years (except Albania and Montenegro), in the Southern and Eastern shores, the median age is less than 30 years, resulting in a much younger age structure. This favourable demographic situation, known as a youth bulge, has great potential from an economic point of view: according to the demographic dividend theorists, it may cause rapid economic growth due to a higher level of education and labour market participation (Bloom et al., 2017). However, countries of the Southern and Eastern region of the Mediterranean have not yet benefited from the demographic dividend. The youth population is much more educated and qualified compared to the generations of their parents, nonetheless, the economic opportunities for these generations are still yet to come. Indeed, the labour supply is higher than the demand, resulting in high unemployment rates. High inflation rates and increasing income inequalities characterise the economy of most of the countries. Therefore, the young generations belonging to the youth bulge, instead of benefitting from the demographic dividend, were at the heart of the protests, which culminated in the so-called Arab Spring, at the beginning of the second decade of the 2000 (Martin & Bardak, 2011). Political and economic problems affecting the Arab Mediterranean countries act as a major driver of migration to European and Near Eastern countries (Etling et al., 2020).

The Mediterranean Basin has been historically characterised by a regular circulation of people within the region. The period after World War II till today (1948–2022) has been characterised by several changes in the Mediterranean migration system, which were largely driven by economic and political factors (De Haas, 2011). Through a chronological approach, we can identify five periods that synthetise the evolution of migration in the Mediterranean region during this period: 1950–1995 (1950–1963; 1963–1973; 1973–1995), then 1996–2022 (1996–2010; 2011–present).

8.2 Migration in the Mediterranean (1950–1995)

One of the main characteristics of the first period (1948–1963) of this first large period is the post-war reconstruction of Northern and Western European countries. The main region of origin were Southern European countries. In the early 1960s, the number of immigrant residents in Western Europe attained the record number of 7.6 million. Another characteristic of this period is that migration in the Southern and Eastern Mediterranean countries was mostly internal.

The main characteristic of the following period (1963–1973) is a sharp decrease in the flows from Southern Europe to Western European countries and an increase in migration flows from Southern and Eastern Mediterranean countries to this region. More specifically France, Germany, Switzerland, Belgium and Austria were the main destination countries. France and Germany were the main receiving countries in Europe during this phase: in France there was a strong presence of migrants from the Maghreb, while in Germany the number of migrants from Turkey steadily increased, replacing migrants from Southern European countries, in particular from Italy.

The early 1970s, characterised by the oil crisis of 1973 mark a slowdown of migration flows in the Mediterranean and correspond to the beginning of the third period (1973–1995). These major changes were largely affected by the process of globalisation, implying a restructuring of the world economy (De Haas et al., 2020). One of the main consequences of this process has been the growth of inequalities within and between regions. The new economic and political configurations had a huge impact on international migration leading to new trends. Coming back to the Mediterranean area, the most important new trend is the change of migration policies in the European countries that have traditionally received migrants. Strongly affected by the economic crisis, they are no longer able (or at least do not have the political will) to receive foreign workers. This new political (and economic) configuration in the Northern shore of the Mediterranean is characterised by restrictive entry policies with the aim of stimulating *en masse* return of migrants to their countries of origin. This policy change has a massive impact in the nature and destination of migration flows. From the 1980s onwards, there is a strong increase in the flow of refugees and asylum seekers to Europe. Family reunification becomes very important because it allows to circumvent the restrictive entry regulations. Migration to this region does not stop, however it changes dramatically assuming different forms compared to the past. One of the main consequences of the new policy configuration is the transformation of the countries of Southern Europe from countries of origin into countries of destination of international migrations. Indeed, the countries of Southern Europe, long-standing labour exporters to other European countries and to America and Oceania, became host countries for migrants originating from countries on the Southern shore of the Mediterranean, from sub-Saharan Africa, from Latin America and, after the fall of the Berlin Wall, from Eastern Europe. Another important (unintended) consequence of the oil crisis is the emergence of Persian Gulf countries and Libya as important poles of attraction for international migration, particularly from South-East Asia and the Arab countries, due to strong economic growth. Moreover, in this period Egypt became one of the main regional labour suppliers because of the opening (*infitah*) to emigration decided by Anwar Sadat and the strong population growth.

Two important political changes, the fall of the Iron Curtain and the first Gulf War, characterised the end of the 1980s and the beginning of the 1990s, generating new migration flows and weakening existing ones. During this period, the countries of Southern Europe, particularly Italy and Spain, have become the favourite destination countries for several populations originating from the Southern shore of the Mediterranean, especially from the Maghreb countries.

Another important political event has characterised the mid-1980s. In 1985, member countries of the European Union signed the Schengen Agreements marking an important breakthrough for the region's migration: a zone of free movement was established within Europe (the effective implementation of the agreements only began in 1995). The internal borders of the Union no longer existed (except for the United Kingdom and Ireland): the internal space of the EU thus became a migration system that includes 26 countries (including non-EU European countries: Iceland, Norway, Switzerland and Liechtenstein). On the other hand, the EU's external borders became increasingly controlled and inaccessible to all those subject to the Schengen visa regime, particularly for countries of the Southern and Eastern shores of the Mediterranean (Wihtol de Wenden, 2013). From this period onwards, there is the emergence of a new phenomenon, as a direct consequence of the entry restrictions in the Schengen zone, significant flows of irregular migration was followed by massive regularisations.

Lastly, high skilled migration is also increasing; it is characterised not only by the mobility of highly skilled workers but also by the increasing mobility of students.

8.3 Migration in the Mediterranean in the XXI Century

A new migration phase in the Mediterranean region (1996–2010) started at the turn of the late 1990s and the first decade of the 2000s; thanks to a positive economic situation, a new migration sequence began (Fig. 8.2). It is a period during which new poles of attraction emerge beyond traditional ones.

In the Northern shore of the Mediterranean, Spain and Italy confirmed their role as poles of attraction for unskilled labour, especially migrants from Southern shore countries employed in agriculture, family services, restaurant services, small retail trade and construction. In the first decade of the 2000s, Spain and Italy became host countries for migration flows, particularly from Maghreb countries and Egypt. On the other hand, in these new hosting countries, there is a low incidence of migrants coming from the Eastern shore of the Mediterranean, in particular of migrants from Turkey. The other European countries that traditionally import foreign labour continue to welcome family migration and highly qualified migrants.

Important changes are taking place on the Southern and Eastern shores of the Mediterranean. In some cases, major transformations are taking place: for example, Turkey is turning into a destination country for migration flows. Other countries in the region are becoming transit countries to Europe for migrants from Sub-Saharan Africa and Asia. Migration to the Arab countries of the Gulf and to Jordan continues to be central, especially for Egypt and the Palestinian territories.

The first decade of the 2000s ends with two disruptive events that could have dramatically altered migration flows: the global economic crisis of 2008 and the Arab Spring in 2010. Contrary to the crisis of 1973, the global economic crisis that began in 2008 did not have a strong impact on migration: the decline in migration flows was rather small. Labour migration to Southern European countries, especially

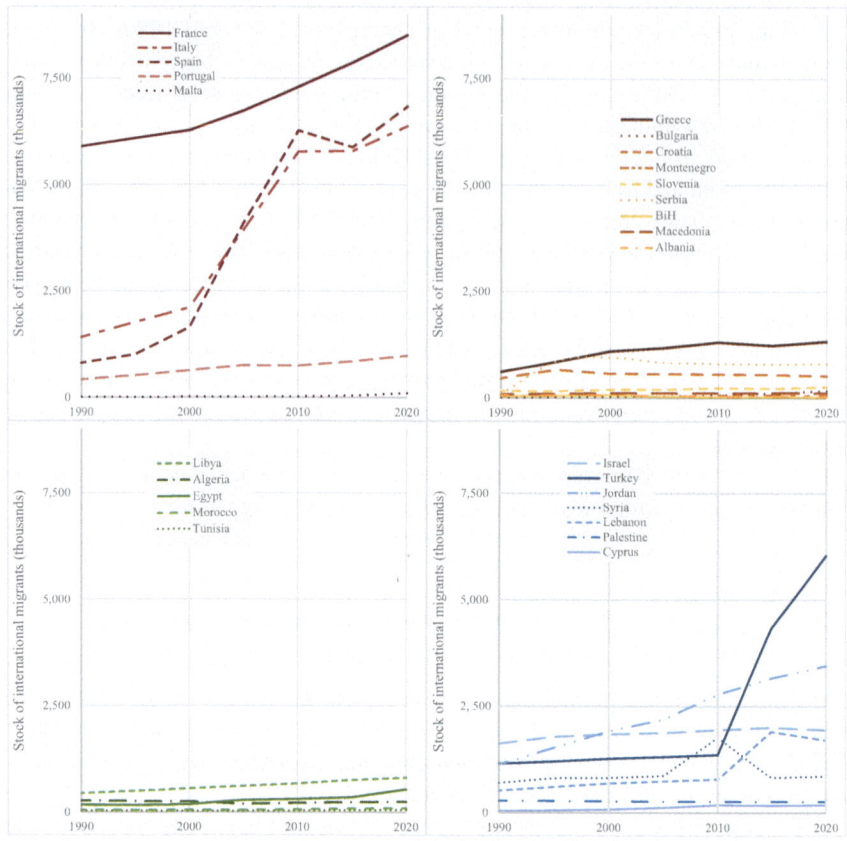

Fig. 8.2 Stock of international migrants in the Mediterranean countries (1990–2020) (*Source* International Migrant Stock [2020])

Spain was largely affected by the crisis. However, other kinds of migration (family, asylum, etc.) did not change or even increase because of the crisis (Bonifazi & Strozza, 2019).

A major disruptive factor for the entire Mediterranean region (and beyond) involving migration and mobility is linked to the season of institutional transition, known as the Arab Spring, that began in 2010. The political unrest in several countries on the Southern and Eastern shores of the Mediterranean has radically changed the institutional landscape of the area. It has triggered non-linear and on-going regime-change processes and structured, in essence, the so called "refugee crisis". In other words, while some policy makers have claimed that economic migrants make up the majority of those arriving, the wars in Syria and Iraq, as well as continuing violence and instability in Afghanistan and Eritrea, were the "real" main drivers of the crisis.

The new political configuration marks the beginning of the ongoing new era of migration (2011–present). At the beginning of the period, thousands of Tunisians

(60,000) and Libyans (26,000) escaped from their home countries which were undergoing a period of political instability to Europe. The Italian Island of Lampedusa become the main entry channel to Europe. The so-called "refugees crisis" has shaken the entire region. Between 2011 and 2014, the significant reduction of the state's control on the socio-economic settings of most of North African countries has acutely affected the regional and international migration flow dynamics, further growing the relevance of the Central Mediterranean Route (CMR) the itinerary referred to as the migration flows coming from Northern Africa towards Italy and Malta across the Mediterranean Sea. In the first stage of the new period, Italy and Malta in the CMR have been at the front stage for rescuing and welcoming migrants.

However, the CMR became much less relevant in terms of flows by the end of Operation Mare Nostrum (OMN), a year-long naval and air search-and-rescue operation promoted by the Italian government in October 2013. Indeed, during 2015, Greece served as the main portal of entry to Europe.

The International Organization for Migration's (IOM) Displacement Tracking Matrix flow-monitoring system counted 1,005,504 irregular arrivals across the Mediterranean in 2015, including migrants journeying by a or sea to Greece, Bulgaria, Spain, Italy, Malta or Cyprus, with just 3% coming by land. To contrast, there were 280,000 arrivals by land or sea for the whole of 2014. The 2015 surge of migration into Europe (going far beyond EU countries bordering the Mediterranean) was unprecedented in scope, producing a massive humanitarian crisis and creating a political and moral impasse for European governments.

From 2011 onwards, refugee flows toward Europe—which had recorded a declining trend since 2005, have increased: the European countries most affected by these new waves have been Germany, Sweden, Italy and France. According to the UN High Commissioner for Refugees (UNHCR) data, the main countries of origin of asylum seekers in 2019 were Syria, Iraq, Afghanistan, Serbia and Kosovo and Eritrea. It is important to stress that migrants are often taking unsafe journeys to Europe: according to IOM estimates, more than 8,000 people died in the Mediterranean Sea between 2014 and 2021 in an attempt to reach Europe (Missing Migrants Project, 2023).

Despite the large attention received by the new and unprecedented number of arrivals and asylum applications faced by European countries, in reality the countries on the Southern and Eastern shores of the Mediterranean were the most affected, not only numerically speaking, by the crisis. First of all, from the numerical point of view, they have received the largest part of refugees and asylum seekers from neighbouring countries. More specifically Lebanon, Turkey, Jordan and Egypt are the countries welcoming the highest number of refugees. These countries have been in the past a major recipient of refugees from Palestine, Iraq and Sudan, and they are now hosting Syrians, Palestinians and Somalis. Overall, in the Mediterranean region, there was a steady increase of the total stock of refugees and asylum seekers during the last 10 years: in 2010 they were around 3 million, while in 2017 they reached the record figure of 14.8 million (Fig. 8.3).

As already mentioned, the major receiving countries are located in the Southern and Eastern shore of the region: most of them are internally displaced in Syria

Fig. 8.3 Stock of refugees in the Mediterranean countries (1951–2021) (*Source* Refugees/Migrants Emergency Response, UNHCR [2023])

(7 million) or hosted in Lebanon (over 1 million), Turkey (almost 4 million), Egypt (almost 300 thousand) or Libya (around 375 thousand). In reality, only a minority of asylum seekers and refugees succeeded in reaching the richer countries of the Northern Shore: France (400 thousand) and Italy (354 thousand) being the major host countries among those bordering the Mediterranean. The top countries sending refugees are mainly Syria, Iraq, the horn of Africa (through Libya), Afghanistan, Kosovo and Albania. With the current crisis, Ukraine should also be added to the list of major sending countries at least for Northern Mediterranean receiving countries.

The unbalanced share of asylum seekers and refugees hosted in the Mediterranean countries is in part the results of political and economic agreements. For instance, Turkey has become from 2015–2016 a major receiving country of refugees in the Mediterranean region, together with Lebanon (and Jordan). Turkey has become more involved than ever in the reception of refugees because of the agreement made by the Turkish government with the European Union (EU) in March 2016. According to the so-called EU-Turkey "Joint Action Plan", in exchange of its assistance in controlling EU borders from irregular migration, Turkey has received from the EU up to 6 billion euros, has been granted visa liberalisation and has been able to reinvigorate talks about its accession to the EU (Panebianco, 2022; Wihtol de Wenden, 2019). The agreement allows EU countries to send back to Turkey irregular migrants who crossed the Turkish borders to reach an EU country. Another important agreement was a bilateral one, involving Italian and Libyan governments. In 2017 the Italian government and Libyan authorities signed a Memorandum of Understanding (MoU) in order to train the Libyan Coast Guard and to control land borders. The MoU has been endorsed by the EU, thus the Libyan Coast Guard is trained by European forces (not only Italian). These agreements with third countries were deemed necessary because the new configuration of migration in the region has caused a great discontent among EU states. In 2015, the countries most affected by the arrivals of refugees, namely EU countries on the Mediterranean shore (Italy, Greece, Malta, etc.) have been asking for a burden-sharing scheme for welcoming refugees among EU countries according to their wealth and population. After long negotiations the then EU commission President Jean-Claude Junker, proposed in May 2015 to implement a burden-sharing agreement. However, far from being cooperative, the response of the EU non-Mediterranean countries, and more specifically of Eastern European countries belonging to the Visegrad group (Poland, Hungary, Czech Republic and Croatia), was to close their borders to the entrance of newcomers across the Balkan route. Only after the summer of 2015, the proposal to relocate 160,000 refugees, was finally accepted by EU member states.

The agreements signed with Libya and Turkey are not new to EU policies; on the contrary, they are part of the well-established European migration policy of the past two decades. Indeed, migration policies of EU countries were based on the signature of bilateral and multilateral agreements with third countries, with the aim to externalise migration control (Triandafyllidou, 2013). This process is also characterised by a policy of border externalisation, implemented by externalising to third transit and sending countries some migration control responsibilities (Sterkx, 2008). Therefore, we have to stress that the EU approach has focused predominantly on "securitised" elements such as cooperation agreements on irregular immigration, external border controls making use of logistical and surveillance technologies, and development cooperation in third countries designed to stop irregular migration. However, given the enduring reality of gross global inequalities and continued economic and political instability in the Global South, we hypothesise that this approach will continue to push forced migrants to rely on smugglers, thereby increasing the risk of exploitation, abuse and death. The recent past has shown that in the presence of durable crisis, fighting off migrants and refugees will come to a dead end. We should be aware that there is a continuity (of migration flows) notwithstanding the crises of different nature. The Mediterranean area can be defined by a migration system (Ambrosetti and Strangio, 2016): a system of principles and rules of admission for aliens that is resilient to changes in economic conditions and other exogenous shocks.

8.4 Two Emerging Phenomena: High Skilled and Irregular Migration

More recent migration flows in Europe are characterised by high skilled migration. A common legislation on high skilled migration was adopted by the European Council with the Directive on the EU Blue Card (Directive 2009/50/EC of 25 May 2009 recently reformed by Directive (EU) 2021/1883 of 20 October 2021). The Directive aims at facilitating the entry and the mobility of highly skilled migrants and of the members of their families and to harmonise procedures for entry and residence in the member countries. High skilled migration has increased in all EU countries since 2010. However it declined in 2020 because of the COVID-19 pandemic. Among the EU countries, those belonging to the Northern shore of the Mediterranean do not attract a lot of skilled migrants: among those countries only France is attractive for the category of researchers. A large part of EU Blue Cards are issued in Germany. Highly skilled migrants are mainly of Chinese, Indian, American and Russian origin.

Undocumented migration has been identified as one of the main characteristics of the "Southern European model of migration" (King, 2000). As such, undocumented migration is a phenomenon largely widespread and debated in the Mediterranean region. However, estimating the number of undocumented migrants is a complex exercise, made on the basis of several sources of data, including the number of applications for regularisation.

Estimates of undocumented migration is complicated by its very nature, additionally at the European level, the definitions and categories are not uniform. In the past, the European Commission has funded the Clandestino project (between 2007 and 2009). The project was responding to a specific need for reliable information; at that time, media and the public had a growing interest in this type of migration, who is using "creative" figures. The aim of the project was to harmonise data sources and methodology used to study undocumented migration, in order to build a database on undocumented migration and to guide policies on this difficult topic in Europe.

The Frontex Agency (the European Agency for the Management of Operational Cooperation at the External Borders of the Member States of the European Union) was created in 2004 by the European Council and it is operational since October 2005 with the aim to promote, coordinate and develop European border management. Within its tasks, Frontex collects data on flows of illegal crossings of external borders and flows of illegal migrant detections reported within European borders. According to Frontex data, illegal crossing of the external EU borders has been stable between 2009 and 2013 (around 100,000 passages). In 2014, because of the worsening of the Syrian crisis, approximately 283,000 illegal crossings were spotted by Frontex, with 60% (170,000) crossing the maritime border of the centre-road Mediterranean (Italy and Malta) (Frontex, 2015). Illegal border crossing increased in 2015, because of the above-mentioned refugees crisis, and it has reached the record figures of 1.82 million in 2015. Starting from 2016 on, the figures started to decrease when 511,047 illegal border crossings were detected. In 2017, the drop in illegal border crossing continued, decreasing by 60% with respect to 2016, reaching 204,719 detections. The figures followed a decreasing trend in 2018 with 150,114 illegal border crossings. In 2019 and 2020, the number of illegal border crossing was even smaller than 2018, reaching its lowest record in 2020 because of the COVID-19 pandemic. In 2021, the numbers of illegal border crossing increased to about 200,000.

It should be stressed that the data provided by Frontex refer to detections of illegal border crossings, rather than the number of persons, as the same person may cross the external EU border several times. Since 2015, with the worsening of the so-called "refugees crisis", the European Commission and international organisations such as the UNHCR and the IOM, put additional efforts in the data production in the Mediterranean region. Data on death at seas and on flows of individuals crossing the borders are nowadays more systematically collected by these agencies. Therefore from 2015, arrivals by sea and land borders in the Northern shore of the Mediterranean are collected by UNCHR and available on their portal, broken down by country of origin, age and gender.[1] 2015 was, as already mentioned in the previous section, a record year for illegal border crossings: more than 1 million. From 2016, there has been a continuous decrease in border crossings because of the above-mentioned agreements with Turkey and Libya. The lowest figures were recorded in 2020 because of the COVID-19 pandemic (95,720). A slow recovery has characterised the last two years with respectively 123,540 and 160,057 sea and land arrivals recorded.

Missing Migrants Project (2023) is an project of IOM aiming to record people who die in the process of migrating to an international destination, regardless of their legal status. It has been implemented in various regions of the world, including the Mediterranean region since 2014.[2] Since 2014, 25,405 missing migrants and 8,216 deaths of migrants were recorded in Mediterranean by the Missing Migrants Project.

8.5 Conclusions

The Mediterranean migration system has undergone many changes since 1948. While migration from the Southern and Eastern shores to Western Europe was numerous from the 1960s onwards, European countries implemented restrictive entry policies with the oil crises of the 1970s. We are witnessing the emergence of new poles of attraction for international migration, such as the countries of Southern Europe, which have long been labour exporters, but also Libya, Turkey and Jordan. International migration is changing, with an increase in the migration of highly skilled people, including students. More recently, the Arab Spring of the 2010 decade has brought the Mediterranean into the "refugee crisis". Migration flows of asylum seekers and refugees are becoming unprecedented, with a peak of almost 15 million in the late 2010s. The countries most affected by this "refugee crisis" are those on the Southern and Eastern shores.

Given the demographic, economic and political situation, the Mediterranean region's migration scenario of the future could be characterised by a strong migration pressure, particularly by young adults from the South-East to Europe. This migration of young adults could be beneficial for the ageing countries of the Northern shore of the Mediterranean. This would, for example, cope with their domestic labour shortages, in particular with the segmentation of the labour market and the need to find care workers to partially respond to structural demographic ageing. Even if international migration will not be able to deal with the massive demographic ageing of the Northern shore countries, it will certainly be able to do so in a partial way in certain

---

[1] https://data.unhcr.org/en/situations/mediterranean.

[2] https://missingmigrants.iom.int/region/mediterranean.

sectors. To realise this benefit, one path to follow could involve (re-)opening the legal channels of migration, for both humanitarian and economic migrants, making immigration a structural and not a transitory phenomenon. For European countries, this would be an alternative to the migration policy paradigm based on securitisation and solidarity with the poor, and would mitigate political discourse and policy actions dominated by security and emergency issues.

References

Ambrosetti, E., & Strangio, D. (2016). Migration in the Mediterranean across disciplines. In E. Ambrosetti, D. Strangio, & C. W. de Wenden (Eds.), *Migration in the Mediterranean: Socio-economic perspectives* (pp. 3–14). Routledge Studies in the European Economy. Routledge.

Bloom, D., Kuhn, M., & Prettner, K. (2017). Africa's prospects for enjoying a demographic dividend. *Journal of Demographic Economics, 83*, 63–76. https://doi.org/10.1017/dem.2016.19

Bonifazi, C., & Strozza, S. (2019). International migrations in the northern countries of the Mediterranean. Continuity and changes, before and after the crisis. In S. Capasso & E. Ferragina (Eds.), *Mediterranean migration and the labour markets: Policies for growth and social development in the Mediterranean area* (26 p.). Routledge.

De Haas, H. (2011). Mediterranean migration futures: Patterns, drivers and scenarios. *Global Environmental Change, 21*, S59–S69. https://doi.org/10.1016/j.gloenvcha.2011.09.003

De Haas, H., Castles, S., & Miller, M. (2020). *The age of migration: International population movements in the modern world* (6th ed.). The Guilford Press.

Etling, A., Backeberg, L., & Tholen, J. (2020). The political dimension of young people's migration intentions: Evidence from the Arab Mediterranean region. *Journal of Ethnic and Migration Studies, 46*, 1388–1404. https://doi.org/10.1080/1369183X.2018.1485093

Frontex. (2015). *Annual risk analysis 2015*. European Agency for the Management of Operational Cooperation at the External Borders of the Member States of the European Union. https://frontex.europa.eu/assets/Publications/Risk_Analysis/Annual_Risk_Analysis_2015.pdf

International Migrant Stock 2020. (2020). United Nations, Department of Economic and Social Affairs, Population Division. https://www.un.org/development/desa/pd/content/international-migrant-stock

King, R. (2000). Southern Europe in the changing global map of migration. In R. King, G. Lazaridis, & C. Tsardanidis (Eds.), *Eldorado or Fortress? Migration in Southern Europe* (pp. 3–26). Palgrave Macmillan UK. https://doi.org/10.1057/9780333982525_1

Martin, I., & Bardak, U. (2011). *Union for the Mediterranean regional employability review. The challenge of youth employment in the Mediterranean*. European Training Foundation.

Missing Migrants Project. (2023). International Organization for Migration. https://missingmigrants.iom.int/

Operational Data Portal Refugee Situations. Mediterranean Situation. (2023). UNHCR (United Nations High Commissioner for Refugees). https://data.unhcr.org/en/situations/mediterranean

Panebianco, S. (2022). The EU and migration in the Mediterranean: EU borders' control by proxy. *Journal of Ethnic and Migration Studies, 48*, 1398–1416. https://doi.org/10.1080/1369183X.2020.1851468

Sterkx, S. (2008). The external dimension of EU asylum and migration policy: Expanding fortress Europe? In J. Orbie (Ed.), *Europe's global role: External policies of the European Union* (pp. 117–138). Routledge.

Triandafyllidou, A. (2013). *Circular migration between Europe and its neighbourhood: Choice or necessity?* Oxford University Press.

References

Venier, P., & Oliveau, S. (2023). Populations en mouvement: comment se redessine le peuplement mondial? In Y. Doignon & S. Oliveau (Eds.), *Dynamique du peuplement mondial. Comment la population habite le monde*, Encyclopédie Des Sciences. ISTE Editions.

Wihtol de Wenden, C. (2013). Migrations en Méditerranée, une nouvelle donne. *Confluences Méditerranée, 87*, 19–30. https://doi.org/10.3917/come.087.0019

Wihtol de Wenden, C. (2019). Migration flows in the Euro-Mediterranean region. The challenge of migration and asylum crisis in contemporary Europe and the global compact. In F. Francesca, A. Masi, C. Wihtol de Wenden, & D. Strangio (Eds.), *Migrations. Countries of immigrants, countries of migrants. Canada, Italy* (pp. 21–37). Migrazioni/Migrations. Edizioni Nuova Cultura.

Open Access This chapter is licensed under the terms of the Creative Commons Attribution 4.0 International License (http://creativecommons.org/licenses/by/4.0/), which permits use, sharing, adaptation, distribution and reproduction in any medium or format, as long as you give appropriate credit to the original author(s) and the source, provide a link to the Creative Commons license and indicate if changes were made.

The images or other third party material in this chapter are included in the chapter's Creative Commons license, unless indicated otherwise in a credit line to the material. If material is not included in the chapter's Creative Commons license and your intended use is not permitted by statutory regulation or exceeds the permitted use, you will need to obtain permission directly from the copyright holder.

Chapter 9
Population Dynamics and Their Components

Abstract The Mediterranean has an average annual population growth rate of around 1%, which is about the same as the world population growth rate. With a few rare exceptions, this growth is not principally fuelled by migration flows. However, it is closely linked to the demographic transition still underway in many Southern and Eastern Mediterranean Countries, i.e. by the excess of births over deaths (natural balance). In these countries, average annual natural change of about 1.6% (higher than the world average and a fortiori that of the Mediterranean as a whole) have been observed. This chapter gives an account of the evolution of the differentiated growth rates of the populations of the Mediterranean region since the 1950s, distinguishing between the development of natural, migration and overall growth rates. This will make it possible to characterise the countries whose growth has been stimulated more by natural than migration growth depending on the period, thus heralding the sustainability of future growth rates. To achieve this, the chapter will propose a ranking of growth rates for different countries over time, as well as the expected developments in terms of projections while discussing the assumptions.

Keywords Natural dynamics · Migration dynamics · Population dynamics · Population growth · Projections · Mediterranean

9.1 Introduction

The Mediterranean has an average annual population growth rate of around 1%, which is about the same as the world population growth rate. With a few rare exceptions, this growth is not principally fuelled by migration flows. However, it is closely linked to the demographic transition still underway in many Southern and Eastern Mediterranean Countries, i.e. by the excess of births over deaths (natural balance). In these countries, average annual natural change of about 1.6% (higher than the world

---

The original version of the chapter has been revised: Figure 9.3 has been replaced. A correction to this chapter can be found at https://doi.org/10.1007/978-3-031-37759-4_12

© The Author(s) 2023, corrected publication 2024
Y. Doignon et al., *Population Dynamics in the Mediterranean*,
SpringerBriefs in Population Studies,
https://doi.org/10.1007/978-3-031-37759-4_9

average and a fortiori that of the Mediterranean as a whole) have been observed. This chapter gives an account of the evolution of the differentiated growth rates of the populations of the Mediterranean region since the 1950s, distinguishing between the development of natural, migration and overall growth rates. This will make it possible to characterise the countries whose growth has been stimulated more by natural than migration growth depending on the period, thus heralding the sustainability of future growth rates. To achieve this, the chapter will propose a ranking of growth rates for different countries over time, as well as the expected developments in terms of projections while discussing the assumptions.

9.2 Evolving Power Relations

The population of the Mediterranean countries amounted to approximately 571 million inhabitants in 2020. It has increased 2.5 times in 70 years. The annual rate of growth was on average very strong until the mid-1980s (exceeding rather continuously 1.4% per year) before beginning to decline (Fig. 9.1). At the start of the twenty-first century, the growth rate of the Mediterranean population was around 0.9% per year, the same rate as that of the world population. While all countries are experiencing a slowdown in their growth, the heterogeneity between major regional clusters is still notable. North Africa and the Near East still have annual population growth above 1.3%, despite a steady decline since the mid-1980s. In 1950, growth was of the order of 2% per year, a significant rate, because it represents a doubling of the population in 35 years. The evolution of population growth in the Near East highlights the impact of cyclical events, such as the insurgency in Syria (1978–1982), the war in Iraq in the 2000s and the reception of refugees in several Near Eastern countries. In contrast, Southern Europe and the Balkans have zero and negative growth respectively (-0.4%). The period when several Southern European countries became receiving countries with a positive net migration (see Chap. 8) can be seen on the graph with a significant increase in population growth in the 2000s, followed by a decrease after the 2007 crisis.

If we focus on countries with more than 10 million inhabitants, we notice that the 3 most populated countries in the Mediterranean in 1950 are all Southern European countries (Italy, France, Spain), ahead of Egypt and Turkey (Table 9.1). There are only 5 countries with more than 10 million inhabitants in the 27 Mediterranean countries. In 1980, two new countries (Morocco and Algeria) joined the group of most populous countries, while the demographic breakthrough of Turkey and Egypt was already visible, with Spain moving up from third to fifth place. In 2020, the order of the shores reversed since Egypt and Turkey were the two most populous countries in the Mediterranean largely ahead of the three Southern European countries, with respectively about 109 and 85 million inhabitants (Blöss-Widmer, 2022). Together, they represent 34% of the Mediterranean population, the same order of magnitude as India and China represent in the world population. 5 new countries exceeded the threshold of 10 million inhabitants in 2021: Syria, Tunisia, Jordan, Greece and Portugal. Seven of the 12 countries with more than 10 million inhabitants are located

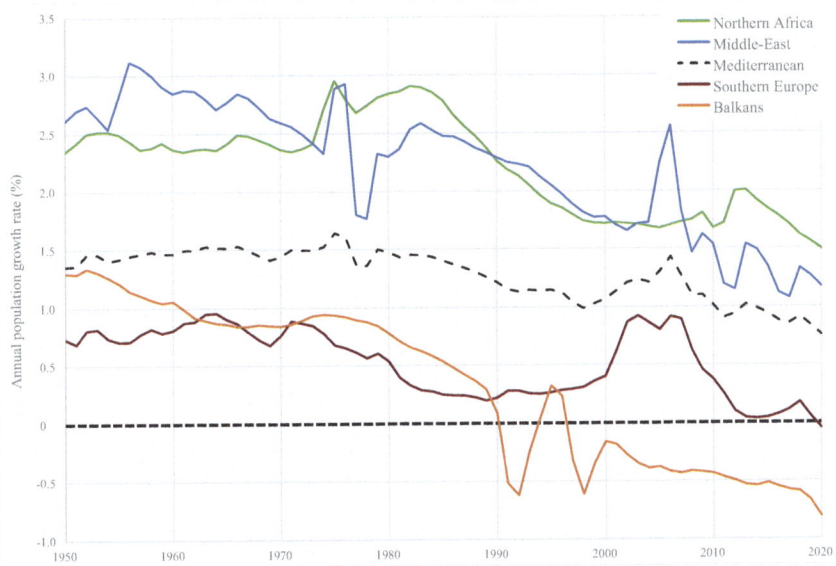

Fig. 9.1 Mediterranean comparative annual growth rate (%) by regional groups (1950–2020) (*Source* World Population Prospects, 2022. Calculations made by the authors)

on the Southern and Eastern shores. This ranking highlights the reversal of the demographic order that prevailed in the 1950s. As a result of the demographic transition (see Chap. 4), the populations of the Southern and Eastern shores have increased sharply and their weight in the Mediterranean population has increased considerably. Indeed, the Northern shore represented 68% of the Mediterranean population in 1950, and the Southern and Eastern shores 32%. These proportions stood at 39% and 61% respectively in 2020. In other words, while the majority of the Mediterranean population was on the Northern shore in 1950, the situation is exactly the opposite at present where 60% of the Mediterranean population is on the Southern and Eastern shores. It should be noted that almost 40% of the Mediterranean population is located in North Africa, 24% in the Near East, 32% in Southern Europe, and only 7% in the Balkans.

Some countries have therefore experienced an impressive increase in their population since 1950 (Fig. 9.2). Egypt and Turkey have experienced growth rates of more than 2% per year for more than 30 years. Their population has multiplied by 5 and 4, respectively. The most spectacular trajectory is that of Jordan, which had less than 500,000 inhabitants in 1950, but more than 11 million in 2021. This increase represents a more than 25-fold increase in the population in 70 years. The countries of the Southern and Eastern shores have seen their population growth by more than 4 times since 1950, compared to 1.5 for the countries of the Northern shore.

This growth is largely a consequence of the various demographic transitions described in Chap. 4. It depends firstly on the level of the natural balance (number of births minus number of deaths), a component that varies according to the stages of the demographic transition. The rate of population change also increases by the size

Table 9.1 Countries with more than 10 million inhabitants in 1950, 1980 and 2021 (population numbers in millions)

1950		1980		2021	
Italy	46	Italy	56	Egypt	109
France	42	France	54	Turkey	85
Spain	28	Turkey	44	France	65
Egypt	21	Egypt	44	Italy	59
Turkey	21	Spain	37	Spain	47
		Morocco	20	Algeria	44
		Algeria	19	Morocco	37
				Syria	21
				Tunisia	12
				Jordan	11
				Greece	10
				Portugal	10

(*Source* World Population Prospects, 2022)

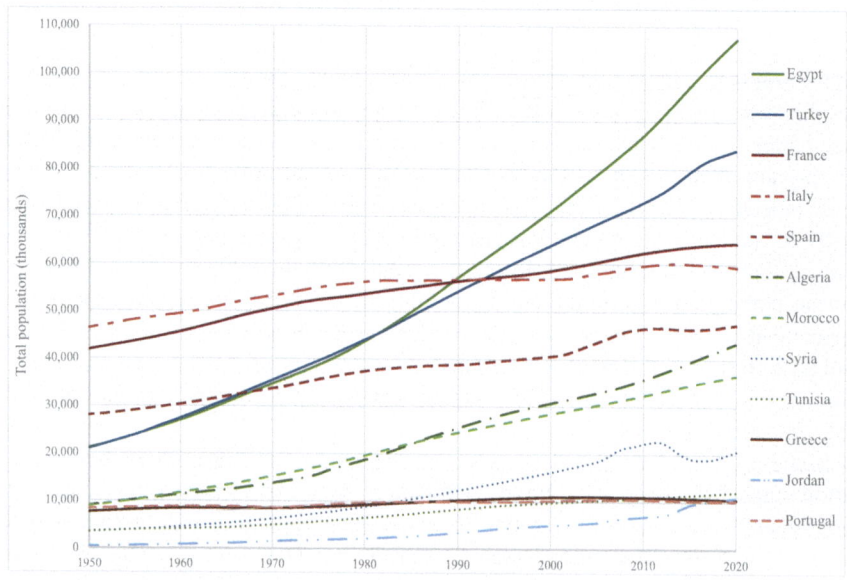

Fig. 9.2 Comparative population evolution in Mediterranean by country (1950–2021) (*Source* World Population Prospects, 2022)

of the net migration (estimate of the difference between arrivals and departures from each country for each period). These two elements, the components of population dynamics, can jointly stimulate growth (positive natural balance and positive net migration), work against each other (positive natural balance/negative net migration or vice versa) or contribute to a general decline (negative natural and net migration).

In order to fully understand the population dynamics of the Mediterranean countries, it is therefore necessary to analyse its two components (natural and migration) in order to derive several profiles of dynamics.

9.3 Natural and Migration Dynamics: Which Combinations Exist in the Mediterranean?

With regard to the natural component, the average annual rates of all countries have fallen considerably since 1950. The demographic transition generates an undeniable phenomenon of convergence of rate of natural change towards lower levels (see Chap. 4). However, there are still marked differences from one shore to the other: several demographic regimes still coexist in the Mediterranean. As for migration dynamics, they cannot be easily summarised for many countries, as they are essentially linked to the economic situation (economic, reception of refugees, etc.) and to specific migration policies (see Chap. 8). It can sometimes be of relative importance for the total population dynamics for certain countries. Figure 9.3 presents the two demographic components of the Mediterranean countries for 3 periods (1950–1954, 1990–1995 and 2015–2019).

9.3.1 Natural Dynamics: South and East

The majority of Mediterranean countries have been in constant natural growth since the 1950s. The level of this natural growth averaged over 2% per year until the early 1990s and then halved on average. These countries, stimulated by their natural growth, belong very much to Northern Africa (Morocco, Algeria, Tunisia, Egypt, Libya) and the Near East (Palestine, Turkey, Syria). The majority of these countries are therefore, logically, those whose demographic transition began later, but much more rapidly, than the others (Chap. 4). The gains in life expectancy due to declining mortality in Northern Africa and the Near-East have been concentrated among the youngest and adults, increasing their probability of survival and thus automatically lowering deaths at all ages (see Chap. 7). This phenomenon, which increases the probability of survival for everyone, contributes to a structural increase in births from generations of fertile age newly preserved from death. It is also combined with a fertility decline that occurs on a delayed mortality timing, still generating many births (Chap. 5). The natural growth levels of Northern Africa and Near East countries

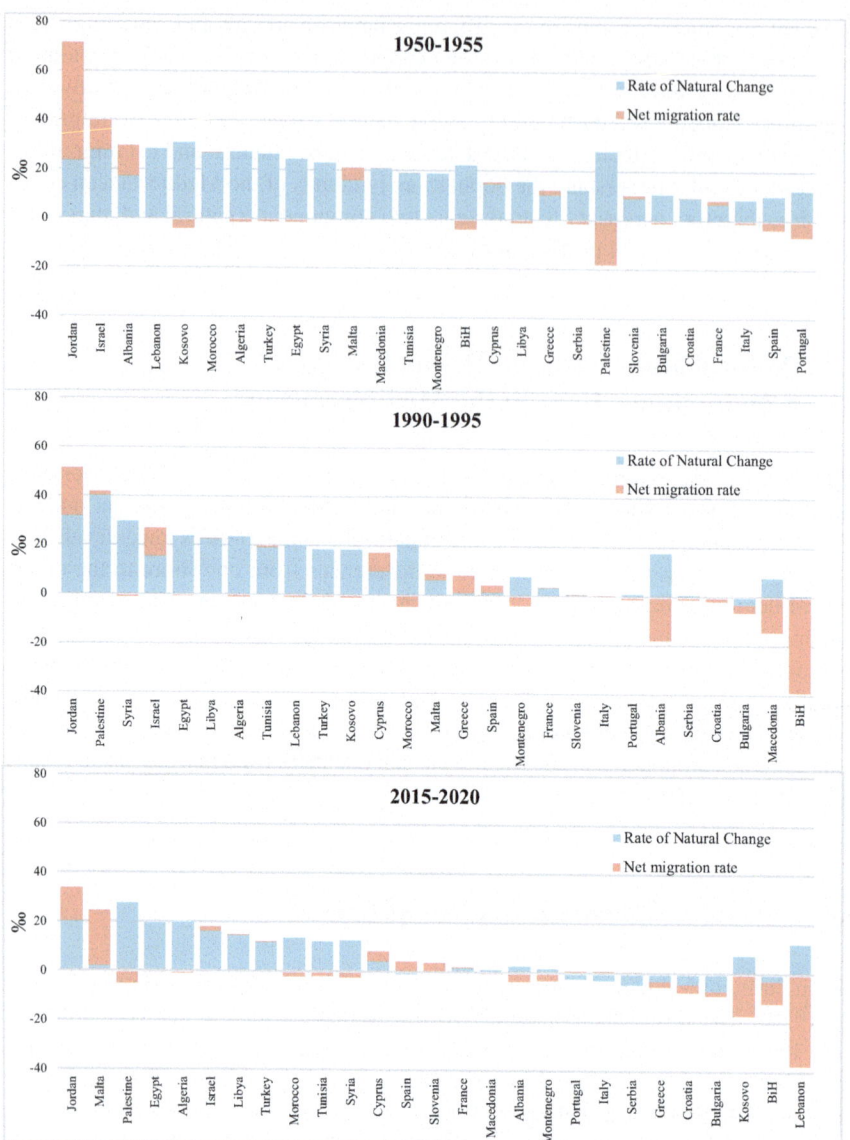

Fig. 9.3 Participation of natural and migration components on total growth for Mediterranean countries at different periods (1950–1955, 1990–1995, 2015–2020) (*Source* World Population Prospects, 2022)

are relatively high and similar, rising over the period from 2.6% per annum to 1.7% per annum.

Some countries have not broken with natural growth, despite the fact that demographic ageing started earlier. France, Cyprus, Malta, Montenegro, Macedonia, Kosovo and Albania have managed to maintain positive natural growth for reasons related to higher fertility by age of women, combined with age structures that are still favourable. However, with rates of no more than 0.5% per year for decades (except for Kosovo), the level of natural growth in these countries is much lower than in the Near-East or Northern Africa.

In contrast to the previous countries, nine Mediterranean countries have experienced a weak and downward natural dynamic since the 1950s, with episodes of natural decline (excess of deaths over births) that have appeared and continued for some for as long as 30 years (Chap. 4). None of these less dynamic countries are located on the Southern and Eastern shores, all are on the Northern shore: Slovenia, Spain, Italy, Bulgaria, Bosnia-Herzegovina, Serbia, Portugal, Greece, and Croatia. Their average annual rate of population dynamics over the period contrasts with previous countries, having increased from about 1.2% on average in the 1950s to −0.3% in 2015–2020. These countries are experiencing a slowdown in their natural dynamics as their populations age and younger generations reduce their fertility. Gap age effects have sometimes accentuated the phenomenon. It is from the years 1990–1995 that negative natural dynamics began to be observed in Italy, Croatia and Bulgaria, rapidly followed by Slovenia and Serbia (1995–2000), Portugal (2005–2010), Greece and Bosnia-Herzegovina (2010–2015) and Spain (2015–2020). Thus, while these 9 countries all had moderate but positive natural growth in the early 1990s, they were all (except Slovenia) in 2020 remarkable for their negative natural dynamics.

9.3.2 Migration Dynamics: Sending Versus Receiving Countries

Although the Southern and Eastern Mediterranean countries are known more as sending countries (negative migration balances) and those of Southern Europe as receiving countries (positive migration balances) (Chap. 8), a detailed analysis makes it possible to show this, to measure the temporalities and to reveal exceptions (Fig. 9.3).

Among the countries that have been in continuous natural growth for 70 years, a large part has been, at the same time and over a large part of the period, more senders of migrants than receivers (negative net migration). This includes Palestine, Egypt, Algeria, Turkey, Morocco, Tunisia, Macedonia, Montenegro, Albania, Kosovo and the Syrian. The intensity of negative net migration has been variable since the 1950s, contributing more or less to tempering the pace of total growth. All these countries, which are naturally dynamic but have had largely negative net migration since the

1950s, are therefore in North Africa, the Near East and some in the Balkans. No Southern European country has had a consistently negative net migration for 60 years, this regional grouping being more characterised by periods of migration alternation (receivers or senders in balance depending on the period) (Chap. 8).

Only 3 countries out of 17 with positive natural growth in the three periods also had positive migration growth: Israel, France and Jordan. France is truly an exception, since it is not only one of the three Mediterranean countries whose two components (natural and migration) are positive, but it is the only Southern European country to have this characteristic.

The countries of Southern Europe and the Balkans have experienced a natural downward trend over the past 60 years. Their migration attractiveness is often erratic, and partially (or not at all) compensates for periods of decline. A rather critical demographic dynamic of decline has thus gradually taken hold in Southern Europe and the Balkans. Two countries, for example, combine their natural dynamics (sustained until the 1990s and then much weaker, or even negative) with a migration dynamic that has constantly been negative for 60 years: Bulgaria and Bosnia-Herzegovina. These countries lost more people than they gained through migration over the whole period, which did not help to offset their negative natural dynamics. Other situations with negative net migration combined with depopulation (negative natural balances) have been noted in recent periods, such as in Serbia, Greece, Croatia, followed closely by Portugal, Slovenia, Spain and Italy where one of the components is negative. Depending on the economic situation, these countries are sometimes attractive and sometimes repulsive from a migration point of view. Positive migration balances over a few periods almost never compensate in level for the low number of births in view of the rise in deaths recorded as a result of demographic ageing.

9.4 Growth Outlook to 2060: What Can We Expect?

By 2060, the median scenario of the United Nations projections forecasts a Mediterranean population of nearly 685 million. Less than half of the countries are experiencing this growth, with the other half projected to lose more of its population each year than it gains from low fertility and population ageing. For the latter countries of Southern Europe and the Balkans, which are in decline, even the hypothesis of a net migration attraction forecast for some (Portugal, Italy, Greece, Spain, Slovenia and Malta) would not be enough to compensate for the negative natural balance that has lasted for a long time (Fig. 9.4).

As a result, the weight of the Southern and Eastern shores would continue to increase, since they will represent 72% of the Mediterranean population, compared to 61% at present (Table 9.2). One in two inhabitants of the Mediterranean by 2060 will be in Egypt, Turkey or Algeria. As for Italy, Spain, Portugal and Greece, all four would lose inhabitants, with the last two even falling back below the 10 million mark. Southern Europe would then represent less than 30% of the Mediterranean population, compared with 39% in 2020 and the Balkans less than 5%. According

9.4 Growth Outlook to 2060: What Can We Expect?

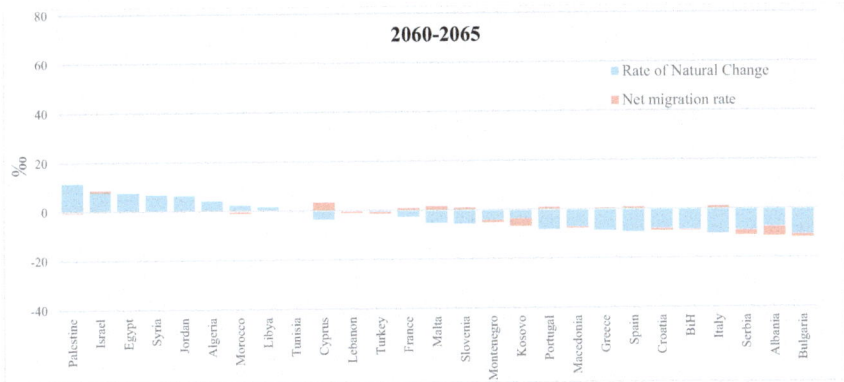

Fig. 9.4 Projection of participation of natural and migration components on the total growth for the Mediterranean countries (2060, median variant) (*Source* World Population Prospects, 2022)

to the median scenario, many countries would have fewer inhabitants in 2060 than in 2020, the vast majority being on the Northern shore, but Lebanon also falls into this category.

Chapter 5 on fertility trends, however, has shown how much uncertainty still exists when it comes to making projections over somewhat distant horizons. Indeed: "Not only is there no longer a general theory capable of indicating the direction in which fertility should significantly evolve, but the future of mortality, which as we have seen weighs heavily on the projections, is the subject of a lively debate, without mentioning migration" (Vallin & Caselli, 2006). Demographic projections are less subject to uncertainty than economic projections, due to the nature of the projected quantities, the inertia of demographic phenomena, and the heavy trend they represent. However, as noted again recently by Adam (2021) in the article entitled "How far will global population rise? Researchers can't agree", it is common for the methods and scenarios used by the different research teams to[1] lead to quite contrasting results.[2]

---

[1] We are thinking in particular of the scenarios of the United Nations (World Population Prospects 2022), of those of CEPAM (Joint Research Centre [European Commission], 2018), of Lutz et al. (2014) and of Vollset et al. (2020).

[2] For example: "World population projections for the twenty-first century as produced by the United Nations Population Division and by the International Institute for Applied Systems Analysis (IIASA) have changed quite a bit over time as a function of different long-term fertility and mortality assumptions, and the incorporation of most recent observed empirical trends and analysis. In their most recent assessments, the UN (2017) projects continuous growth of world population for their medium variant, reaching more than 11 billion people by the end of the century. Whereas IIASA (…) with its medium scenario (SSP2), projected a peak population of 9.4 billion in 2065–2075, followed by a slight decline to 9 billion by the end of the century (…) This difference is mostly due to different methods of deriving long-term fertility assumptions for the different parts of the world, where the UN relies primarily on statistical extrapolation models and IIASA gives more weight to expert arguments and scientific reasoning" (Joint Research Centre [European Commission], 2018, 117).

Table 9.2 Population (in thousands) and share of Mediterranean population (in %) in 2020 and 2060, by countries and regional area

Countries	Population (in thousands)		Share of Mediterranean population (in %)	
	2020	2060	2020	2060
Egypt	107,465	174,311	19	25
Turkey	84,135	96,017	15	14
France	64,480	64,903	11	9
Algeria	43,452	63,554	8	9
Italy	59,501	48,233	11	7
Morocco	36,689	46,214	6	7
Spain	47,364	41,257	8	6
Syria	20,773	41,042	4	6
Jordan	10,929	16,131	2	2
Tunisia	12,162	14,512	2	2
Israel	8,757	14,332	2	2
Palestine	5,019	10,036	1	1
Libya	6,654	8,762	1	1
Portugal	10,298	8,683	2	1
Greece	10,512	8,506	2	1
Serbia	7,358	5,238	1	1
Lebanon	5,663	4,947	1	1
Bulgaria	6,979	4,656	1	1
Croatia	4,097	3,067	1	0
BiH	3,318	2,523	1	0
Albania	2,867	2,218	1	0
Slovenia	2,118	1,920	0	0
Macedonia	2,111	1,784	0	0
Kosovo	1,671	1,575	0	0
Cyprus	1,238	1,404	0	0
Montenegro	629	560	0	0
Malta	515	507	0	0
Northern Africa	206,421	307,354	37	45
Near-East	136,514	183,909	24	27
Balkan countries	39,989	30,471	7	4
Southern Europe	182,158	163,582	32	24
Southern and Eastern Shores	342,935	491,263	61	72
Northern Shore	222,147	194,053	39	28
Mediterranean	565,083	685,317	100	100

(*Source* World Population Prospects, 2022)

9.4 Growth Outlook to 2060: What Can We Expect?

Although assumptions are difficult to make and subject to discussion, we have nevertheless identified groups of countries whose fertility does not seem, for the time being at least, to reach low fertility levels (Chap. 5). Consequently, the growth dynamics of the regional clusters of Northern Africa and Near East could be more sustained than what all the recent projections predict. Conversely, the projections of decline for the countries of Southern Europe and the Balkans seem less uncertain, as they are part of an inevitable context of ageing and a preference for small families. And if declining countries were to shift their fertility upwards to counter the rate of growth of the elderly, they would have to reach levels of around 3 children per woman (Blanchet, 2001). However, this does not seem to be consistent with the number of desired children reported by families in international comparative surveys.[3]

With regard to migration, Chap. 8 showed the importance of the movements to be anticipated towards ageing Southern Europe. However, regardless of the size of net immigration to these countries over the next 40 years (the evolution of which is the most unpredictable of all the components), this solution would not, a priori make it possible to halt the expected phenomena of decline, because the ageing of the population leads to the observation of too rapid an increase in the number of deaths. As early as the 2000s, a United Nations report (Population Division et al., 2000) modelled an adjustment of imbalances by migration flows. The main conclusions were that controlling ageing through migration would require migration balances twice as high as those experienced by the most attractive countries in the world such as the United States; and some simulations of migration balances needed to maintain dependency ratios in ageing developed countries are even described as "totally unrealistic"[4] (Blanchet, 2001, 523), because certainly not acceptable to the populations of these same countries, nor realistic.

In conclusion, in the Mediterranean, the average annual growth rates have continued to decline in all countries since the 1950s with the spread of the demographic transition towards the countries on the Southern and Eastern shores. While growth differentials have narrowed, on average much faster rates are still recorded in the Near East and Northern Africa compared to Southern Europe and especially in the Balkan countries. The population dynamics of the vast majority of countries are mainly due to the natural component (excess of births over deaths). If migration dynamics temper the demographic dynamics of sending countries,[5] it is expected to sustain, but with difficulty, that of the receiving countries with the lowest fertility

---

[3] We are thinking in particular of the responses given to surveys such as: The European Values Study (EVS), International Social Survey Program (ISSP), World Values Survey (WVS), Generations and Gender Survey (GGS), Afrobarometer and Anna Lindh Foundation.

[4] This text has been translated into English by the authors. The original text in French is as follows: "totalement irréalistes".

[5] "Anyway, according to CEPAM Medium (SSP2) scenario, migration would not be able to affect significantly the MENA population size and structure: (…) It implies that population changes would be mainly driven by fertility and mortality behaviours under this scenario" (Joint Research Centre [European Commission], 2018, 69).

and the highest life expectancies, since most of them are expected to lose inhabitants by 2060.[6]

References

Adam, D. (2021). How far will global population rise? Researchers can't agree. *Nature, 597*, 462–465. https://doi.org/10.1038/d41586-021-02522-6

Blanchet, D. (2001). L'impact des changements démographiques sur la croissance et le marché du travail: Faits, théories et incertitudes. *Revue D'économie Politique, 111*, 511–564. https://doi.org/10.3917/redp.114.0511

Blöss-Widmer, I. (2022). Make way for numbers: The age race in the Mediterranean. *IEMed Mediterranean yearbook 2022*. European Institute of the Mediterranean (IEMed). https://www.iemed.org/wp-content/uploads/2022/10/Make-Way-Numbers-Age-Race-Mediterranean-Bloss-Widmer-IEMedYearbook2022.pdf

Joint Research Centre (European Commission). (2018). *Demographic and human capital scenarios for the 21st century: 2018 assessment for 201 countries*. Publications Office. https://data.europa.eu/doi/10.2760/41776

Lutz, W., Butz, W. P., & Samir, K. C. (2014). World population and human capital in the twenty-first century. *Oxford University Press*. https://doi.org/10.1093/acprof:oso/9780198703167.001.0001

Population Division, Department of Economic and Social Affairs, and United Nations Secretariat. (2000). *Replacement migration: Is it a solution to declining and ageing populations?* https://www.un.org/development/desa/pd/sites/www.un.org.development.desa.pd/files/unpd-egm_200010_un_2001_replacementmigration.pdf

Vallin, J., & Caselli, G. (2006). The United Nations' world population projections. In G. Caselli, J. Vallin, & G. J. Wunsch (Eds.), *Demography: Analysis and synthesis* (Vol. III, pp. 197–234). Elsevier.

Vollset, S. E., Goren, E., Yuan, C.-W., Cao, J., Smith, A. E., Hsiao, T., Bisignano, C. et al. (2020). Fertility, mortality, migration, and population scenarios for 195 countries and territories from 2017 to 2100: A forecasting analysis for the global burden of disease study. *The Lancet* 396. Elsevier: 1285–1306. https://doi.org/10.1016/S0140-6736(20)30677-2

World population prospects. (2022). United Nations, Department of Economic and Social Affairs, Population Division. https://population.un.org/wpp/

---

[6] "If the current demographic trends continue as in the presented scenarios the main driver of change in population size of EU-28 countries would be migration" (Joint Research Centre [European Commission], 2018, 33).

References

Open Access This chapter is licensed under the terms of the Creative Commons Attribution 4.0 International License (http://creativecommons.org/licenses/by/4.0/), which permits use, sharing, adaptation, distribution and reproduction in any medium or format, as long as you give appropriate credit to the original author(s) and the source, provide a link to the Creative Commons license and indicate if changes were made.

The images or other third party material in this chapter are included in the chapter's Creative Commons license, unless indicated otherwise in a credit line to the material. If material is not included in the chapter's Creative Commons license and your intended use is not permitted by statutory regulation or exceeds the permitted use, you will need to obtain permission directly from the copyright holder.

Chapter 10
Conclusions. An Overview of Population Dynamics in the Mediterranean

Abstract This book has made it possible to review the main demographic developments of the last 70 years. Above all, it has made it possible to highlight the rapid global homogenisation of several demographic behaviours in the Mediterranean, to point out certain exceptions and to identify the global challenges that await Mediterranean populations.

Keywords Mediterranean · Population studies · International comparison · Demographic convergence

10.1 Major Demographic Developments Since 1950

This book has made it possible to review the main demographic developments of the last 70 years. Above all, it has made it possible to highlight the rapid global homogenisation of several demographic behaviours in the Mediterranean, to point out certain exceptions and to identify the global challenges that await Mediterranean populations.

From a geographical point of view, the Mediterranean appears to have extremely heterogeneous populations, since it includes some of the most densely populated regions in the world as well as desert regions. Nevertheless, most of the Mediterranean countries are experiencing a strong coastalisation of its population. In addition, there are several coastal cities. The role of water, the sea and also the rivers in shaping human settlement in the Mediterranean is a characteristic that is present in the entire area studied (the Nile being the most archetypal example). The Mediterranean is undergoing rapid urbanisation, from a predominantly rural population in 1950 to an urban population of 70% by 2020. The urban agglomerations on the Southern and Eastern shores account for most of the Mediterranean's urban population growth between 2000 and 2020. This phenomenon has led to a higher concentration of the population in the area, especially on the coastlines. This human pressure on the natural environment is not without consequences in terms of maritime pollution, the

© The Author(s) 2023
Y. Doignon et al., *Population Dynamics in the Mediterranean*,
SpringerBriefs in Population Studies,
https://doi.org/10.1007/978-3-031-37759-4_10

degradation of the environment and biodiversity, fires, pressures on water resources, etc.

From a demographic point of view, however, the rate of growth has been steadily decreasing for all Mediterranean countries since the late 1970s. However, due to the inertia of the demographic phenomena, the populations of the Mediterranean countries have more than doubled, reaching around 570 million inhabitants in 2020. This increase in Mediterranean populations is mainly driven by the Southern and Eastern shores. Indeed, while the Mediterranean as a whole has gained 110 million inhabitants between 2000 and 2020, the countries on the Northern Shore have only contributed 11 million. This trend explains why today 2 out of 3 Mediterranean people live in a country on the Southern and Eastern shores (compared to 1 out of 3 in 1950), and also why Egypt and Turkey are the most populated Mediterranean countries in 2020, and no longer Italy and France as in 1950.

The slowdown in the rate of population growth in the Mediterranean, which is currently lower than in the past, can be explained by the demographic transition generalising to the whole region. All Mediterranean countries have seen their birth and death rates fall, thus limiting population growth. Nevertheless, we have managed to identify that there are significant disparities behind these overall trends. There is no single demographic transition model in the Mediterranean. On the contrary, there are several types, differing in their pace, course, and post-transitional demographic regime. The transition has been much faster in some countries than in others. Some post-transitional regimes are characterised by declining growth (Bulgaria, Croatia, Italy, etc.), others by low or moderate growth (France, Cyprus, Tunisia, Kosovo, Turkey, etc.), and a few are still experiencing relatively high growth (Egypt, Palestine, Jordan, Algeria, Israel). Thus, the slowdown in the rate of growth is leading some countries to lose population, while others continue to gain population.

If the Mediterranean is increasing its number of inhabitants, it is above all, experiencing a rapid transformation in the composition of its population. In fact, the most striking development noted is that of demographic ageing, with an increase in the number of elderly people in the population and a decrease in that of the young. Currently, the elderly (65 years of age or older) represent 12% of the Mediterranean population, and the young (under 15 years of age) about 24%. In general, the populations of the countries on the Northern shore are older than those on the Southern and Eastern shores: in 2020, people aged 65 or over represented 21% on average for the former, and 6% for the latter. However, the gap between countries is slightly smaller today than it was in 1950. This phenomenon will continue at an even faster pace in the coming decades, with demographic ageing definitively establishing itself as a concern shared by all Mediterranean countries. Indeed, the UN projections (median scenario) will expect that people aged 65 or over represent about 22% of the entire Mediterranean population in 2060, with about 34% for the Northern shore and 17% for the Southern and Eastern shore.

With the demographic transition process, fertility levels have been reduced in all Mediterranean countries. Despite this convergence towards lower levels than those of the pre-transitional regimes, fertility differences still persist in the Mediterranean. Our analyses reveal first of all that some countries have reached a fertility level well below the population replacement level (2.1 children per woman). With the exception of Cyprus, all of these very low fertility countries are not on the Southern and Eastern shores. Other groups of countries have a fertility level around the replacement level, such as France, Tunisia, Turkey or Lebanon; and finally, other fertility situations are noted as remaining fixed well above this threshold (more than 3 children per woman), such as Jordan, Egypt, Israel and Palestine. In light of the predicted convergence of the demographic transition, our analyses suggest that Mediterranean countries could stabilise at different fertility levels, potentially generating different demographic regimes in the future. For example, two groups can be distinguished in terms of fertility timing: countries where the childbearing age is lower and those for which it is higher. However, this is not a shore-based divide, as there are countries from all shores in both groups. The determinants of these birth timing seem to be very heterogeneous from one country to another, thus fuelling the possibility that fertility in the Mediterranean will not fully converge in the end.

However, family formation and dissolution behaviours have converged in some ways over the last 70 years. In the Mediterranean, there has not only been a decrease in the frequency of marriages and a reduction in the disparities in divortiality, but also an increase in the age at marriage and in permanent celibacy. These contemporary family changes have been interpreted as a profound challenge to the institution of marriage in Western Europe, and as a marriage revolution in Arab-Muslim countries. However, lifelong commitment is still expressed in various forms in Europe and marriage continues to endure and structure family models on the Southern and Eastern shores. Permanent celibacy and postponement of the age of marriage may then be less about questioning the institution of marriage itself than of worsening socio-economic conditions, such as high youth unemployment, greater precariousness and uncertainty about the future, or the cost of housing or marriage being too high. Similarly, not being married does not imply the same social reality. In Arab-Muslim societies, this means waiting longer for social independence and economic autonomy, or being unable to start a family. Thus, similar trends in demographic indicators may conceal very different social situations.

The Mediterranean has also seen a broad convergence of mortality, with a historic increase in life expectancy at birth for all countries. The disparities of the 1950s have narrowed considerably, with countries with the lowest life expectancy at birth catching up rapidly. However, convergence has not been observed for about 30 years. The control of infectious diseases, and later of cardiovascular diseases, has led to a reduction in infant and adult mortality. On the other hand, the unequal capacity of Mediterranean countries to fight against societal diseases, neurodegenerative diseases and cancers, has led to a divergence in life expectancy at age 65. Massive ageing will therefore inevitably lead to a significant increase in the number of deaths in these countries, as survival probabilities at older ages are unlikely to increase rapidly.

Finally, with regard to international migration, the book showed that the Mediterranean constitutes a real migration system, and above all one of the largest migration areas in the world. Migration from the Southern and Eastern shore countries to European countries was intense in the 1960s. However, the various economic crises from the 1970s onwards led to increasingly restrictive entry policies in Europe. Southern

European countries have been gradually becoming host countries. Since the 2000s, there has been a recomposition of the poles of attraction in the Mediterranean, with the emergence of Turkey for example. Finally, the number of refugees and asylum seekers has increased considerably since the "Arab Spring" and the various ensuing conflicts, to the point of talk of a "refugee crisis". The issue of international migration is, along with that of the urbanisation/littoralisation of the common sea and the ageing of populations, a challenge shared by the entire Mediterranean area.

10.2 An Assessment of the Book's Overall Approach

The introduction to this publication set out a number of approaches, including the implementation of a comparative approach. Now that the project is drawing to a close, what heuristic lessons can we draw from it? First of all, regarding out choice to study Mediterranean populations over a long demographic period (i.e., over the last 70 years), we can commend ourselves, which has proven particularly fruitful. It is indeed by putting recent trends into perspective within long-term developments that has allowed us, for example, to identify the broad movements of convergence that have taken place in various fields. Situating the present in a historical perspective allows for an account of underlying trends rather than short-term fluctuations. Thanks to this approach, it is also possible to affirm that the disparities have been reduced over time, and that the Mediterranean populations are closer and more similar today than in the past. The Mediterranean is therefore well and truly in the process of demographic homogenisation on the whole, despite persistent heterogeneities in certain areas.

This choice of studying it over the long term has also made it possible to show that the demographic history of the Mediterranean countries is not always monotonous, but on the contrary is sometimes punctuated by changes in pace, breaks in trends or even reversals. This historical perspective sometimes makes it possible to put certain recent economic developments into perspective and to interpret them more accurately and also makes it possible to avoid considering demographic developments as being one-way or predetermined. Indeed, recent reversals in trends have again reminded us of this, such as the decline in life expectancy at birth with the COVID-19 pandemic. Some of these may be surprising at first glance, but are less so when hewed from an historical perspective. Increases in fertility in Egypt and Algeria, for example, may appear as notable exceptions to the theory of demographic transition. However, fertility increases have already taken place in the past in the Mediterranean, with baby booms observed in many European countries in the 1950s and 1960s, and in Egypt in the 1980s, putting the current increases or surges in fertility into perspective. The question is to what extent these trend reversals reflect backtracking, a temporary change or even a new behavioural trend.

Our second approach was to implement an overall international comparison, with countries as the level of analysis, rejecting any predefined geographical framework. The analyses in this publication have therefore not sought to reiterate the classic

10.2 An Assessment of the Book's Overall Approach

contrasts,[1] such as the Northern shore vs. the Southern and Eastern shores, or the Balkans, Southern Europe, North Africa vs. the Near East. On the contrary, we opted for a bottom-up approach, allowing groups from all Mediterranean countries to emerge, regardless of their geographical location.

This choice showed the extent to which the Mediterranean is a complex region that cannot be reduced to a simple demographic opposition between two blocks (Northern Shore/Southern and Eastern shore). Beyond the traditional contrasts, this method made it possible to highlight the internal diversity of each of the blocks in many areas. Surprisingly, some countries are closer to countries on other shores than to their neighbours. For example, Tunisia has a demographic regime closer to France than Algeria or Morocco. Similarly, the demographic regime of France is more similar to that of Tunisia than to those of Italy or Spain. This is also the case for certain Balkan countries (Serbia, Montenegro, etc.) whose life expectancy at birth is similar to that of countries on the Southern and Eastern shores (Turkey, Lebanon).

This option, which consists of taking all the countries without first grouping them together, has made it possible to show once again that the overall contrast between the shores of the Mediterranean is still coherent for a certain number of demographic phenomena. However, even when contrasts between shores are noted, the situations are less often caricatured and there are exceptions for each shore. Indeed, in several chapters, our analyses highlight countries or particular groups of countries that would not have been identified by any other method. This concerns, for example, the particular position of specific Balkan countries (Kosovo, Albania, Macedonia, etc.), which are quite systematically closer to the countries of the Southern and Eastern shores than to the other Balkan countries in terms of several demographic phenomena. This characteristic had already been highlighted for Albania by Attané and Courbage (2004). The same applies to Israel, Cyprus, and sometimes Lebanon, for the Southern and Eastern shores, which stand out as atypical in the region.

In addition, certain demographic phenomena reveal contrasts between countries from different shores. This is the case, for example, for adult mortality, age at childbearing or age at marriage. It is by refusing to perpetuate existing regional categories that it has been possible to obtain a renewed understanding of the Mediterranean, we have identified trans-Mediterranean formations (grouping together countries from different shores), and regionalisations beyond the Northern shore and the Southern and Eastern shores divide.

This publication is therefore not a juxtaposition of regional monographs, or a bibliographic synthesis of national studies. It is an integrated, bottom-up demographic and geographical approach based on data. This approach has been fruitful in proposing an original synthesis of the major demographic phenomena over the last 70 years, and thereby offering up-to-date insights of demography in the Mediterranean.

The aim of this publication was to provide an overview of the demographic trends over the last 70 years for all populations of the Mediterranean. To this end, we chose to analyse the classic demographic phenomena. On the other hand, some aspects have

---

[1] Throughout the publication, only the graphical representations have used broad regional groupings, for reasons related to practicality and consistency.

not been developed or have only been partially developed. These are all avenues to be developed further with an approach similar to that of this publication. We mention three of them here, but there are obviously many others.

Firstly, we did not focus enough on educational progress and the status of women. Both have considerable influence on demographic behaviour, in particular on the decline in fertility and the nuptiality rate. The Mediterranean area is varied from the point of view of women's place in society, whether one compares the countries or the different social and geographical sub-areas specific of each country studied. The status occupied by women varies between and within societies, just as the place of residence (urban or rural) or the community to which they belong influences a couple's plans to have children.

Secondly, it is imperative to obtain an improved understanding of representations and values in the Mediterranean countries, particularly those associated with the couple, the family, motherhood and children. We are thinking of, for example, the ideal number of children,[2] the importance of family life, the acceptability of giving birth to a child out-of-wedlock, the importance of work for a woman, the values transmitted from parents to children, etc. It is rather difficult, despite opinions being collected via relevant international comparative surveys, to construct a complete picture of the Mediterranean situation. However, there are some elements that can provide food for thought. A number of opinion questions are asked to male and female respondents from different countries. As such, it is possible to pinpoint and measure the transformation of norms and the conception of marriage and the family in the Mediterranean and to imagine their future.

Finally, this publication mainly uses countries as the level of analysis, as it was already rich enough to offer a synthesis of demographic phenomena in the Mediterranean. However, we are aware that the lessons learned at the national level mask regional inequalities. The analyses carried out at the sub-national level in this publication, for population density or age structure for example, have shown the extent to which very contrasting situations can co-exist within the same country, and that homogeneous geographical groupings can include regions of several countries. There is now a desire to encourage international comparative studies at a sub-national level, as has been done for demographic ageing in the Mediterranean (Doignon, 2016, 2020). However, this approach remains painstaking for several reasons. This is because international databases only cover countries. It would therefore be necessary to obtain data from national statistical offices, international institutions (e.g. Eurostat) or major international surveys. This raises the question of data access, as well as data availability and comparability. All these aspects are unequal from one Mediterranean country to another and vary according to the topic. While it would therefore be time-consuming to study all the Mediterranean countries at the sub-national level, it seems to us that the analytical potential of such an approach is very high. We would thus be highly supportive of any initiative aiming to undertake a systematic sub-national demographic comparison.

---

[2] See Ambrosetti et al. (2021) for the case of Egypt.

References

Ambrosetti, E., Angeli, A., & Novelli, M. (2021). Childbearing intentions among Egyptian men and women: The role of gender-equitable attitudes and women's empowerment. *Demographic Research 44*, 1229–1270. https://doi.org/10.4054/DemRes.2021.44.51

Attané, I., & Courbage, Y. (2004). *Demography in the Mediterranean region: Situation and projections.* Économica.

Doignon, Y. (2016). *Le vieillissement démographique en Méditerranée: convergences territoriales et spatiales.* Ph.D. in Geography, Aix-Marseille University. https://tel.archives-ouvertes.fr/tel-01471133/

Doignon, Y. (2020). Demographic ageing in the Mediterranean: The end of the spatial dichotomy between the shores? *Spatial Demography, 8*, 85–117. https://doi.org/10.1007/s40980-019-00054-2

Open Access This chapter is licensed under the terms of the Creative Commons Attribution 4.0 International License (http://creativecommons.org/licenses/by/4.0/), which permits use, sharing, adaptation, distribution and reproduction in any medium or format, as long as you give appropriate credit to the original author(s) and the source, provide a link to the Creative Commons license and indicate if changes were made.

The images or other third party material in this chapter are included in the chapter's Creative Commons license, unless indicated otherwise in a credit line to the material. If material is not included in the chapter's Creative Commons license and your intended use is not permitted by statutory regulation or exceeds the permitted use, you will need to obtain permission directly from the copyright holder.

Correction to: Mortality Profiles

Correction to:
Chapter 7 in: Y. Doignon et al., *Population Dynamics in the Mediterranean*, **SpringerBriefs in Population Studies,**
https://doi.org/10.1007/978-3-031-37759-4_7

In the original version of the book, Figures 7.5 and 7.6 have been replaced. The book has been updated with the changes.

The updated version of this chapter can be found at
https://doi.org/10.1007/978-3-031-37759-4_7

© The Author(s) 2023
Y. Doignon et al., *Population Dynamics in the Mediterranean*,
SpringerBriefs in Population Studies,
https://doi.org/10.1007/978-3-031-37759-4_11

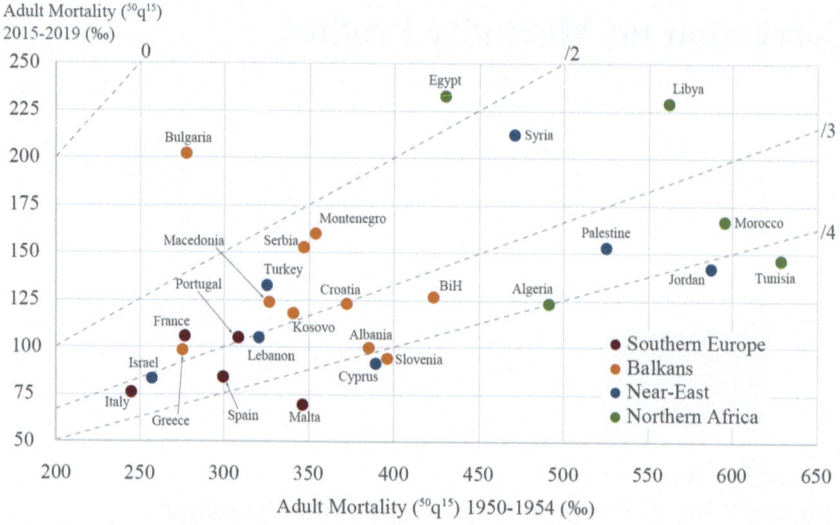

Fig. 7.5 Adult mortality in the Mediterranean (1950–2019) (*Source* World Population Prospects 2022. Graphic developed by the authors. *Reading tip* The dotted lines represent the change between 1950–1954 and 2015–2019. For example, points on the "/4" line have an adult mortality that has been divided by 4 between the two periods. The colour of a dot represents the regional area to which a country belongs)

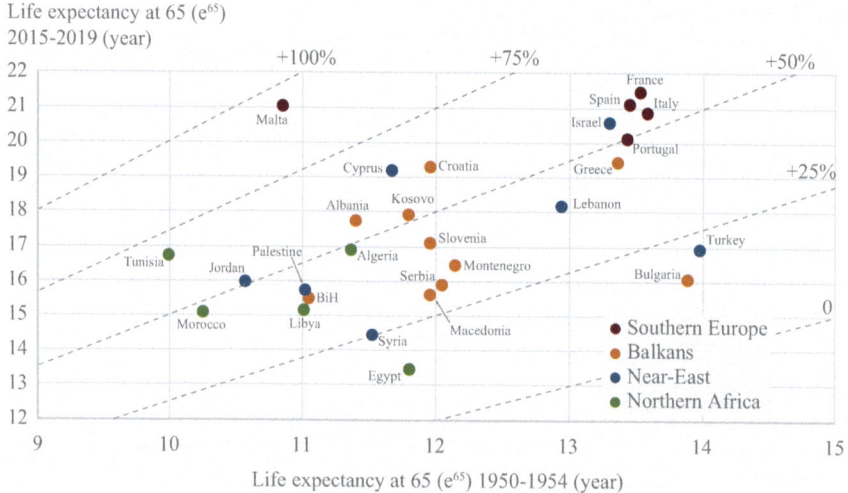

Fig. 7.6 Life expectancy at age 65 in the Mediterranean (1950–2019) (*Source* World Population Prospects 2022. Graphic developed by the authors. *Reading tip*: the dotted lines represent the change between 1950–1954 and 2015–2019. For example, points on the "+75%" line have a life expectancy at age 65 that was increased by 75% between the two periods. The colour of a dot represents the regional area to which a country belongs)

Correction to: Population Dynamics and Their Components

Correction to:
Chapter 9 in: Y. Doignon et al., *Population Dynamics in the Mediterranean*, **SpringerBriefs in Population Studies, https://doi.org/10.1007/978-3-031-37759-4_9**

In the original version of the book, the initially published version of Figure 9.3 has been removed and replaced. The book and the chapter have been updated with the changes.

The updated version of this chapter can be found at
https://doi.org/10.1007/978-3-031-37759-4_9

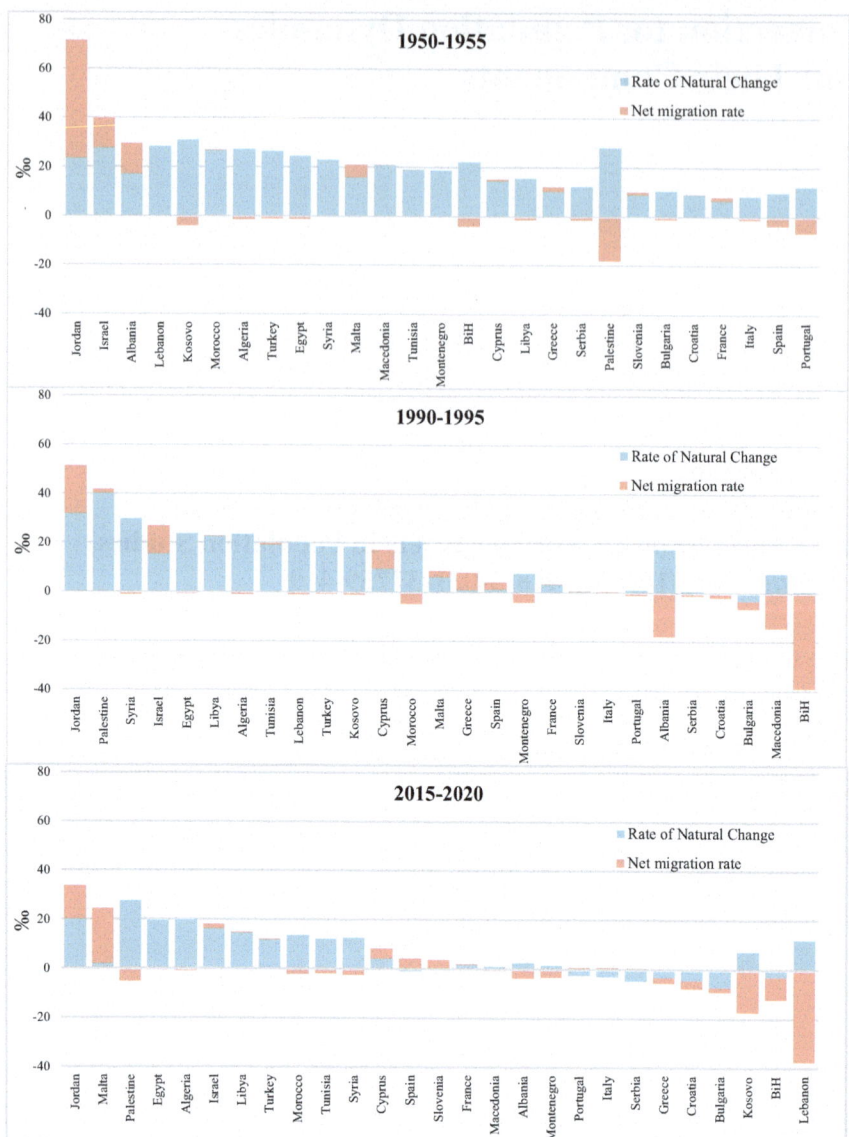

Fig. 9.3 Participation of natural and migration components on total growth for Mediterranean countries at different periods (1950–1955, 1990–1995, 2015–2020) (*Source* World Population Prospects, 2022)

Correction to: Chapter 9 in: Y. Doignon et al., *Population Dynamics* …

Open Access This chapter is licensed under the terms of the Creative Commons Attribution 4.0 International License (http://creativecommons.org/licenses/by/4.0/), which permits use, sharing, adaptation, distribution and reproduction in any medium or format, as long as you give appropriate credit to the original author(s) and the source, provide a link to the Creative Commons license and indicate if changes were made.

The images or other third party material in this chapter are included in the chapter's Creative Commons license, unless indicated otherwise in a credit line to the material. If material is not included in the chapter's Creative Commons license and your intended use is not permitted by statutory regulation or exceeds the permitted use, you will need to obtain permission directly from the copyright holder.

References

Adam, D. (2021). How far will global population rise? Researchers can't agree. *Nature, 597*, 462–465. https://doi.org/10.1038/d41586-021-02522-6
Al Zalak, Z., & Goujon, A. (2017). Exploring the fertility trend in Egypt. *Demographic Research, 37*, 995–1030. https://doi.org/10.4054/DemRes.2017.37.32
Albera, D. (2006). Anthropology of the Mediterranean: Between crisis and renewal. *History and Anthropology, 17*, 109–133. https://doi.org/10.1080/02757200600633272
Alessi, E., & Di Carlo, G. (2018). *Pollution plastique en Méditerranée. Sortons du piège !* WWF. https://www.wwf.fr/sites/default/files/doc-2018-06/180608_rapport_plastiques_mediterranee.pdf
Ambrosetti, E. (2011). *Égypte, l'exception démographique*. Les cahiers de l'INED 166. Institut National d'Études Démographiques. https://books.openedition.org/ined/1778?lang=en
Ambrosetti, E. (2020). Demographic challenges in the Mediterranean. *IEMed Mediterranean Yearbook 2020*. European Institute of the Mediterranean (IEMed). https://www.iemed.org/wp-content/uploads/2021/01/Demographic-Challenges-in-the-Mediterranean.pdf
Ambrosetti, E., Angeli, A., & Novelli, M. (2021). Childbearing intentions among Egyptian men and women: The role of gender-equitable attitudes and women's empowerment. *Demographic Research, 44*, 1229–1270. https://doi.org/10.4054/DemRes.2021.44.51
Ambrosetti, E., & Strangio, D. (2016). Migration in the Mediterranean across disciplines. In E. Ambrosetti, D. Strangio, & C. Wihtol de Wenden (Eds.), *Migration in the Mediterranean: Socio-economic perspectives* (pp. 3–14). Routledge Studies in the European Economy. Routledge.
Ambrosetti, E., Strangio, D., & Wihtol de Wenden, C., (Eds.). (2016). *Migration in the Mediterranean: Socio-economic perspectives*. Routledge Studies in the European Economy. Routledge.
Anastasiou, E., Doignon, Y., Karkanis, D., Léger, J. F., Parant, A., & Sahraoui, S. E. (2020). *Tendances et perspectives démographiques en Méditerranée*. Les Cahiers du Plan Bleu 21. Plan Bleu. https://planbleu.org/wp-content/uploads/2020/10/PLAN-BLEU-CAHIER-21-Tendances-demographiques-en-Mediterranee.pdf
Attané, I., & Courbage, Y. (2004). *Demography in the Mediterranean region: Situation and projections*. Économica.
Ausubel, J., Kramer, S., Shi, A. F., & Hackett, C. (2022). Measuring age differences among different-sex couples: Across religions and 130 countries, men are older than their female partners. *Population Studies, 76*, 465–476. https://doi.org/10.1080/00324728.2022.2094452
Avdeev, A., Eremenko, T., Festy, P., Gaymu, J., Le Bouteillec, N., & Springer, S. (2011). Populations and demographic trends of European countries, 1980–2010. *Population, 66*, 9–133. https://doi.org/10.3917/popu.1101.0009

Blanchet, D. (2001). L'impact des changements démographiques sur la croissance et le marché du travail: faits, théories et incertitudes. *Revue D'économie Politique, 111*, 511–564. https://doi.org/10.3917/redp.114.0511

Bloom, D., Kuhn, M., & Prettner, K. (2017). Africa's prospects for enjoying a demographic dividend. *Journal of Demographic Economics, 83*, 63–76. https://doi.org/10.1017/dem.2016.19

Blöss, T. (Ed.). (2018). *Ageing, lifestyles and economic crises: The new people of the Mediterranean*. Routledge Studies in the European Economy. Routledge, Taylor & Francis.

Blöss-Widmer, I. (2019). Pour une connaissance statistique de la Méditerranée. In T. Blöss & I. Blöss-Widmer (Eds.), *Penser le vieillissement en Méditerranée: données, processus et liens sociaux* (pp. 19–24). L'atelier méditerranéen. Karthala; MMSH.

Blöss-Widmer, I. (2022). Make way for numbers: The age race in the Mediterranean. *IEMed Mediterranean Yearbook 2022*. European Institute of the Mediterranean (IEMed). https://www.iemed.org/wp-content/uploads/2022/10/Make-Way-Numbers-Age-Race-Mediterranean-Bloss-Widmer-IEMedYearbook2022.pdf

Bonifazi, C., & Strozza, S. (2019). International migrations in the northern countries of the Mediterranean. Continuity and changes, before and after the crisis. In S. Capasso & E. Ferragina (Eds.), *Mediterranean migration and the labour markets: Policies for growth and social development in the Mediterranean area* (26 p.). Routledge.

Borderon, M. (2023). Migrations, changements environnementaux et climatiques. In Y. Doignon & S. Oliveau (Eds.), *Dynamique du peuplement mondial. Comment la population habite le monde*, Encyclopédie Des Sciences. ISTE Editions.

Bourguet, M.-N., Lepetit, B., Nordman, D., & Sinarellis, M. (Eds.). (1998). *L'invention scientifique de la Méditerranée: Egypte, Morée, Algérie*. Recherches d'histoire et de Sciences Sociales, 77. École des Hautes Études en Sciences Sociales.

Braudel, F. (1949). *La Méditerranée et le monde méditerranéen à l'époque de Philippe II*. Armand Colin.

Bromberger, C., & Durand, J.-Y. (2001). Faut-il jeter la Méditerranée avec l'eau du bain? In A. Blok, D. Albera, & C. Bromberger (Eds.), *L'anthropologie de la Méditerranée* (pp. 733–756). L'atelier méditerranéen. Maisonneuve et Larose, Maison Méditerranéenne des Sciences de l'Homme. https://www.researchgate.net/publication/32233079_Faut-il_jeter_la_Mediterranee_avec_l%27eau_du_bain

Brunet, R. (1995). Modèles de méditerranées. *L'espace Géographique, 24*, 200–202. https://doi.org/10.3406/spgeo.1995.3389

Buisson, I. (2016). *Déséquilibre de sexes et conflits: une étude du territoire yougoslave entre 1981 et 2011*. Master's Thesis in Geography, Aix-Marseille University. https://dumas.ccsd.cnrs.fr/DEMOMED/dumas-01383003v1

Carella, M., & Parant, A. (2016). Age-structural transition and demographic windows around the Mediterranean. In R. Pace & R. Ham-Chande (Eds.), *Demographic dividends: Emerging challenges and policy implications* (pp. 83–113). Population Studies. Springer. https://doi.org/10.1007/978-3-319-32709-9

Chesnais, J.-C. (1992). *The demographic transition: Stages, patterns, and economic implications*. Clarendon Press ; Oxford University Press.

Clément, C. (2002). Une mer des hommes: les limites du monde méditerranéen. In D. Borne & J. Scheibling (Eds.), *La Méditerranée* (pp. 28–48). Carré géographie 8. Hachette.

Coale, A. J., & Watkins, S. C. (1986). *The decline of fertility in Europe*. Princeton University Press.

Costemalle, V. (2021). Bayesian probabilistic population projections for France. *Economie et Statistique/Economics and Statistics, 29*, 47. https://doi.org/10.24187/ecostat.2020.520d.2031

Coudert, E. (2013). Une approche régionale de la population et de l'urbanisation en Méditerranée, rétrospective et projections à 2025. In J.-P. Carrière (Ed.), *Villes et projets urbains en Méditerranée* (pp. 21–31). Perspectives Villes et Territoires. Presses universitaires François-Rabelais.

Courbage, Y. (1997). La démographie en rive sud de la Méditerranée au XXIe siècle: changement de perspectives. *Espace Populations Sociétés, 1997/1*, 11–26. https://doi.org/10.3406/espos.1997.1786

References

Courbage, Y. (1999). *New demographic scenarios in the Mediterranean region*. Travaux et documents 142. Institut National d'Etudes Démographiques-Presses Universitaires de France.

Courbage, Y. (2006). Les enjeux démographiques en Palestine après le retrait de Gaza. *Critique Internationale, 31*, 23–38. https://doi.org/10.3917/crii.031.0023

Courbage, Y. (2008a). Démographie des communautés chrétiennes au Proche-Orient. *Confluences Méditerranée, 66*, 27–44. https://doi.org/10.3917/come.066.0027

Courbage, Y. (2008b). La guerre des berceaux. *Les collections de l'Histoire*. https://www.lhistoire.fr/%C2%AB-la-guerre-des-berceaux-%C2%BB

Courbage, Y. (2015a). The political dimensions of fertility decrease and family transformation in the Arab context. *DIFI Family Research and Proceedings, 2015:3*. https://doi.org/10.5339/difi.2015.3

Courbage, Y. (2015b). Tunisie: la contre-transition démographique. Interview by Khadija Mohsen-Finan. *Orient XXI*. https://www.youtube.com/watch?v=FBxRclm8wnA

Courbage, Y. (2015c). Egypte, une transition démographique en marche arrière. *Orient XXI*. http://orientxxi.info/magazine/egypte-une-transition-demographique-en-marche-arriere,0956

Courbage, Y., & Todd, E. (2014). *A convergence of civilizations: The transformation of Muslim societies around the world*. Columbia University Press.

D'Addato, A. (2010). Tendances démographiques, développement économique et mobilité des populations en Méditerranée. *Migrations Société, 6*, 13–30. https://doi.org/10.3917/migra.132.0013

De Haas, H. (2011). Mediterranean migration futures: Patterns, drivers and scenarios. *Global Environmental Change, 21*, S59–S69. https://doi.org/10.1016/j.gloenvcha.2011.09.003

De Haas, H., Castles, S., & Miller, M. (2020). *The age of migration: International population movements in the modern world* (6th ed.). The Guilford Press.

Delbès, C., Gaymu, J., & Springer, S. (2006). Women grow old alone, but men grow old with a partner. A European Overview. *Population & Societies, 419*. https://doi.org/10.3917/popsoc.419.0001

Demographic Statistics Database. United Nations Statistics Division. https://unstats.un.org/unsd/demographic-social/products/dyb/index.cshtml

Deprest, F. (2002). Notes on the Geographic Invention of the Mediterranean. *L'espace Géographique, 31*, 73–92. https://doi.org/10.3917/eg.311.0073

Deslondes, O. (2004). Les populations des Balkans depuis 1990: Aspects géographiques de la crise. *Espace Populations Sociétés, 2004/3*, 487–498. https://doi.org/10.4000/eps.336

Doignon, Y. (2016). *Le vieillissement démographique en Méditerranée: convergences territoriales et spatiales*. Ph.D. in Geography, Aix-Marseille University. https://tel.archives-ouvertes.fr/tel-01471133/

Doignon, Y. (2019). Transitions démographiques et vieillissements en Méditerranée: le Sud rattrapera-t-il le Nord? In T. Blöss & I. Blöss-Widmer (Eds.), *Penser le vieillissement en Méditerranée: données, processus et liens sociaux* (pp. 151–177). L'atelier méditerranéen. Karthala; MMSH.

Doignon, Y. (2020a). Les transitions démographiques des pays méditerranéens depuis 1950. *Géoconfluences*. http://geoconfluences.ens-lyon.fr/doc/etpays/Medit/MeditScient.htm

Doignon, Y. (2020b). Demographic ageing in the Mediterranean: The end of the spatial dichotomy between the shores? *Spatial Demography, 8*, 85–117 https://doi.org/10.1007/s40980-019-00054-2

Doignon, Y. (2023). Dépeuplement et dépopulation dans un monde en croissance. In Y. Doignon & S. Oliveau (Eds.), *Dynamique du peuplement mondial. Comment la population habite le monde*. Encyclopédie Des Sciences. ISTE Editions.

Doignon, Y., Ambrosetti, E., & Miccoli, S. (2021). The spatial diffusion of fertility decline in Egypt (1950–2006). *Genus, 77*, 23. https://doi.org/10.1186/s41118-021-00131-9

Doignon, Y., Blöss-Widmer, I., & Oliveau, S. (2017). Half a century of ageing in France. Dynamics and specificities of the Mediterranean coastline. In T. Blöss (Ed.), *Ageing, lifestyles and economic crises: The new people of the Mediterranean* (pp. 82–100). Routledge Studies in the European Economy. Routledge, Taylor & Francis Group.

Doignon, Y., & Oliveau, S. (2015). Territorial grids in the Mediterranean: Space versus population. *Bollettino dell'Associazione Italiana di Cartografia, 154*, 46–63. https://doi.org/10.13137/2282-472X/11827

Doignon, Y., Oliveau, S., & Blöss-Widmer, I. (2016). L'Europe méridionale depuis 20 ans: Dépeuplement, dépopulation et renouveau démographique. *Espace Populations Sociétés, 2015/3-2016/1*, 23. https://doi.org/10.4000/eps.6171

Dubresson, A., Moreau, S., Raison, J.-P., & Steck, J.-F. (2011). *L'Afrique subsaharienne: une géographie du changement* (3rd ed.). Armand Colin.

Engelen, T., & Puschmann, P. (2011). How unique is the Western European marriage pattern? A comparison of nuptiality in historical Europe and the contemporary Arab world. *History of the Family, 16*, 387–400. https://doi.org/10.1016/j.hisfam.2011.07.004

Etling, A., Backeberg, L., & Tholen, J. (2020). The political dimension of young people's migration intentions: Evidence from the Arab Mediterranean region. *Journal of Ethnic and Migration Studies, 46*, 1388–1404. https://doi.org/10.1080/1369183X.2018.1485093

Fargues, P. (1986a). Traditions matrimoniales dans les sociétés arabes. *Population et Sociétés, 198*. https://www.ined.fr/fichier/s_rubrique/18983/pop_et_soc_francais_198.fr.pdf

Fargues, P. (1986b). Un siècle de transition démographique en Afrique méditerranéenne 1885–1985. *Population, 41*, 205–232. https://doi.org/10.2307/1533059

Fargues, P. (1989). The decline of Arab fertility. *Population, 44*, 147–175. http://www.jstor.org/stable/2949078

Fargues, P. (1990). Algérie, Maroc, Tunisie: vers la famille restreinte? *Population et Sociétés, 248*. https://www.ined.fr/fichier/s_rubrique/18984/pop_et_soc_francais_248.fr.pdf

Fargues, P. (1995). Les données démographiques de la paix au Proche-Orient. In L. Blin & P. Fargues (Eds.), *L'économie de la paix au Proche-Orient* (pp. 61–90). Maisonneuve et Larose, CEDEJ.

Fargues, P. (2000a). *Générations arabes: l'alchimie du nombre*. Fayard.

Fargues, P. (2000b). La démographie et la Méditerranée ou les faits contre les représentations. In E. Kienle (Ed.), *La reconstruction d'un espace d'échanges: la Méditerranée* (pp. 53–69). CEDEJ—Égypte/Soudan. https://doi.org/10.4000/books.cedej.758

Fargues, P., & Salinari, G. (2011). Flux migratoires et transition démographique. Evolution et scénarios pour l'avenir. In C. Jolly & "Mediterranean 2030" Consortium (Eds.), *Demain, la Méditerranée. Scénarios et projection à 2030* (pp. 71–113). Construire La Méditerranée. IPEMED—Institut de prospective économique du monde méditerranéen.

Frenk, J., Bobadilla, J. L., Stern, C., Frejka, T., & Lozano, R. (1991). Elements for a theory of the health transition. *Health Transition Review, 1*, 21–38. http://www.jstor.org/stable/40608615

Frontex. (2015). *Annual risk analysis 2015*. European Agency for the Management of Operational Cooperation at the External Borders of the Member States of the European Union. https://frontex.europa.eu/assets/Publications/Risk_Analysis/Annual_Risk_Analysis_2015.pdf

Gastineau, B. (2012). Transition de la fécondité, développement et droits des femmes en Tunisie. *Les Cahiers d'EMAM, 21*, 75–94. https://doi.org/10.4000/emam.521

Goode, W. J. (1963). *World revolution and family patterns*. Free Press.

Goody, J. (1983). *The development of the family and marriage in Europe*. Past and Present Publications. Cambridge University Press. https://doi.org/10.1017/CBO9780511607752

Goujon, A., & Zalak, Z. A. (2018). Why has fertility been increasing in Egypt? *Population & Societies, 551*. https://doi.org/10.3917/popsoc.551.0001

Guilmoto, C. Z., & Duthé, G. (2013). Masculinization of births in Eastern Europe. *Population & Societies, 506*. https://doi.org/10.3917/popsoc.506.0001

Guilmoto, C. Z., & Oliveau, S. (2007). Sex ratio imbalances among children at micro-level: China and India compared. In *Population Association of America 2007*. http://paa2007.princeton.edu/papers/71096

Hajnal, J. (1965). European marriage patterns in perspective. In D. V. Glass & D. E. C. Eversley (Eds.), *Population in history: Essays in historical demography, Volume I: General and Great Britain* (pp. 101–143). Edward Arnold; Aldine Publishing.

Herzfeld, M. (1987). *Anthropology through the looking-glass: Critical ethnography in the margins of Europe.* Cambridge University Press.

Horden, P., & Purcell, N. (2000). *The corrupting sea. A study of Mediterranean history.* Blackwell Publishers.

Huebner, S. (2016). A Mediterranean family? A comparative approach to the Ancient World. In S. Huebner & G. Nathan (Eds.), *Mediterranean families in antiquity: Households, extended families, and domestic space* (pp. 3–26). John Wiley & Sons.

Human Life-Table Database (HLD). Max Planck Institute, University of California at Berkeley (USA), French Institute for Demographic Studies (France). http://www.lifetable.de

Human Mortality Database (HMD). Max Planck Institute, University of California at Berkeley (USA), French Institute for Demographic Studies (France). www.mortality.org

Huntington, S. P. (1993). The clash of civilizations? *Foreign Affairs, 72*, 22–49. https://doi.org/10.2307/20045621

Ilbert, R. (2006). Questionner le concept Méditerranée. Presentation presented at the Ateliers méditerranéens, MMSH. https://cinumed.mmsh.univ-aix.fr/collection/item/96810-questionner-le-concept-mediterranee?offset=2

International Migrant Stock 2020. (2020). United Nations, Department of Economic and Social Affairs, Population Division. https://www.un.org/development/desa/pd/content/international-migrant-stock

ITAN. (2015). *Integrated territorial analysis of the neighbourhoods. main report.* European Union. ESPON Programme. https://www.espon.eu/sites/default/files/attachments/02_ITAN-FR-Main_report_FINAL_v15.pdf

Joint Research Centre (European Commission). (2018). *Demographic and human capital scenarios for the 21st century: 2018 assessment for 201 countries.* Publications Office. https://data.europa.eu/doi/10.2760/41776

Jones, G. W. (2006). A demographic perspective on the Muslim world. *Journal of Population Research, 23*, 243–265. https://doi.org/10.1007/BF03031818

Kayser, B. (1996). *Méditerranée. Une géographie de la fracture.* Encyclopédie de La Méditerranée 2. Edisud.

King, R. (2000). Southern Europe in the changing global map of migration. In R. King, G. Lazaridis, & C. Tsardanidis (Eds.), *Eldorado or Fortress? Migration in Southern Europe* (pp. 3–26). Palgrave Macmillan UK. https://doi.org/10.1057/9780333982525_1

Lacoste, Y. (2001). La Méditerranée. *Hérodote, 103*, 3–39. https://doi.org/10.3917/her.103.0003

Kirk, D. (1966). Factors affecting moslem natality. In B. Berelson (Ed.), *Family planning and population programs* (pp.149–154). University of Chicago Press.

Landry, A. (1934). *La révolution démographique: études et essais sur les problèmes de la population.* Sirey.

Laria, S. (2008). L'avenir en Méditerranée se jouera dans les villes. *Annales Des Mines—Responsabilité Et Environnement, 49*, 56–61. https://doi.org/10.3917/re.049.0056

Laslett, P. (1983). Family and household as work group and kin group: Areas of traditional Europe compared. In R. Wall, J. Robin, & P. Laslett (Eds.), *Family forms in historic Europe* (pp. 513–563). Cambridge University Press.

Le Bris, A. (2021). Enfants nés hors mariage au Maghreb: l'influence du genre sur leurs trajectoires. In M. Jacquemin, M. Pilon, D. Bonnet, C. Deprez, & G. Pison (Eds.), *Être fille ou garçon: Regards croisés sur l'enfance et le genre* (pp. 127–149). Questions de Populations. Ined Éditions.

Lerch, M. (2018). Fertility and union formation during crisis and societal consolidation in the Western Balkans. *Population Studies, 72*, 217–234. https://doi.org/10.1080/00324728.2017.1412492

Lesthaeghe, R. (2014). The second demographic transition: A concise overview of its development. *Proceedings of the National Academy of Sciences, 111*, 18112–18115. https://doi.org/10.1073/pnas.1420441111

Lévêque, É. (2017). *L'éducation efface-t-elle les frontières? L'exemple de la fécondité en Méditerranée*. Master's Thesis in Geography, Aix-Marseille University. https://dumas.ccsd.cnrs.fr/dumas-01612919

Lévêque, É., & Oliveau, S. (2019). La transition de la fécondité autour de la Méditerranée: convergence générale et hétérogénéités spatiales, un éclairage par l'éducation. *Espace Populations Sociétés, 2019/2*. https://doi.org/10.4000/eps.9025

Liziard, S. (2013). *Littoralisation de la façade nord-méditerranéenne: analyse spatiale et prospective dans le contexte du changement climatique*. Ph.D. Thesis in Geography. Nice Sophia Antipolis University. https://tel.archives-ouvertes.fr/tel-00927492/document

Locoh, T., & Ouadah-Bedidi, Z. (2014). *Familles et rapports de genre au Maghreb, Evolutions ou révolutions*. Document de travail 213. Institut National d'Etudes Démographiques. https://www.ined.fr/fichier/s_rubrique/22779/document.travail.2014.213.magreb.genre.fr.pdf

Lutz, W., Butz, W. P., & Samir, K.C. (2014). *World population and human capital in the twenty-first century*. Oxford University Press. https://doi.org/10.1093/acprof:oso/9780198703167.001.0001

Martin, I., & Bardak, U. (2011). *Union for the Mediterranean regional employability review. The challenge of youth employment in the Mediterranean*. European Training Foundation.

Matthijs, K., Neels, K., Timmerman, C., & Haers, J. (Ed.). (2016). *Population change in Europe, the Middle-East and North Africa. Beyond the demographic divide*. International Population Studies. Routledge. https://doi.org/10.4324/9781315601496

Meslé, F., & Vallin, J. (2006). The health transition: Trends and prospects. In G. Caselli, J. Vallin, & G. J. Wunsch (Eds.), *Demography: Analysis and synthesis* (Vol. II, pp. 247–260). Elsevier.

Missing Migrants Project. (2023). International Organization for Migration. https://missingmigrants.iom.int/

Moriconi-Ebrard, F., & Pascal, R. (2020). Peuplement et urbanisation de la Libye: construction d'une information cartographique. *Géoconfluences*. http://geoconfluences.ens-lyon.fr/informations-scientifiques/dossiers-regionaux/la-mediterranee-une-geographie-paradoxale/articles-scientifiques/demographie-libye

Muñoz-Pérez, F., & Recaño-Valverde, J. (2011). A century of nuptiality in Spain, 1900–2007. *European Journal of Population, 27*, 487–515. https://doi.org/10.1007/s10680-011-9234-1

Notestein, F. W. (1945). Population: The long view. In P. T. Schultz (Ed.), *Food for the world* (pp. 36–57). University of Chicago Press.

Oliveau, S., & Doignon, Y. (2014). Ever closer to the water. Recent developments in Mediterranean settlement patterns. *South-East European Journal of Political Science, II*, 22–30. https://halshs.archives-ouvertes.fr/halshs-01070622

Oliveau, S., Doignon, Y., & Blöss-Widmer, I. (2023). Population distribution: Follow the Nile. In H. Bayoumi & K. Bennafla (Eds.), *An atlas of contemporary Egypt* (pp. 56–57). CNRS éditions. https://books.openedition.org/editionscnrs/58390

Oliveau, S., Larue, Q., Doignon, Y., & Blöss-Widmer, I. (2019). Mapping foreign nationals in Spain: An exploratory approach at local level. *Genus, 75*, 5. https://doi.org/10.1186/s41118-018-0047-5

Omran, A. R. (1971). The epidemiologic transition: A theory of the epidemiology of population change. *The Milbank Memorial Fund Quarterly, 49*, 509–538. https://doi.org/10.1111/j.1468-0009.2005.00398.x

Operational Data Portal Refugee Situations. Mediterranean Situation. (2023). UNHCR (United Nations High Commissioner for Refugees). https://data.unhcr.org/en/situations/mediterranean

Ouadah-Bedidi, Z., Vallin, J., & Bouchoucha, I. (2012). Unexpected developments in Maghrebian fertility. *Population & Societies, 486*. https://doi.org/10.3917/popsoc.486.0001

Panebianco, S. (2022). The EU and migration in the Mediterranean: EU borders' control by proxy. *Journal of Ethnic and Migration Studies, 48*, 1398–1416. https://doi.org/10.1080/1369183X.2020.1851468

References

Péguy, C.-P. (1986). L'univers géographique de Fernand Braudel. *Espaces Temps, 34*, 77–82. https://doi.org/10.3406/espat.1986.3355

Peristiany, J.-G. (1966). *Honour and shame: The values of Mediterranean society*. University of Chicago Press.

Peristiany, J.-G., (Ed.). (1968). *Contributions to Mediterranean sociology: Mediterranean rural communities and social change*. Mouton&Cie.

Peristiany, J.-G. (Ed.). (1976). *Mediterranean family structures*. Cambridge University Press.

Pfirsch, T. (2011). Une géographie de la famille en Europe du Sud. *Cybergeo: European Journal of Geography*. https://doi.org/10.4000/cybergeo.23669

Pina-Cabral, J. (1989). The Mediterranean as a category of regional comparison: A critical view. *Current Anthropology, 30*, 399–406. https://www.jstor.org/stable/2743537

Pitt-Rivers, J. (Ed.). (1963). *Mediterranean countrymen. Essays in the social anthropology of the Mediterranean*. Mouton.

Population Division, Departement of Economic and Social Affairs, and United Nations Secretariat. (2000). *Replacement migration: Is it a solution to declining and ageing populations?* https://www.un.org/development/desa/pd/sites/www.un.org.development.desa.pd/files/unpd-egm_200010_un_2001_replacementmigration.pdf

Pouget, B. (2021). La Méditerranée et les grandes épidémies. Retour sur un demi-siècle de travaux historiques. *Cahiers de la Méditerranée, 103*, 173–189. https://doi.org/10.4000/cdlm.15133

Puschmann, P., & Matthijs, K. (2016). The demographic transition in the Arab world: The dual role of marriage in family dynamics and population growth. In K. Matthijs, K. Neels, C. Timmerman, J. Haers, & S. Mels (Eds.), *Population change in Europe, the Middle-East and North Africa. Beyond the demographic divide* (pp. 119–165). International Population Studies. Routledge, Taylor & Francis Group. https://doi.org/10.4324/9781315601496

Pyramus de Candolle, A. (1820). *Essai élémentaire de géographie botanique*. Imprimerie de F.G. Levrault.

Rashad, H. (2015). Demographic transition in Arab countries: A new perspective. *Journal of the Australian Population Association, 17*, 83–101. https://doi.org/10.1007/BF03029449

Rashad, H., Osman, M., & Roudi-Fahimi, F. (2005). Marriage in the Arab world. Population Reference Bureau, 8. https://u.demog.berkeley.edu/~jrw/Biblio/Eprints/PRB/files/MarriageInArabWorld_Eng.pdf

Reba, M., Reitsma, F., & Seto, K.C. (2018). *Historical urban population: 3700 BC–AD 2000*. NASA Socioeconomic Data and Applications Center (SEDAC). https://doi.org/10.7927/H4Z G6QBX

Reclus, E. (1876). *La Terre et les Hommes: l'Europe méridionale*. Nouvelle Géographie Universelle Tome 1. Hachette.

Roncayolo, M. (2002). Relire la Méditerranée de Fernand Braudel. In D. Borne & J. Scheibling (Eds.), *La Méditerranée* (pp. 216–231). Carré géographie 8. Hachette.

Sacchi, P., & Viazzo, P. P. (2014). Family and household. In P. Horden & S. Kinoshita (Eds.), *A companion to Mediterranean history* (pp. 234–249). Wiley Blackwell Companions to History. Wiley & Sons. https://doi.org/10.1002/9781118519356

Salvini, M. S. (2023). *Le popolazioni del Mediterraneo. Storia, cultura e demografia*. @racne.

Sardon, J.-P. (2001). Demographic change in the Balkans since the end of the 1980s. *Population, 13*, 49–70. https://www.jstor.org/stable/3030275

Sebti, M., Courbage, Y., Festy, P., & Kurzac-Souali, A.-C. (2009). Maghreb, Morocco, Marrakech: Demographic convergence, socioéconomic diversity. *Population & Societies, 459*. https://www.cairn-int.info/journal-population-and-societies-2009-8-page-1.htm

Seklani, M. (1960). La fécondité dans les pays arabes: données numériques, attitudes et comportements. *Population, 15*, 831–856. https://doi.org/10.2307/1526919

Smith, R. (1990). Monogamy, landed property and demographic regimes in pre-industrial Europe: Regional contrasts and temporal stabilities. In J. Landers & V. Reynolds (Eds.), *Fertility and resources* (pp. 164–188). Society for the Study of Human Biology Symposium Series 31. Cambridge University Press.

Sobotka, T., & Beaujouan, É. (2014). Two Is best? The persistence of a two-child family ideal in Europe. *Population and Development Review, 40*, 391–419. https://doi.org/10.1111/j.1728-4457.2014.00691.x

Sorre, M., & Sion, J. (1934). *Géographie Universelle, Tome VII. Méditerranée, péninsules méditerranéennes* (P. V. de la Blache & L. Gallois, Eds.). Armand Colin.

Speziale, S. (2018). Les médecins européens, médiateurs scientifiques et culturels en Afrique méditerranéenne entre le XVIIIe et le XIXe siècle. *Cahiers De La Méditerranée, 96*, 231–248. https://doi.org/10.4000/cdlm.10953

Sterkx, S. (2008). The external dimension of EU asylum and migration policy: Expanding fortress Europe? In J. Orbie (Ed.), *Europe's global role: External policies of the European Union* (pp. 117–138). Routledge.

Tabutin, D., & Schoumaker, B. (2005). The demography of the Arab world and the Middle East from the 1950s to the 2000s. *Population, 60*, 611–724. https://doi.org/10.3917/popu.505.0611

Tabutin, D., Vilquin, E., & Biraben, J.-N. (2002). *L'histoire de la population de l'Afrique du Nord pendant le deuxième millénaire*. Document de Travail 15. Centre de recherche en démographie.

Thornton, A. (2001). The developmental paradigm, reading history sideways, and family change. *Demography, 38*, 449–465. https://doi.org/10.2307/3088311

Tolosana, C. (2001). The ever-changing face of honour. In A. Blok, D. Albera, & C. Bromberger (Eds.), *L'anthropologie de la Méditerranée* (pp. 133–147). L'atelier méditerranéen. Maisonneuve et Larose, Maison Méditerranéenne des Sciences de l'Homme.

Triandafyllidou, A. (2013). *Circular migration between Europe and its neighbourhood: Choice or necessity?* Oxford University Press.

Troisi, J., & Von Kondratowitz, H.-J. (Eds.). (2013). *Ageing in the Mediterranean*. Policy Press.

Vallin, J., & Caselli, G. (2006). The United Nations' world population projections. In G. Caselli, J. Vallin, & G. J. Wunsch (Eds.), *Demography: Analysis and synthesis* (Vol. III, pp. 197–234). Elsevier.

Vallin, J., & Meslé, F. (2004). Convergences and divergences in mortality. A new approach to health transition. *Demographic Research, 2*, 10–43. https://doi.org/10.4054/DemRes.2004.S2.2

Vallin, J., & Meslé, F. (2014). De la transition épidémiologique à la transition sanitaire: l'improbable convergence générale. In D. Tabutin & B. Masquelier (Eds.), *Ralentissements, résistances et ruptures dans les transitions démographiques* (pp. 257–290). Actes de La Chaire Quetelet (2010). Presses Universitaires de Louvain.

Venier, P., & Oliveau, S. (2023). Populations en mouvement: comment se redessine le peuplement mondial? In Y. Doignon & S. Oliveau (Eds.), *Dynamique du peuplement mondial. Comment la population habite le monde*, Encyclopédie Des Sciences. ISTE Editions.

Verdeil, E., Faour, G., & Velut, S. (2007). Population et peuplement. In Atlas du Liban: Territoires et société (pp. 64–90). Contemporain Co-Éditions. Presses de l'Ifpo, CNRS Liban. https://books.openedition.org/ifpo/402?lang=en

Vollset, S. E., Goren, E., Yuan, C.-W., Cao, J., Smith, A. E., Hsiao, T., Bisignano, C., et al. (2020). Fertility, mortality, migration, and population scenarios for 195 countries and territories from 2017 to 2100: A forecasting analysis for the Global Burden of Disease Study. *The Lancet, 396*, 1285–1306. https://doi.org/10.1016/S0140-6736(20)30677-2

Von Kondratowitz, H. J. (2013). Squaring the circle: Demographic outlook and social development as determinants of ageing in the Mediterranean. In J. Troisi & H.-J. Von Kondratowitz (Eds.), *Ageing in the Mediterranean* (pp. 3–32). Policy Press.

Weeks, J. (2020). *Population: An introduction to concepts and issues* (13th ed.). Cengage.

Wihtol de Wenden, C. (2013). Migrations en Méditerranée, une nouvelle donne. *Confluences Méditerranée, 87*, 19–30. https://doi.org/10.3917/come.087.0019

Wihtol de Wenden, C. (2019). Migration flows in the Euro-Mediterranean region. The challenge of migration and asylum crisis in contemporary Europe and the global compact. In F. Francesca, A. Masi, C. Wihtol de Wenden, & D. Strangio (Eds.), *Migrations. Countries of immigrants, countries of migrants. Canada, Italy* (pp. 21–37). Migrazioni/Migrations. Edizioni Nuova Cultura.

References

Wilson, C. (2001). On the scale of global demographic convergence 1950–2000. *Population and Development Review, 27*, 155–171. https://doi.org/10.1111/j.1728-4457.2001.00155.x

Wilson, C. (2005). Transitions démographiques en Europe et dans le bassin méditerranéen. In P. S. Cassia & T. Fabre (Eds.), *Les défis et les peurs: entre Europe et Méditerranée* (pp. 21–48). Etudes Méditerranéennes. Actes Sud—Maison Méditerranéenne des Sciences de l'Homme.

Wilson, C. (2011). Understanding global demographic convergence since 1950. *Population and Development Review, 37*, 375–388. https://doi.org/10.1111/j.1728-4457.2011.00415.x

WHO Mortality Database. World Health Organization. https://platform.who.int/mortality

World Marriage Data 2019. (2019). United Nations, Department of Economic and Social Affairs, Population Division. https://population.un.org/MarriageData/Index.html

WorldPop. (2018). WorldPop (School of Geography and Environmental Science, University of Southampton; Department of Geography and Geosciences, University of Louisville; Departement de Geographie, Universite de Namur) and Center for International Earth Science Information Network (CIESIN), Columbia University. Global High Resolution Population Denominators Project—Funded by The Bill and Melinda Gates Foundation (OPP1134076). https://www.worldpop.org/

World Population Prospects. (2022). United Nations, Department of Economic and Social Affairs, Population Division. https://population.un.org/wpp/

World Urbanization Prospects. (2018). United Nations, Department of Economic and Social Affairs, Population Division. https://population.un.org/wup/

Zagaglia, B. (2013). Demographic transitions and social changes in the Mediterranean region. *IEMed Mediterranean Yearbook*. European Institute of the Mediterranean (IEMed). https://www.iemed.org/wp-content/uploads/2021/04/Anuari-2013-EN.pdf

The manufacturer's authorised representative in the EU is Springer Nature Customer Service Centre GmbH, Europaplatz 3, 69115 Heidelberg, Germany. If you have any concerns regarding our products, please contact ProductSafety@springernature.com

Printed and bound by CPI Group (UK) Ltd, Croydon, CR0 4YY

23/03/2026

02076360-0019